Two in a Boat

Two in a Boat

THE TRUE STORY OF A
MARITAL RITE OF PASSAGE

Gwyneth Lewis

HarperCollins*Publishers*

HarperCollins books may be purchased for educational, business, or sales promotional use. For information, please write: Special Markets Department, HarperCollins Publishers, 10 East 53rd Street, New York, NY 10022.

Extract from C. S. Forester's *Lieutenant Hornblower* © Cassette Productions, 1952, 1954, reproduced by permission of Penguin Books Ltd. Extract from Felipe Fernández-Armesto's *Civilizations* reproduced by permission of Pan Books. Extract from Peter Whybrow's *A Mood Apart* reproduced by permission of Macmillan Ltd. Extract from *Green Guide: Portugal (2001 edition)* © Michelin et Cie, 2005, authorization no. 0501003. Extract from *Shipwreck* by John Fowles reproduced by permission of The Random House Group.

Maps by Leslie Robinson

First published in Great Britain in 2005 by Fourth Estate.

FIRST EDITION

Printed on acid-free paper

Library of Congress Cataloging-in-Publication Data
Lewis, Gwyneth.
    Two in a boat : the true story of a marital rite of passage / Gwyneth Lewis.—1st ed.
      p. cm.
    ISBN-10: 0-06-082323-2
    ISBN-13: 978-0-06-082323-8
    1. Ocean travel. 2. Lewis, Gwyneth, 1959—Travel—Atlantic Ocean. 3. Poets, Welsh—20th century—Biography. 4. Atlantic Ocean—Description and travel. 5. Lewis, Gwyneth, 1959—Marriage. I. Title.
    G550.L49 2006
    910'.9163'0902—dc22
    [B]   2005050327

06 07 08 09 10 RRD 10 9 8 7 6 5 4 3 2 1

The water is wide,
I cannot get o'er,
And neither have I wings to fly.
Give me a boat that will carry two,
And both shall row, my love and I.

Folk song

Marriage is a long journey at close quarters.

Iris Murdoch

CONTENTS

Two in a Boat

1   Leighton and Gwyneth

CHAPTER ONE

Call me Sea Bitch

We purchased our first sailing boat by accident.

I could blame it all on Mrs Rubenstein. She lived in Cardiff, a short way down the hill from us, had a hedgehog shelter in her front garden and was known for reading tarot cards. I was restless, just about to return to work after over a year of being seriously ill with depression. I phoned.

'Come down, my dear. All I ask is a donation for the animals.'

I sat with her and her pungent white Westie dog on the sofa as she read my tarot and chain-smoked. Mrs Rubenstein told me many things about work and love and what I should do about my health. She also gave free tax advice between cards. The main thrust of her reading was that I wasn't living my life to the full. My ears pricked up at one particular aside.

'And by the way, dear, you should buy a boat.'

Then she moved on swiftly to tell me what we should do for my husband's lower back pain.

Leighton, my husband, was full of scorn when I told him where I'd been. 'What a load of rubbish, I don't believe a word of it,' he said. 'And I haven't even got a bad back.'

By the end of the week he did. But, even more surprisingly for a tarot atheist, he came home from work the following day and announced, 'I've found a boat!' She was a twenty-three-foot racing boat called *Nitro*, had a yellow hull and was totally unsuitable for beginners, so we bought her and started to learn how to sail in the Bristol Channel. Not long afterwards we were talking about renting out the house and sailing round the world.

Less than a month after I'd seen Mrs Rubenstein, I applied for voluntary redundancy from my job. I went to see a financial adviser, who made the usual suggestions. Rather than investing my pay-off and remortgaging the house, I decided to pay cash for a thirty-year-old Nicholson 35 yacht called *Jameeleh*. Having jumped from my job without a parachute, and with no gainful employment, we were soon astonished to find that the prospect of being able to sail away had become financially viable. A book contract and a fellowship meant that I would be able to work as a freelance writer even if we were away from home. We put our house in the hands of a letting agent, placed our belongings in storage, and went to live on the boat. We planned to spend the first year travelling in Europe and then, when we were more experienced sailors, to cross the Atlantic to Brazil and on into the Pacific through the Panama Canal. This was a dream journey for both of us, our reward for having come through a difficult couple of years together and for having been such good troupers.

In my mind's eye, I had a clear image of what a true seaman or –woman should be. The sea dog (or sea bitch, as I wanted to be called) always had blue eyes, feet planted firmly on the ground and a calm grip on his internal horizon. The seaman had faced many terrors but was a person of few words. He or she had the same taciturnity as monks or nuns, a quality that comes from knowing that words won't help you to ride out your worst fears or to survive contact with forces much stronger than yourself. Speech had been superseded by faith in countless tiny acts of seamanship and discipline, which may be the closest we can ever come to real safety. I was ready to varnish wood, splice ropes or grease winches – anything that might help me change from a messy depressive, often overwhelmed by my own emotions, into one of these self-contained sailors. I wanted to be cool, unaffected by tumult, unbowed by internal or external storms. I wanted a glint of the sea in my eyes.

Unfortunately, whenever we sailed in the Bristol Channel, I was either asleep or seasick. When we first started going out into the tea-coloured waters of the Severn Estuary, I was still so lethargic from prolonged clinical depression that the rocking of the boat sent me instantly to sleep. I completely understood why Marcel Proust had fantasised about living on a yacht, so that he could travel the world without having to get out of bed. I'd crawl under a duvet in one of the bunks below and be lulled by the white noise of water against the boat's hull and the swell underneath her. Leighton learned how to sail virtually single-handed, although he'd always wake me when he was ready to come in.

The Bristol Channel is a challenging place to learn to sail because the estuary has one of the largest tidal ranges in the world. Every six hours a huge body of water shoulders its way up into the mouth of the Severn and then, after a short period of slack, rushes back down to the open sea. The difference between the level of the water at high and low tide in Cardiff can be as much as forty feet, so particular care needs to be taken in reading the Bristol Channel tide tables. One day, Leighton and I found ourselves alone in the Cardiff Barrage lock. This was unusual, but we congratulated ourselves on our good luck at not having to avoid other boats in the confined space. In the sunlight above us a couple of weekday spectators were staring down at us from the barrage wall. The sluices opened, the pontoons groaned and we fell into shadow. We sank further still and, surrounded by dripping walls at the bottom, watched the friendly faces above us gradually disappear, bored with waiting for the lock to empty. Finally, the huge gates opened. We were expecting water but instead saw gulls walking on exposed mudbanks in the estuary. Not liking the look of the narrow channel in between the sand flats, we asked politely if we could come back in. The lock-keeper chuckled, closed the sluice gates, and the water lifted us slowly back into daylight.

Having a boat meant that we could visit the mid-Bristol Channel islands of Flat Holm and Steep Holm, which I'd seen all my life from the shore. We'd depart, full of hope, leaving the turquoise roof of Penarth pier behind us. We'd charge across the channel towards Somerset, sure that we were covering a lot of ground. Half an hour later we'd tack triumphantly, but, after an hour's sailing, we'd find that the tidal stream had pushed us back up the channel and that we were still dead level with Penarth. No matter in which direction we set off, we always seemed to end up in exactly the same spot. I thought we'd never get away from that pier.

Despite the difficulties of sailing in the Severn Estuary, I found that being on the water was slowly bringing me back to life. It was wonderful to go out on a winter's morning into the ugly but subtle brown waters of the Bristol Channel and just move in the open air. We'd look over to the Somerset and Devon coasts and know that, if they suddenly appeared much closer to us, rain was certainly on the way. The Severn brings down a huge amount of silt suspended in its waters.

This detritus is set down on Cefn-y-Wrach – the witch's back – a notorious bank just outside the entrance to Cardiff. Steep Holm island in mid-channel glowed red like Ayers Rock. The endlessly shifting light turned the waters lavender, pink and terracotta, as if they were full of minerals. Winter sun played a silver spotlight on distant water, turning the tide pewter.

It is alleged by some that Tiger Bay, the docks area in Cardiff, was given its name by Portuguese sailors who described sailing in the rough waters along the Severn Estuary as sailing in *uma bahia de tigres*, a bay of tigers. This is my preferred myth about the origin of the name because it makes me see the powerful feline muscles of the tide rippling under the feral waters, the exact colours of a semi-precious tiger's-eye stone.

In its heyday, Cardiff was the largest coal-exporting port in the world, fuelling the British Empire by stacking mountains of Welsh coal at strategic points all round the globe. It was even rumoured that Welsh coal was being burned in the *Titanic* the night she sank. In 1913, its peak year, Cardiff exported over 10.5 million tons of black energy. The first ever million-dollar cheque was raised on a consignment of Cardiff coal bought in 1905 by the American Navy. By 1910, forty-eight different countries had consular representatives in Cardiff, including the US, Russia, Argentina, Spain, Turkey, Sweden and Brazil. When Captain Scott left Cardiff in the same year for his final voyage to the Antarctic, he requested a large supply of patent fuel made in the city because it suited the extreme conditions he was to face. His men were to experience temperatures so low that their teeth cracked and the water in their eyes froze, but Cardiff coal blazed so brightly at that time that it literally burned on ice.

I have visited the docks regularly since I was a child because my father worked for the Port Health Authority. The soundtrack of my childhood was the clanking as miles of coal trucks were pulled down from the valleys to the docks by rail. If Cardiff exported to the rest of the world, it also imported the exotic into Wales. Once, on a school visit, warehousemen in a shed began to roll oranges at us across the floor, like sweet planets. I also remember one particular day in the early seventies when my father brought home a piece of fresh ginger root from a ship. We gathered round the strange vegetable, glad to be able to put a face to a spice's name, as it were, but we had no idea what to do with it. Eventually, the ginger was placed on a kitchen shelf until it shrivelled to look like the mummified member of an African monkey.

I had spent a lot of time in my childhood looking at ships passing in the Bristol Channel and longing to be on board one of them. Now, as an adult, I wanted to sail out of Cardiff and trace some of the trade routes that had spread Welsh coal around the world. I also wanted to see what had become of the romance of the sea in the twenty-first century, with its container ships, skeleton crews and roll-on roll-off freight.

Out sailing one day, Leighton and I passed Lavernock Point and reached Watchet in Somerset, where the channel starts to open out. We were both on deck and, for once, I was awake and not feeling sick. Our spirits lifted as we looked south-west into a larger sky. We gazed at the open horizon and were knocked breathless by the gust of freedom that it offered. Then we looked at one another and knew we'd been hit by the same urge to head for the high seas.

'Come on – let's go now. Let's just go!' I cried.

It was very hard having to point the boat's bows back towards Cardiff and acknowledge that we simply weren't ready. But that glimpse of the open sea had changed us. From then on we were determined to head westwards and out into the Atlantic.

My relationship with Leighton began in 1989 under difficult circumstances. We had met when I was twenty-nine, shortly after my life had fallen to pieces. Creeping depression and self-medication with alcohol had left me pretty much in a personal gutter. Leighton, who himself had given up drinking two and a half years earlier, played a huge part in my recuperation. At one point, when I would pace the streets of Cardiff at night suffering from alcohol withdrawal, he said an astonishing thing to me: 'If I could, I'd give my recovery to you. I know I can get well, but you're struggling.' I wasn't used to such selflessness in a relationship. Here was a man who was willing to give me his own health. Uncharacteristically for me, I had the sense to stick with him.

Twenty-three years older than me, Leighton is a loud and cheerful man, who looks much younger than he really is. He bears a strong resemblance to a happy Samuel Beckett, with his shock of white hair, long face and Afghan nose. He is immensely sociable, can cook and iron (like all good mariners), and knows how to skin a pheasant. Wherever we go, people warm to him instantly. I was invited to read at the Sydney Literature Festival in 1998 and Leighton came with me. Before a session on devolution at the City Hall with Colum McCann and Irvine Welsh, we went to talk to the Scotsman, who had turned up magnificently drunk. When I suggested a cup of coffee and some aspirin, Welsh said that

2   My Leighton

nothing short of the Betty Ford Clinic was going to help him. After we'd moved on he turned to the organiser of the festival and declared Leighton to be 'the coolest man in Australia, no, the whole world'.

Leighton and I were married in 1993. Aged fifteen, he had gone to sea from Cardiff, and had spent ten years in the merchant navy. At one point he was the youngest bosun to have sailed out of the Bristol Channel. When he came ashore and married his first wife, he worked first as a rigger in steel-works, and later as a roofer. He and his wife were ten-pound emigrants to Australia. He had dug for opals in the outback, and for copper in Iran before the fall of the Shah. He had worked as a salesman, had a diamond-drilling business (that is, drilling *with* diamonds, not *for* them) in Cardiff, before running his own cleaning company. At his lowest, he had washed dishes in the local Chinese restaurant for drink. Once he gave up alcohol, however, he was, unusually for a white man, trusted with money by the Chinese community and used to take a lorry back and forth to London twice a week to buy meat and fish from the city's markets.

Like Leighton, I had been brought up in Cardiff, but had a completely different background. Brought up Welsh-speaking, I was a poet and a swot. Before I sobered up, I'd spent years in further education both here and in America, before finally becoming a television producer at the BBC. But the sea had played its tricks on me as well. During the worst of my drinking, someone had told me that Scandinavian shipping lines recruited female communications officers. I instantly resolved to go to sea as a radio operator. Late at night, after a lot of Smirnoff Blue Label, I could just see myself in overalls, listening through headphones to other vessels reporting heavy weather in the North Sea. This pipe dream never survived my Herculean hangovers, but the seed was sown.

Ours was not an obvious marriage, but we were thrilled with one another, and continuously astonished at our mutual good luck in being together. Now we were about to undertake an adventure that would have been impossible for us individually. Had it not been for Leighton, I would never have had the courage even to attempt making my dream of going to sea a reality. As a former bosun with ten years' experience, he had a practical and invaluable knowledge of what was required at sea. He had never sailed before, but he knew what was safe to do and could read the weather extremely accurately.

It was harder to see what I had to offer on this adventure. Having a good job had enabled me to buy the boat for us, but I had no practical skills whatsoever. Not only that, I was cack-handed: any knots I tied instantly came undone, and I was soon black and blue from knocking myself against the unfamiliar boat. Temperamentally I was far from being an ideal crew member. I was opinionated, stubborn, used to being in charge of my own projects and always ready to argue with a given order. I was also still forgetful after the searing depression from which it had taken me eighteen months to recover. Some days I couldn't even remember which side of the boat was port and which starboard. I felt brain-damaged, either from the illness or the anti-depressant medication. Plus there was the seasickness. But, I told myself, the main thing was that I was there.

Leighton and I decided to educate ourselves as sailors. We went to night school, perching on high chairs in a technical-drawing classroom, and passed the Royal Yachting Association's Day Skipper Theory course. I went on to gain my Yachtmaster Theory qualification, so I could navigate, read charts and plan passages on paper, but hands-on sailing was another matter. On *Jameeleh* we tackled the Day Skipper Practical course with John Hart, a former coxswain of the Barry lifeboat and now a sailing instructor and examiner.

We decided to do the practical part of our ticket in early spring, when strong winds were still whipping up the Bristol Channel. The estuary looked as though it were composed of liquid rock strata, rippling under the wind. When the swell rolls in from the Atlantic and hits the shallows surrounding the British Isles, the energy in the waves disperses, making the water turbulent. In an estuary, the waves bounce off the shores and shallows to create a short, sharp chop. Add to this the movement of the tides and you have an unpredictable, uncomfortable sea, a nightmare for anybody who suffers from seasickness.

There's nothing like nausea for blotting out the rest of the world. We were out in mid-channel, heading for Portishead.

The others watched the beautiful paddle steamer, the *Waverley*, pass us on a run to Avonmouth. I was too busy being sick. This malaise wasn't confined to my stomach: I even felt it in the palms of my hands. The sickness was so overwhelming that I didn't know what to do with myself. I tried a stint at the helm, which is usually restorative. I looked at the horizon, very hard. Then I meditated, focusing on my breath.

I thought of Sir Henry Bessemer, whose process for manufacturing steel had helped transform the industrial landscape of South Wales, and who once designed a ship with an anti-seasickness saloon. The room was hung on gimbals so that its pitch could be adjusted to keep the room level in rough seas. This was to be done through hydraulics by an engineer dedicated to the task, and who took his cue for adjustments from a spirit level. The idea was tried out on a ship called the *Bessemer*, built in 1875, but a Channel crossing showed that the engineer, through no fault of his own, was always fractionally behind the waves in his corrections. This delay must have made susceptible passengers even more nauseous.

Back in the Bristol Channel I'd begun to lose interest in life. My internal gyroscope was so confused that even my vision was blurring. In between bouts of retching over the side I'd look disinterestedly at the rest of the crew, who were continuing to work the boat. At that moment I couldn't recall why on earth being out in a boat was a good idea. I was trapped on an infernal fair ride. Couldn't we call the emergency services?

I tried staying out in the cockpit but became freezing cold. Stoically, I decided to go below, and lowered myself gingerly on to our forepeak bunk. I could move so little that I didn't even take down the hood of my red and lime-green waterproof coat, so I lay down still fully dressed, heavy-weather trousers and all. Soon I was sweating as well as feeling seasick.

I couldn't have picked a worse place to rest. A boat's pivot, its most stable point, is usually behind its mast, but the forepeak – in the bows of the boat, where I was lying – moves more than any other place on board. The short Bristol Channel chop made the boat see-saw up and down violently. I felt as though I were being tossed in a blanket.

Nearly demented now with nausea, I began to plot my escape from the boat. It seemed to me entirely reasonable that Leighton should stop a passing freighter and get me transferred from this fairground ride, or at least bring *Jameeleh* close enough to a rock so that I could step off. I no longer knew which way was up, and I certainly didn't care what happened to the boat. I was sure I could make my own way back from Porlock to Cardiff if they gave me some cash – anything as long as this horrible motion stopped.

Suddenly I knew for sure that I was going to be sick again. But in what? I cast my mind frantically around the forepeak. The bathroom sink? Too far. The heads? The same. I could feel it coming. The only remotely vomit-tight thing I could find was my shower cap. Happily, this didn't have any holes in it but, alas, it wasn't big enough. Leighton manfully carried the sloshing cap out of the saloon and threw it, a steaming orange jellyfish, into the Bristol Channel.

Later, when we had anchored in Porlock Bay behind a headland and the water was sufficiently calm for me to gather my wits, I had a chat with our instructor about how I was doing.

'John, tell me: am I going to fail?'

I blinked at the withies – branches stuck into the mud by local sailors to mark the channel into Porlock.

'Well,' said John gently, 'it's difficult to be skipper if you're being sick all the time.'

Still smelling of vomit, I cried with frustration.

Of course I failed. I was bitterly disappointed that I couldn't do in practice what I knew backwards on paper. Seasickness came between me and even seeing straight, so I didn't know how I was going to be fit enough to do anything more than lean precariously over the side, losing weight.

On the way back to Cardiff the wind died down and we sailed on a different, smoother point of sail. Although my stomach muscles were still aching from vomiting, I no longer felt sick and so sat, breathing deeply on deck, euphoric with relief. This was my first night sail and I found it ravishing.

As we approached Penarth again I saw a shooting star and made a wish.

Even before I had set foot on a boat, I had been fascinated by the idea of seamanship. When I was a child I liked looking at a photograph of my father as a young sailor. He had volunteered for the navy when he was eighteen and, after a year as a seaman, had trained to become a radar mechanic. He subsequently became a petty officer. He was posted out to the Far East and one of the highlights of his Second World War was being responsible for a slave transmitting station on one of the Admiralty Islands. Such transmitters were operated remotely but their frequencies had to be altered manually before they could relay messages from central HQ. The station was reached by a path through the forest and the sailors had been warned never to leave the track, as it might be impossible to find it again. Men had been lost, even though those who were searching for them could hear their voices in the vegetation. One night my father was on duty and, on his way in the tropical moonlight, he became convinced that his eyes were playing tricks on him. The path looked as if it were seething. He peered closer. In front of him a stream of land crabs stretched for twenty yards. They were the size of dinner plates and had vicious claws. My father was wearing only thin plimsolls. Then the thought of Winston Churchill relying on him to establish the correct frequency, so that he could consult with President Roosevelt, galvanised the young Welshman. He plucked up his courage and sprinted through the heaving crabs.

Over centuries, the tradition of seamanship has developed to enable sailors to pass safely through huge force fields of wind, tide and weather. I too wanted to learn how to use external weather systems to travel long distances. Part of a seaman's knowledge has always been how to deal with the internal hazards of fear, panic and carelessness. This, I thought, might help me to move further away from the depression I'd suffered at home. Not in the sense of escaping it, which is impossible, but by learning new ways of navigating emotionally. My old patterns had let me down badly, so I was searching for alternative principles of travel that would both show me different landscapes and get Leighton and me to our destinations safely. It's no accident that, in *The Anatomy of Melancholy*, Robert Burton suggests that one cure for depression is 'at seasonable times to be seasick'. If nausea was the cost of letting go of my fixed ideas and moving on, then I was ready to feel sick for as long as it took.

The British public was transfixed a few years ago by the case of Eric Abbott in his twenty-five-foot yacht *Plus VAT*.

3 Gwilym Lewis, Petty Officer Radar Mechanic, 1946

Abbott had spent eighteen years building his boat but had neglected to learn anything about navigation or seamanship. He decided he would make his way using a road atlas, the *Daily Telegraph* map of Europe and an Ordnance Survey map of the Mountains of Mourne. In 1999, he was rescued three times by the lifeboat services on his way from Liverpool to Abergele in North Wales. The coastguard log notes that 'the owner appeared to lack any ability whatsoever'. Undaunted by his incompetence, Abbott set sail the following year from Anglesey to the Isle of Man which he couldn't find. This trip required five lifeboat rescues in all. Still not put off, he set sail (if that's the term) for Strangford Lough, equipped with only a Second World War chart of the area and a compass, which he didn't know how to use. He reported to the Belfast coastguard that he could see what looked like mountains, but that he had no idea where he was. Here was a man who went to sea but refused to let go of the landmarks by which he was used to making his way in the world. After little more than a year sailing, Abbot was estimated to have cost the rescue services £30,000.

If ever an object was designed to test the distance between fantasy and reality, a small boat is it. Clearly, our voyage was not going to be an athletic venture of any note. What interested and excited me was the journey into the state of mind that sailing induces in a good sailor. I had a hunch that this was a place where one might become teachable and able to break out of the compulsive maps of old behaviour that had led me to shipwreck time and again.

Leighton and I barely made up one moderate sailor between us: a dyslexic pensioner and an innumerate poet. But we were willing to learn and to try out new ways of travelling. As Leighton said to me, 'This could be the best thing we ever did. But it could also kill us.'

It was a tremendous gamble but, in the end, we just went.

For our first voyage alone, Leighton could have chosen an easy sunny run to Ilfracombe or Swansea, but, no, he wanted to do a night sail up the channel to Bristol. In this, we were unconsciously mimicking the earliest trade routes from Cardiff up the Severn and into the River Avon. Between 1882 and 1912 the Marquis of Bute and his successors ran the Cardiff & Bristol Steam Ship Company, a twice-weekly steamer service between the two cities. This carried passengers, cargo and livestock. Records show that a cargo of elephants was once transported this way.

After the fiasco of the Day Skipper course, I was taking no chances with seasickness. The chemist sold me Stugeron, a popular anti-motion-sickness medication, so, just before we left the house, I took the suggested dose. We prepared the boat and did our passage plan, working out the bearings and distances, the influence of the tide on our course, and making sure that we stayed in water deep enough for our keel. We checked the weather forecast for any gale warnings, made a list of the buoys we would pass, noting their light characteristics so that we could recognise them in the dark, and looked up the lock times at Bristol. Only after checking our projected courses on the GPS plotter was it safe to go.

As we made these preparations I was aware of feeling rather tired. Under the pressure of leaving, Leighton was becoming hyperactive but all I wanted to do was sleep.

Drowsiness is one of the noted side effects of the medication but my desire to crash out became irresistible. Leighton found me collapsed on the saloon couch. When it was time to go he woke me with difficulty. Even upright, I was stupid with sleep.

'Let go for'ard!' said Leighton brightly.

I looked at the rope. I knew I'd done this all before but I couldn't for the life of me work out how to free the rope from its cleat. I took some deep breaths and fumbled in slow motion with the figure-of-eight knots. With a supreme intellectual effort I managed to untie the lines and we were under way.

We had plotted our route to Bristol from the North Cardiff buoy, which marks the top of the Cefn-y-Wrach shoal. I was in charge of buoys. I don't know what happened but I missed the first one and, as a result, nearly took us into Newport – completely the wrong direction. I swore that someone had moved the buoy, but it must have been my Stugeron-induced confusion. As it grew dark, though, we found the South Mid Grounds buoy and rejoined our original passage plan. I vowed I'd never take Stugeron again, unless I was suffering from insomnia. On a two-handed sailing boat, seasickness pills were clearly a recipe for double suicide.

Leighton was in his element, which was just as well because I was still spaced out. His years at sea gave him confidence in interpreting the lights we saw: that one was a ship going away from us, that red another going out to sea, well out of our way. Being out on the water in the dark, especially in my state, was like entering a subatomic world. We saw the lights of vessels on different courses and heard conversations from unseen bridges. A ship called the *State of Manipoor* made arrangements to take a pilot on board. Behind us, a yacht, the *Cruise Missile*, was trying to book a lock into Bristol but would, by our calculations, be too late on the tide.

At night you have to adjust your vision and employ a different mental filter from the one that you normally use to exclude irrelevant information from your brain. Sea marks are very difficult to see against the light pollution on shore. Car headlights behind a long avenue of trees can look like a flashing buoy, but you follow that guide at your peril. The driver reaches a roundabout and turns for home. What you thought was a reliable mark is exposed as an illusion, leaving you lost in relation to the shallows you know lie somewhere ahead. At sea you have to know that appearances can deceive and that, sailing at night, the difference between how things *look* and how they actually *are* can cost you your life.

We made good speed on the rising tide. As we approached the port of Avonmouth, we started to look for the entrance to the River Avon. This was a single red light, hidden among a polka-dot collection of street lights, houses, road illuminations and we didn't know what else. I had begun to wake up a bit in the cold air and thought I could see the port light. Leighton couldn't, so I tried to describe its location to him.

'See those harbour lights there on the left? Come over to your right and past that big black hole . . .'

'Big black hole?' said Leighton dreamily.

Then, a moment later, as if dredging something from deep in his memory, he cried, 'Shit! That's no big black hole, that's a bloody great ship between us and the land! The red is its port light! It's coming straight at us! Turn to starboard, quick!'

At that moment we heard someone on the VHF radio, calling the 'small yacht on my port side'. That was us. A supremely cool and polite voice enquired would we like to pass port to port? We would, yes, thank you; we would like to do that very much. We sat in silence as the 100,000-ton tanker passed on our port side, like a moving fortress, its powerful engines chilling us with their discreet roar.

This experience shook us, and made us keep a doubly sharp lookout from then on. 'At sea,' John Hart had told us, 'trust your eyes more than anything else.' Another sailor told us how he'd once sailed into Gosport at night, only to find that there was nothing but blackness where he'd expected to see the city's lights. He checked and rechecked his position on his charts and still couldn't understand what he was seeing. At a loss for an explanation the sailor had to conclude that Gosport had simply disappeared from the face of the earth. He even wondered about a nuclear strike. He wasn't right in his conclusion, but he wasn't wrong either. What he'd seen was a flotilla of Royal Navy ships anchored outside Gosport. As part of an exercise they had switched off their navigation lights, so they completely blocked the usual view of the illuminated town. As the tide turned, all the vessels swung in unison on their anchors, revealing Gosport, all safe and sound, in the gaps between the blacked-out ships. At sea, it's easy to see the story you expect, but the truth might be very different.

Shocked by our encounter with the bulk carrier, we lost our way completely in the Avonmouth lights. Not proud, I called Avonmouth Radio on the VHF to ask for advice.

'Wait a minute, I'll put the strobe light on. Keep that ten metres to your port side and you should be fine.'

And, indeed, like a parent putting on the landing lights so that you don't trip in the dark, we saw our own personal discotheque marking the entrance into the River Avon.

We passed under the Clifton Suspension Bridge at midnight, just making it into the last Bristol lock. We found that we'd managed to lose all the fresh water from our tank but the lock-keeper kindly filled a celebratory kettle for us. We were so excited to have completed our first passage that neither of us – seasickness pills or not – could fall asleep till after four in the morning.

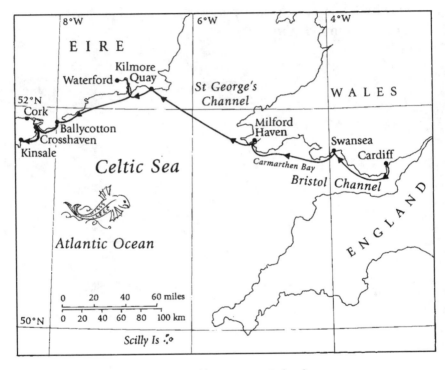

4   *Jameeleh*'s voyage to Ireland

CHAPTER TWO

A Bosun's Chimp

Before setting off for distant waters, Leighton and I decided that we should undertake a shakedown voyage. This would enable us to iron out any problems with the boat and see if we could live together on *Jameeleh*. From Wales, the obvious destination was Ireland.

Things started badly.

'Gwyneth! Grab that rope!' Leighton screamed at me.

I turned. 'I'm not sure I like your tone of voice,' I countered, haughtily.

The scene that followed the crash was ugly. I watched, horrified, as Leighton – my sweet, funny Leighton – turned into a monster. 'When I say jump, I don't mean maybe. You've just got to *do* it.'

In my imaginary navy, chirpy and precise orders were given with a pleasant note of authority to which I would have been happy to reply, 'Aye aye, skipper!' What had happened to 'please' and teamwork? Couldn't he see I was doing my best? The shock of Leighton's rage made me start crying.

'Your people skills are terrible,' I said with as much dignity as I could muster, and turned my Now You've Really Upset Me back on him.

In Penarth lock the morning we left, there were three boats,

5   Leaving Penarth Marina

each with a married couple on board. I was sulking on deck, fiddling with ropes that I couldn't even tie, fuming with Leighton for being so unnecessarily nasty to me. I looked round the lock and was astonished to see this scene repeated on every single boat. The husbands were muttering angrily to themselves and the wives, furious, were as far away as it was physically possible to be on a small pleasure boat. The atmosphere was dreadful. We all tried to keep our voices down, but nobody could hide what was going on.

Later, Leighton and I tried to be adult and talk it through. I had been studying the *Manual of Seamanship* which my father had been given in 1938 when he joined the Royal Navy. I read out a section entitled 'Method of Giving Orders':

It will generally be found that an order will be carried out in the same way as it is given. For this reason, orders to be obeyed sharply should be given sharply, and this will be emphasised if orders not to be obeyed sharply are slightly drawled. As an example take the case of hoisting a boat. The first order is 'Haul taut singly' followed by 'Marry', both orders should be given sharply . . . 'Ease to the life lines' can be drawled. 'Light to', the final order, should again be given sharply.

Now here was a method, I said to Leighton. How could I know what he wanted me to do when he was just screaming something about a rope at me? If he was to be skipper, he needed to learn how to speak to his crew.

'There are no bad crews, only bad skippers,' I added, pushing my luck.

Leighton, faced with the full might of Royal Navy culture, paused but came back: 'Is there a section about how to *take* orders in your book?'

Many wives refuse, with good reason, to have anything to do with boats. I was intrigued by why this should be. In his hilarious, if dated, book, *The Artless Yachtsman*, written in 1964, John Davies suggests that the type of woman who happily goes sailing with her husband is

very rare indeed, since the woman in question needs to have certain attributes which are completely foreign to the basic feminine make-up. She needs, specifically, to have a liking for active physical adventure and a natural love of the sea, plus at least a willingness to endure completely unnecessary dangers and discomforts. Women, being sensible creatures, do not often possess these qualities.

Six years later, Joyce Sleightholme asserted in *The Sea Wife's Handbook* that 'a knowledgeable woman on board a short-handed cruiser is as great a safety factor as a set of life jackets'. This was the writer who also thought that hair care should be a high priority for a seagoing wife, 'because no matter how long a woman spends on her face, if her hair is a mess she can do very little about it afloat – and she knows it'. Mrs Sleightholme's advice includes the truism that 'the uses of aluminium foil are endless', and continues, 'the woman who owns a hair-piece and is practised at fixing it herself is way ahead when it comes to ringing the changes for that important visit ashore. However, I would never advocate taking a wig – there isn't room on board the small sailing cruiser for items like this.'

A recent survey of cruising boats reported that the fewest problems were experienced aboard boats sailed by married couples or families. A marriage on a boat can be only as good as it is on land. The sea is a medium that puts constant pressure on a vessel, ruthlessly exposing any structural defects, careless stowing of goods or negligence on the part of its crew. This is even more true for any couple sailing together. Indeed, boats act as catalysts for any resentments or general pettiness sloshing about in a relationship. Under the pressure of bad weather, seasickness and lack of space, small disagreements can easily blow up into serious disputes.

A marriage is, after all, very like a boat. It has to be structurally sound before you can expect it to take you any distance in life. Both marriage and boat need constant attention if they are to remain seaworthy. Small problems ignored can grow into large, life-threatening hazards. Mistakes on a boat can be very expensive, for there are no such things as bargain boats; as world-famous yachtsman Bernard Moitessier wrote, they 'cost you everything you possess, and then some more'.

And yet, when things go well, a boat will allow you to see the world from a stunning new perspective. In order to trust ourselves and our marriage to the sea, Leighton and I would each have to place our life in the hands of the other. By leaving everything that was familiar – even the solid land under our feet – we were testing our own limits. We both knew from the past that we had pretty long tethers, but we wondered how much stretch the experiences of alcoholism and depression had left in them. The main engine of our journey was going to be our marriage and we were hoping for a joyous, exhilarating ride.

Over the years, Leighton and I had come through a good deal of emotional bad weather together and so thought of ourselves as being very close. On board *Jameeleh*, however, this counted for little, because sailing called for us to play entirely unfamiliar roles. While I'd been working on a book, Leighton had spent months labouring over his own work of art, *Jameeleh*, getting her ready for us to sail. He knew how everything worked, whereas I knew very little, and coming on board, finally, to do a proper voyage, I felt like a gooseberry. The balance of power had changed in our marriage and we were now living in a *ménage à trois* – Leighton, me and a Nicholson 35.

Jameeleh (pronounced Ja-*mee*-luh, not Jamie Lee) is Arabic for 'lovely lady'. Her second owner had taken her out to the Gulf, where she had been given her Arabic name. She is a Nicholson 35, 'unquestionably one of the all-time classic cruising designs', according to *Yachting Monthly*. Our Nic was number thirty-seven out of a production run of 228 boats, whose moulds have since been destroyed. We discovered that we had bought into an illustrious line of boat owners, stretching back to 1782, when Camper & Nicholsons had begun making yachts for the rich. When the Prince of Wales, who later became King Edward VII, began to race boats in the Solent in 1876, he did so in *Hildegarde*, a schooner built by Ben Nicholson. Later, Charles Nicholson designed the world-famous *Shamrock IV* and *Shamrock V* for the America's Cup challenger Sir Thomas Lipton. Because the company was so closely involved in yacht racing, Camper & Nicholsons's yard was at the cutting edge of sailing technology and this was reflected in the quality of their boats.

The customers for these yachts were, of course, fabulously rich. One of Camper & Nicholsons's customers was Prince Ibrahim, uncle to King Farouk of Egypt, who commissioned a cruising ketch, *Rakkassa*, in 1959. Prince Ibrahim had a distinguished stomach, which he liked to rest on top of a boat's bulwarks (a ship's side above deck). When he asked for bulwarks to be made high enough for him to do this, the designer told him that this would reduce the performance of the yacht. The Prince replied, 'No bulwarks, no order.' The Camper & Nicholsons joiners had to measure the exact height of the Prince's belly and include it as part of their design so that the Prince could look out at the sea in perfect comfort.

After the Second World War, Camper & Nicholsons became interested in the new sport of offshore yacht racing, which involved solitary sailors travelling long distances in small boats. (This was before the days of satellite beacons and dramatic rescues. Racers were expected to take full responsibility for their own lives. Indeed, it was stipulated in the early race rules that 'any skipper who is unable to remain alive by his own efforts is expected to die with dignity'.) In the mid-sixties, GRP, or fibreglass, became popular as a material for boats, being much less labour-intensive and easier to maintain than the traditional wood. Camper & Nicholsons launched their own line of fibreglass sailing yachts in 1961.

The Nicholson 35 is known not as a racer but as a superb heavy-weather boat. A longish encapsulated lead fin keel makes the design stable. The boat's designer, Raymond Wall, recalled in a letter to me that she was designed as a 'cruising yacht suitable for a couple to take two guests or their family'. The Nic 35 is known as a 20/20 boat because she can sail under full canvas in twenty knots of wind and at an angle of less than twenty degrees. Her only vice is going astern, which, as *Yachting Monthly* noted tactfully, 'is best reserved for relatively wide open spaces'. We found that the best policy was to let the boat go where she wanted and then to look as if that was what we had intended all along.

The Nicholson 35s were all moulded under Lloyd's supervision, meaning that inspectors paid several visits to ensure that the processes were up to Lloyd's standard. We knew this because the man we employed to survey the boat had inspected her when she was built and still had the records. One of the reasons why the small Nicholson yachts were discontinued in the 1980s was that the high spec demanded by the series had priced them out of the market. For example, the early Nicholsons had fibreglass hulls that were, in places, over an inch thick. Today, on new boats, the fibreglass is often so thin that you can see water through the hull. *Jameeleh* had been fitted with two non-standard features: a teak deck and a bow thruster. The last, which is a propeller to move

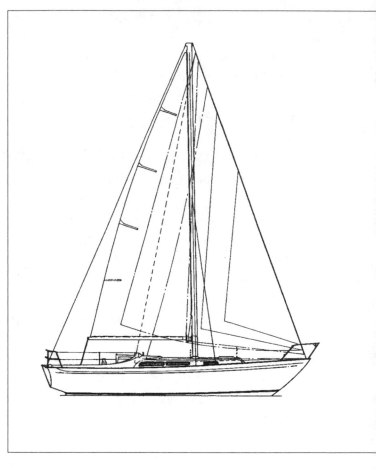

6   Plan of Nicholson 35 yacht

the bows of the boat to port or starboard, is invaluable in tight berthing situations or in the stimulating process of going astern in a Nic 35. Although we were buying a vessel that was thirty years old, we were getting a lot of boat for my redundancy money. We felt like two bums who had landed a Rolls-Royce.

Jameeleh began teaching us seamanship as soon as we took

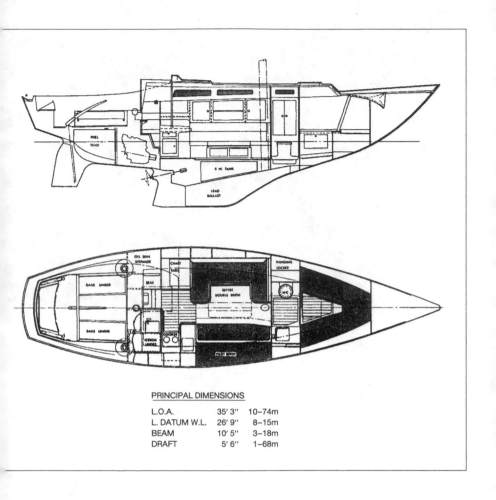

PRINCIPAL DIMENSIONS

L.O.A.	35' 3"	10–74m
L. DATUM W.L.	26' 9"	8–15m
BEAM	10' 5"	3–18m
DRAFT	5' 6"	1–68m

possession of her. When we bought her, she was moored on the Beaulieu River at Buckler's Hard, where Nelson's ship *Agamemnon* was built. Richard, a charming gentleman who helped out at the brokerage, said he would give us a hand to bring *Jameeleh* from her mooring to the quay.

Richard had clearly done a great deal of sailing and he loved the boat, so we gradually relaxed as we motored upriver

7   *Jameeleh* on the hard

in the unfamiliar cockpit. As he prepared *Jameeleh* for docking, Richard did a small thing that made me think hard about
the tradition of British seamanship. When approaching land,
fenders, or heavy plastic balloons, are put out as buffers
between the boat's hull and the dock. We were still a good
way from the quay when Richard tied all the fender ropes
ready on to the stanchions, but kept the fenders themselves
inboard. This, he explained, was so that the boat should look
neat and tidy. He would 'pop them out at the last moment',
if that was all right with us.

Leighton and I looked at one another, speechless. We
would never have thought of making such a distinction
between fenders out and fenders in. Until then we had been
so preoccupied with simply not wrecking any boat we sailed

that we had given no thought to how we or she might seem to others.

At sea, however, a boat can always be judged by her appearance. If you and your vessel don't look good, you're not likely to be a skilful sailor. In this, details like fenders matter. Steaming along in open waters with long plastic balls hanging by ropes over the side not only looks messy but involves the risk of losing fenders in the chop. It spoils the hydrodynamics of your boat, slowing her down and marking you out as a landlubber. 'Popping them out' calmly at the last moment of an approach is a necessary compromise between the elegance and caution required of a true sailor.

This was our first small but important lesson in seamanship, and Richard had given me a glimpse of a nation of seamen. The sea is a vast country that cuts across all nation states, and whose citizens earn their residence papers by serving their chosen vessels. I was desperate to join this group of calm, competent sailors who know how to turn themselves out smartly on a world that just won't stop moving.

We spent one night in Swansea and left the following morning for Milford Haven, our jumping-off point for Ireland. Leaving Swansea at 7 a.m., we motored along in oily water, both dressed optimistically in shorts and T-shirts, as there wasn't enough wind to sail. We passed shoals of kitsch jellyfish patterned with pink rings. They propelled themselves along by vaginal contractions, moving like diaphanous orgasms. I sat and gazed at the limestone bays and inlets of the Gower Peninsula passing in front of me, from left to right –

Brandy Cove, Pwll Du, Three Cliffs, Oxwich Bay, Paviland with its crazy folded strata and cave and then, finally, the Worm rearing its fine head at Rhossili. Having walked the Gower for twenty years, it was thrilling to see such a loved landscape from a new angle. Rather than looking from the inside out to the sea, now I was on the outside looking in.

By the time we hit the steely blue water of Carmarthen Bay, all our sails were up and pulling. The increase in wind speed had been so gradual that we hadn't really noticed, but the weather was changing. Soon we were wearing long trousers and sweaters. When we were level with Tenby we thought about putting in but the wind direction meant that we would have been exposed at anchor. Conditions grew increasingly lively and so we changed into heavy-weather gear and carried on. By the time we had reached St Govan's Head, we could no longer cope with the amount of canvas we had up, so we struggled to put one reef and then a second into the mainsail. It became clear that we were in for some very rough weather.

The wind-speed gauge was now showing speeds of forty knots, which is force eight on the Beaufort scale and technically classed as a gale. Occasionally, it was registering gusts of forty-five, meaning that we were experiencing force nine, a severe gale. Where had this come from? There had been no mention of anything but fine weather on the morning forecast. Leighton pulled down the sail and we motored. This was the wrong thing to do. We would have been much more stable had we put out a storm sail or part of the genoa, but we didn't know this at the time and so had to endure the waves throwing us about like a billiard ball on a newly-wed couple's bedspread.

I had never been out at sea in weather like this. The

horizon, which had been dead level as we left the Mumbles that morning, had developed alarming ridges. First, it looked as though giant egg boxes were coming towards us, then whole estates of houses. Everywhere I looked, I felt sure I could see land, but it was only more ranks of opaque, horribly substantial waves heading our way, it seemed, from all directions. My reaction to all this surprised me. There was no point in being afraid, or even in feeling downcast, because we were on our own and nobody was going to be able to help. It was as if Leighton and I were the sole inhabitants of a wayward planet bucking its course across the universe. *Jameeleh*'s orbit was erratic but she was our only solid land. I wrapped myself round a winch and held on for dear life.

And *Jameeleh* behaved magnificently. This was the first time we had felt the full force of her personality. In a marina she was indistinguishable from other boats, merely a platform on which you could eat and sleep. Out in rough water, however, she came alive. She met the challenge of the waves with aplomb, cutting through each one with ease and a smooth motion that made us laugh with delight. The seas off St Govan's Head came at us chaotically but, rather than banging into them, *Jameeleh* kicked up her heels and skipped over the most turbulent eddies. 'Ah,' she seemed to say, 'now you can see what I can do.' She was gracious in turmoil, a perfect lady in conditions that would have flustered a tugboat.

In my heightened state of alert, I had been seeing imaginary boats and lobster pots in all directions, but suddenly I saw a solid black mast coming at us out of nowhere.

'What on earth is that?' Leighton shouted in horror.

That turned out to be Crow Rock, an unlit hazard marked by a tall pole. We hadn't noticed its tiny dot on the chart because it was so small it didn't seem to matter. Out in a storm, it looked huge and threatening and could have wrecked us. I vowed to be more careful in the future.

By now Leighton had asked me to take the helm but I couldn't keep the boat to the angle he needed to make the entrance to Milford Haven.

'Just put her on a course that's comfortable,' he said.

After an age of washing-machine seas and driving rain, I heard Leighton shout with joy. He'd spotted the Milford Haven fairway buoy; we were going to be able to get in. At that moment I was gloriously sick.

It was bliss to come out of the weather and into the smoother waters of the Haven, even if it did pelt down with hail as we made our way up to Neyland. We passed a tanker called *Tarquin Pride of Panama*, and looked at one another with new respect. Leighton had been entirely competent in the unexpected gale and I had been calm and able to help. More importantly, we now had confidence in *Jameeleh*, who had coped beautifully with the psychotic seas.

Once we reached the marina, we showered, ate and tumble-dried our bedding, which had been soaked in the high seas. 'Leighton,' I asked, 'where exactly is the good time in this? We didn't have lunch, I've been freezing cold, soaked to the skin, I'm black and blue, and I've been sick.'

Leighton laughed. We couldn't have been happier.

Our course down the Bristol Channel had been followed by mariners since prehistoric times. I imagined their wakes like threads running from Cardiff across St George's Channel to Ireland: prehistoric metal traders, the Vikings bartering with

Welsh slaves, Normans exchanging agricultural goods for tanned leather, honey and tar. Later, ships from the Continent brought raisins, wine and exotic oranges and lemons. Nowadays, the vessels moving like metal filings up and down the Bristol Channel are car carriers and small oil tankers. Cardiff now imports orange concentrate in bulk and has a profitable trade in cat litter – a good cargo, provided it doesn't get wet in the hold.

We left Milford Haven for Ireland after fog lifted on a windless July day, with nothing on board to trade but ourselves. Leighton was rapidly becoming a confident skipper. The bad news was that, because of my seasickness, he also had to be the crew.

I sat rigidly on deck, trying to hold my head steady. Going below to boil a kettle or use the heads was out of the question, as it immediately made me ill. All I could usefully do was keep a good lookout on deck and try my best not to be sick. The moment we left the sight of land I cried, 'Look, Leighton! No walls, all floor!' as I looked queasily at the gently heaving, sprung dance floor of the sea.

In a moment of despondency, I told Leighton how badly I felt about being so inactive. I hated being a passenger, but I didn't yet have the energy or the skills to play a larger part than that of witness. He tried to comfort me. 'Don't worry, you're the crew comfort. Just your being here is enough.' But it wasn't enough for me. Leighton had just appointed a depressive as his morale-raiser. Poor man.

Nevertheless, we crossed St George's Channel without incident and made it comfortably into the tiny harbour at Kilmore Quay before dark, edging past trawlers with their crayfish tentacles. Leighton was jubilant. We had completed our first international passage safely. We walked around grinning.

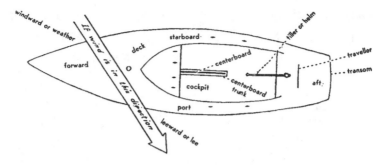

8 Plan of a small half-decked boat

'Admit it, it's killing you, isn't it? I did really well!' he laughed at me.

I had to concede that he had been an exemplary skipper all day. Having to do everything, however, had left him exhausted. He was so tired that he couldn't even flex his muscles to pee. 'It'll have to drip out,' he said happily, before crashing asleep.

If the sea was a new country to which I aspired, learning to sail a boat and living on her was a culture shock to me. Boats, like churches, all possess the same basic layout: the port side is her left as you look towards the bows at the front, starboard her right. Port and starboard are therefore directions only in relation to the boat and not to you.

This is typical of boats, which have a whole language of their own. Before being able to understand even the most basic instructions, I had to learn to speak Sea. Initially, it took a real effort to remember that a boat never goes *backwards*, but *astern*; that the back of a boat is always *aft*; and that a yacht doesn't have *walls* but *bulkheads*. I'm sure that one of the reasons why new sailors are so prone to tantrums is that their lack of language to describe their new world takes them back to the inarticulate rages of childhood. I was, however, very good at sitting on deck and greeting other boats, looking like someone who sailed. I liked the waving in particular, as it implied that I was a part of the special camaraderie of the sea.

My father is a devotee of C.S. Forester's maritime novels and so, over the years, I've read every single one of his hero Hornblower's adventures during the Napoleonic wars. My father is also a stickler for nautical accuracy and, in his copies of the novels, technical terms are annotated in full. It was reading the Hornblower novels that introduced me to my favourite maritime word ever: 'futtock'. The futtock shrouds (derived from 'foothook') are the short chains or hemp lines that support the top on a lower mast (see Figure 9). To climb the futtock shrouds a sailor has to hang backwards and outwards away from the mast. He could, of course, go through the lubber's hole and avoid this snag, but Hornblower would rather die than commit such an unseamanlike act in front of his crew. In a light moment, Leighton and I decided that it would be awful to get your buttocks tangled in the futtocks, but worse still to get your bollocks caught in the 'rollocks' (rowlocks).

When we first met, I used to call Leighton the Ancient Mariner, because he had never recovered from the ten years he'd spent at sea in his youth. He had originally gone to sea in 1951 and his first job was apprentice deck officer on a ship called the *Avon Venturer*, though he later worked on deck. She was an oil tanker on charter to Shell and, although British, she was crewed mainly by German sailors. If ever you need to know which are the poorest nations in the world at any given time, look at the nationalities of merchant seamen. Today's ships' crews, for instance, are often made up of Filipino, Indian or Eastern European sailors. Jobs were scarce in

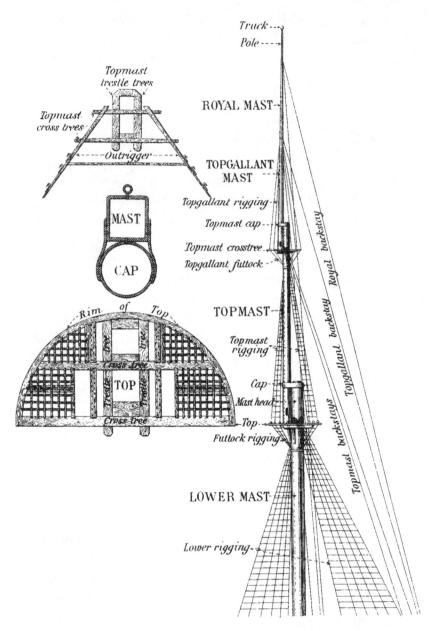

9 Masts and equipment

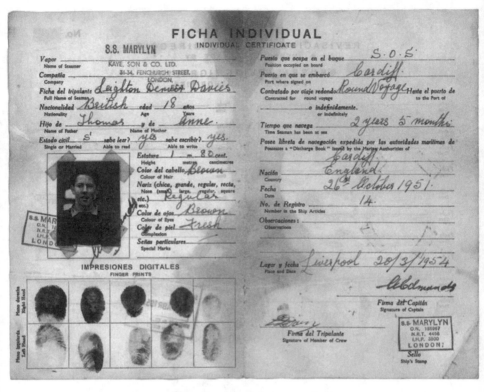

10   Leighton's shore papers in Argentina, 1954

Germany after the war, so labour was cheap, and Leighton even saw men fighting on the quays for work. He joined the *Avon Venturer* in Hamburg and, to this day, speaks fluent Plattdeutsch, the vigorous Hamburg dialect distinct from the more refined Hochdeutsch, or High German.

Hamburg came as a shock to a fifteen-year-old boy fresh from his mother's apron strings. At the first opportunity his fellow sailors took Leighton out on the town and spent his money for him, showing him the sights. He remembers in particular the way prostitutes in the Reeperbahn, St Pauli, had price tags stuck on the soles of their shoes.

It was another incident, however, that stuck most forcibly about his initiation into adult life in port. A big ship, rumoured to be the *Altmark*, moored alongside the *Avon Venturer*. In 1940 the *Altmark* had been seized by the destroyer *Cossack* in a daring raid on the Norwegian coast, thus saving a large number of captured British seamen. The freighter, now manned by Americans, towered over the tanker. Leighton looked up and could see the American bosun looking down at the British deck. By his side was a smaller figure, with a hat set at a jaunty angle and a belt. It was a monkey – the bosun's chimp. Whenever the officer gave orders, the chimp would imitate him, mimicking his gestures and expressions. He even stuck his thumbs in his diminutive belt and swaggered along the deck with all his master's authority.

In my low moments, I felt that I was no more than this chimp, a fraud pretending to be a sailor but able, in fact, to do little but imitate a real seaman. I commented on this when we were in the middle of St George's Channel. There we sat, in between sea and sky, with nothing but ourselves in sight.

Never one to pull his punches, Leighton paused and said, 'Must be difficult out here for you, Gwyneth. You can't even wave to other boats.'

It wasn't long, however, before *Jameeleh* showed us both up for the chimps we were. Triumphant at having crossed St George's Channel, we headed west. There's little room for visiting yachts in Ballycotton's tiny harbour, so six moorings

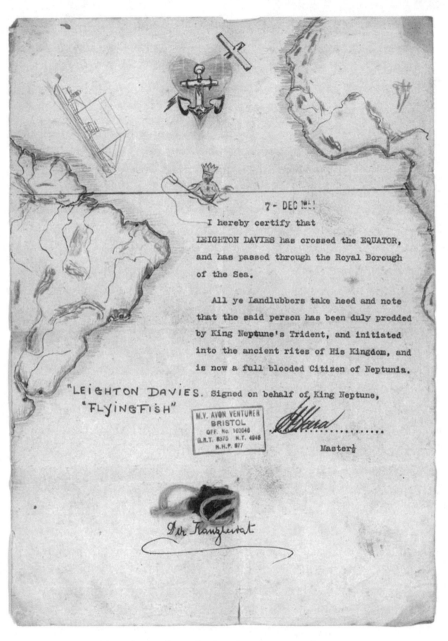

7 - DEC 1951

I hereby certify that
LEIGHTON DAVIES has crossed the EQUATOR,
and has passed through the Royal Borough
of the Sea.

All ye Landlubbers take heed and note
that the said person has been duly prodded
by King Neptune's Trident, and initiated
into the ancient rites of His Kingdom, and
is now a full blooded Citizen of Neptunia.

"LEIGHTON DAVIES. Signed on behalf of King Neptune,
"FLYINGFISH"

M.V. AVON VENTURER
BRISTOL
OFF. No. 162046
G.R.T. 8375   N.T. 4945
R.H.P. 577

Master½

11   Leighton's certificate for his first crossing of the Equator

had been provided outside the quay wall, funded by the EU. In the swell they looked like luminous yellow nipples on a bitch's chest. We'd never picked up this type of mooring before but assumed that it would be easy, especially as there was already a Dutch yacht tied up to one of them. Each mooring consisted of a heavy drum with a large metal eye on top, and they all trailed long ribbons of seaweed, so that they looked like very solid jellyfish. I was sent to for'ard with a boat-hook.

After a few passes I found that I was completely unable to attach a rope to the buoy. Usually a mooring has a smaller ball floating alongside it, enabling you to pick up the thin mooring line easily and attach it to your bow. Then you can pull in the thicker rope and make the boat fast properly. These buoys had no small buoy, no rope, no chain, nothing that you could lift. Whenever I did manage to get the boat-hook into the eye, I couldn't reach it to thread the rope through, nor could I lift the buoy because it weighed a ton. We learned later that there was no rope for you to pick up because this limited the EU's insurance liabilities. The EU might well have provided a mooring but you were to supply the rope with which to hang yourself.

The blue boat-hook I had been using broke. I flung it into the cockpit in disgust. Cursing me, Leighton said, 'Here, let me do it,' so we swapped ends. I wasn't entirely displeased when he promptly left the black boathook in the eye of the mooring he was hunting, like a matador's sword flopping in the back of a bull.

A few people settled down to watch us from the shore. We tried to ignore them and look professional. As we passed the Dutch boat, we asked the sailor on board, 'What's the secret?' The desperation in our voices was clear, and he replied:

'Slowly, slowly. Let the wind take you to it.' Then he confessed, 'I have a special instrument.' We pondered this new information, but before we could beg him to lend it to us, the bastard disappeared below.

By now we'd attracted a small crowd on the Ballycotton quay wall. We were becoming hot and sweaty and extremely flustered. This should be child's play; instead, it was turning into a nightmare version of Jeux Sans Frontières. We were aware of having become the evening entertainment and, in an attempt not to scream, took to hissing at one another.

Once more I brought the boat close in to one of those nipples. Leighton shouted that he had hold of it so I stopped the boat, ran for'ard and flung myself on top of him to help with the struggle. What I didn't realise was that he had nearly broken a rib against one of the stanchions and that he was choking on one of the wire handrails. My weight, added to his own, prevented him even from screaming.

'Don't worry!' I panted. 'I've got you!'

I heard a death rattle underneath me and moved, easing the pressure on Leighton's throat.

Then it all became a bit of a blur. Somehow Leighton managed to thread a thin rope through the mooring's eye but, in a slow-motion moment of horror, while I was meant to be holding the rope, I let it go. I can't explain what happened but we drifted slowly away from the precious buoy. It took me a few moments to gain the courage to tell Leighton what I'd done.

By now the strength had gone out of both of us. After another half-dozen passes with me on the helm and Leighton using even thinner rope, we finally harpooned our yellow Moby Dick. It had taken us an hour and twenty minutes to perform what should have been a perfectly straightforward manoeuvre. The crowd dispersed and went back to their lives in Ballycotton.

That night, a Danish yacht arrived and spent so long fighting with the mooring that it had to be helped on to the troublesome European teat by a local boat. We felt a totally unjustified smugness. I could just imagine the comments in the local harbour: 'Ballycotton Moorings: Two. Visiting Yachts: Nil.'

We may have been novices, but we were teachable. After our humiliation in Ballycotton we sailed to Crosshaven and made a special trip into Cork to visit a chandlery. There we bought a cunning device called a Jolly Hooker, which allows you miraculously to thread a rope through an eye without nearly killing yourself in the process. On our way back home from Kinsale at the end of the season, we made a special detour to Ballycotton in order to spear and kill the yellow mooring that had humiliated us.

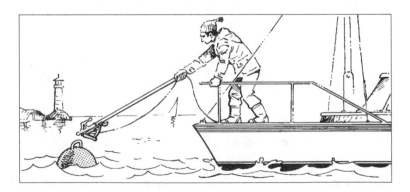

12   Jolly Hooker instruction pamphlet

With me on the helm and Leighton wielding his Jolly Hooker, we caught the bitch in one.

The girl in the Waterford Council Offices admitted that couples often arrived there having had a blazing row on the way up the River Suir. We were, ourselves, tight-lipped when we registered *Jameeleh* and paid for her mooring. There's a prefabricated row that lies in wait for inexperienced couples navigating their way up the river for the first time, and I know exactly where it is.

I was becoming tired of being no more than a passenger on *Jameeleh*, and so had gradually begun to do some of the navigating. Leighton, after all, couldn't be expected to do everything for ever and, as my seasickness started to subside on the trip, I was able to read the charts and pilot the boat into harbour.

Leighton, however, didn't trust me at all.

The city of Waterford is situated about fifteen miles up the River Suir, a spectacular estuary going north from the open sea. As we made our way past the Hook lighthouse, gannets were diving for fish. From the air they would locate their prey, fold their wings and plunge like daggers into the waves. The entrance to the river was challenging, as local fishermen had stretched their nets across the channel and any river traffic had to zigzag its way through the overlapping obstacles. Once past the car ferry, we had stopped shouting at each other in panic and had started to relax.

By now, I had become confident in my reading of the chart, and was ticking off every buoy we passed in the channel up to the city. One of the major features of the river is a large bend sweeping ninety degrees to the left before the cargo terminal. The chart showed me that we needed to keep well to the right at this bend, or we would go aground in shallows. At this exact point, however, Leighton's eye was caught by a series of small buoys that seemed to be telling us we should keep to the left. Looking up from the chart I explained quietly that on no account should we obey those buoys, as they led into a tiny harbour suitable only for shallow-draught boats. We should disregard them and keep well to the right.

Leighton ignored me and continued to steer the boat straight for the shallows. The water looked deep enough for us – in fact, it looked perfectly safe – but I knew from the pilotage book that we would hit bottom at any moment. I couldn't let our beautiful boat be ruined.

So I hit him. He still refused to change course, so I hit him again.

Later that week, in Waterford, we met a couple who had, in fact, gone aground at that point and done a lot of damage to their boat. Our behaviour hadn't been seamanlike but we had brought *Jameeleh* safely into Waterford and that was the bottom line.

The bosun's chimp had learned something, after all.

CHAPTER THREE

Kissing Hornblower

Getting Under Weigh Drill

1. Remove sail cover
2. Hank on headsail
3. Reeve the sheets
4. Check food and drink and stow securely
5. Water, fuel and gas bottle – check levels
6. Check weather forecast. Check navigational gear, instruments, charts and almanacs
7. Check battery charge level and level of electrolyte. Turn on battery switches and main panel switches
8. Turn on valves
   a) heads inlet
   b) heads outlet
   c) cooling water inlet
   d) exhaust outlet
9. Hoist burgee and ensign
10. Stow dinghy
11. Start engine

Nicholson 35 Owners Handbook

There is such a thing as seasickness on dry land. Leaving, like dying, has to be practised. Shedding our old lives was extremely disorientating and we suffered from emotional nausea until we became used to the motion.

When we first decided to live on the boat and do a long voyage, we thought we'd be sensible and take two years to prepare. After all, we were hoping to be away for four in all, and there were a lot of practical arrangements to make to ensure that the boat was safe and that we had everything we'd need for me to continue working while we were abroad.

Six months into this period of preparation, Leighton, for some reason, became very anxious. Things weren't moving quickly enough for him. He'd say to me, 'If we don't go soon, I'm sure that something will happen to mess it all up. I just know we're going to get stuck here, and I couldn't bear it if we didn't go.'

I tried to reassure him, but he feared that a door was closing for us and that we needed to slip through it while it was still ajar. Normally an optimist, Leighton felt a sense of doom in his bones, and because it was rare for him to be pessimistic, I took his intuition seriously. I made some changes to our financial plans and brought the voyage forward by a year. This meant that we would have a great deal to do in a short time, but we were determined to leave while the going was still good.

In order to be able to afford to live on the boat, we had to rent out our house. This meant a radical clear-up, making us, in effect, dispose of our goods before we'd died. This was an act of simplification, of shedding fantasies about ourselves. The image of myself as a potential gardener or gourmet cook had to go. We were narrowing down all of life's possibilities to one choice: living on a boat, where you need neither rose bowls nor three pestles and mortars. I filled forty-four boxes with books, and placed them, along with eight paintings and three bags of clothes, in a storage container. I became very popular at the local charity shops, where the voluntary ladies would thank me for the boxes of discarded clothes and kitchen equipment, but shake their heads in horror when they discovered where we were going. As we packed all our china into cartons for the container we were renting, we recalled how we had acquired each piece. *Desert Island Discs* was on the radio and, as we worked, we considered what we would take as our luxury item. Leighton said decisively, 'You.' I thought for a while and replied, 'I'd have to have you as a necessity. That's the difference between us.'

All this made me think of tombs in ancient societies where death was imagined mythically as a voyage to the underworld. In my mind's eye I saw the king laid in his lavish vessel, loaded with all the supplies and treasures needed on the last, most important, journey to death. On *our* boat, Leighton and I were mainly taking each other. We had very little storage room for clothes – mainly T-shirts and shorts and not much else. I stashed books in the lockers until *Jameeleh* sank so low in the water that Leighton made me promise to dispose of some of my library, as its weight was a safety hazard.

I found some guidance about what to take or, at least, the right attitude to possessions at sea, in the Royal Navy's *Manual of Seamanship* for 1937. In the navy 'a waterproof canvas bag will be issued to every boy on his leaving the training ship, with his name stamped on the bottom of the bag. He will retain the bag until it is worn out or until he leaves the service.'

I desperately wanted one of these bags, an institutionalised way of travelling light. My father had been issued with one

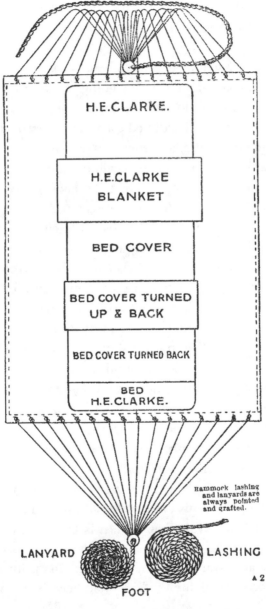

13   Diagram of a Royal Navy hammock

when he volunteered for the navy and he still had it in his garage. The *Manual of Seamanship* also had a diagram indicating how a sailor's bedding should be laid out for inspection. There was no room for hammocks on *Jameeleh* but I was entranced by the neatness and precision of the plan. I wanted to lay out my bed to be inspected every day, with my blankets marked in the correct place with my name. It would help establish where you stood in life – at least, in terms of your hammock.

I found more details about what a sailor would need at sea in a diagram showing the layout of the Royal Navy's compulsory kit. Astonishingly, the kit my father was issued in 1937 was virtually identical to that given to trainee boys at the end of the nineteenth century (see Figure 14). The major changes for 1937 sailors were that prayer books were no longer compulsory and 'blue jean collars' had made an appearance. Apart from that, life at sea had not changed for decades, and probably for much longer.

During our trip to Ireland, I had found in Kinsale Museum a poem written by an unknown English sailor in around 1850, advising young seamen what they would need to take to sea. I found it heartbreaking and deeply encouraging that men could make do with so little:

> A chest that is neither too big nor too small
> Is the first thing to which your attention I'll call
> The things to put in it are next to be named
> And if I omit some I'm not to be blamed.
>
> Stow first in the bottom a blanket or quilt
> To be used on the voyage whenever you wilt
> Thick trousers and shirts, woollen stockings and shoes
> Next your papers and books to tell you the news.

Good substantial tarpaulins to cover your head
Just to say keep it furled n.e. nuff said
Carry paper and ink, pens, wafers and wax
A shoemaker's last, awls and some small tacks,

Some cotton and thread, silk needles and palm
And a paper of pins as long as your arm
Two vests and a thimble, a large lot of matches
A lot of old clothes that will answer for patches.

A Bible and hymn book of course you must carry
If at the end of the voyage you expect to marry
Don't forget to take esseners, pipes and cigars,
Of the sweetest of butter a couple of jars.

A razor you will want, a pencil and slate
A comb and a hairbrush you will need for your pate
A brush and some shaving soap and plenty of squills
And a box of those excellent Richardson's pills.

A podeldoe and painkiller surely you will need
And something to stop the red stream should you bleed.
Some things I've omitted but never mind that
Eat salt junk and hard bread and laugh and grow fat.

The poem still stands as a good checklist for the kinds of things you need for going to sea today. The equipment still falls broadly into two categories – Repairs and Luxuries. I didn't have any Richardson's pills, whatever they were, but they would have fitted right into the first-aid kit I put together. I had antibiotics, first-aid bandages, pills for different kinds of pain and a book telling us how to deliver a baby, should the need arise. I also packed an emergency dental kit. We met a sailing wife who once become so bored on a long voyage that she pulled out the kit and began tinkering with her children's fillings, just for something to do.

As a going-away present my girlfriends compiled a box of goodies that combined practicality and pleasure in equal

1ˢᵀ & 2ᴺᴰ CLASS BOY'S KIT.

Laid out for inspection.

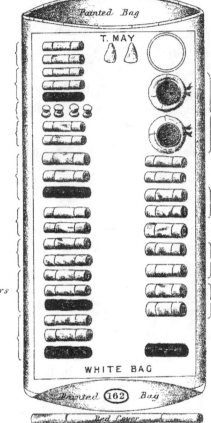

Painted Bag

T. MAY

WHITE BAG

Painted (162) Bag

2 Towels
2 Cap Covers
3 Collars

2 Pair Socks

2 Pair Drawers

3 Flannels

2 Night Shirts

2 Day Shirts

3 Duck working Jumpers

3 Duck Trowers

Cap Box

2 Caps { 1 Serge / 1 Cloth

The Serge Cap is replaced by a Cloth one on a boy being rated 1ˢᵗ Class.

1 Black Silk Handkerchief

1 Comforter

2 Jerseys

1 Serge Frock

2 Serge Jumpers

2 Serge Trowsers

1 Cloth Trowsers

Red Cover
Prayer Book

Your
Clothes Brush

Ditty Box

Scrubbing Brush

2 Pocket Handkerchiefs.

1 Pair Boots, 1 Pair Shoes

2 Brushes and a box of Blacking in duck Bag.

Haversack

2 Manuals { Seamanship / and Signal }
2 Knife Lanyards, 1 Knife
48 Clothes Stops
Soap Bag
1 Housewife
1 Toothbrush

Kit on entry shewn in Blue.
Kit on rating 1ˢᵗ Class shewn in Red and Blue.

14   Contents of a Royal Navy kit bag (1904)

measure. On top of the box was a mask and snorkel and, lower down, a floating keyring, sail-repair tape, two heavy shackles, a tube of plastic padding, marine filler and a packet of plastic eyelets. Underneath them was a tin of escargots cooked in champagne, Altoid mints, stuffed vine leaves, smoked paprika and a packet of hazelnut cream biscuits. The whole box was covered in very unseamanlike Marilyn Monroe paper.

Then, one day in the middle of all the chaos of dismantling our home, the full terror of what we were about to do hit us. Going sailing on *Jameeleh* seemed totally overwhelming, financially impossible, eccentric (if not perverse), unnatural, unreasonable and hopelessly overambitious. We must be out of our minds.

And yet we didn't think of cancelling for one second. The reason we were going was in order to be changed. We were going to trust the sea and our boat to alter us in ways we ourselves never could.

In early summer we moved on to the boat, which was, by now, moored in Milford Haven. While I finished some writing commitments, Leighton worked hard on *Jameeleh*, getting her ready for our voyage. He had radar fitted and a new autohelm, to enable the boat to steer herself without one or other of us having continually to be at the helm, which is very tiring when there are only two on board. A good autohelm can be like having an extra crew member and we named ours Hilda, after a close friend's mother. 'I hope I don't let you down,' said the real Hilda, who had just turned eighty. We were glad to have her benign presence along with us on the boat.

Life on board *Jameeleh*, however, was already harder than I had imagined. Even though we'd been planning for and working towards this voyage for a long time, I wasn't prepared for its reality: I couldn't find anything on the boat and trying to write was very difficult when there was no door between me and Leighton; there were simply too many new things to learn, and nothing was familiar; the pressure to get everything done was making us both bad-tempered; I felt totally lost without my friends. We had left one life but had not yet started on the new one at sea. My fears were running rampant and, of all the things we'd left at home, I missed my washing machine terribly. For the first three months we lived on the boat, I cried every single day.

Nevertheless, during this preparation time we became fond of Milford Haven. The town was created at the end of the eighteenth century, when a 1790 Act of Parliament gave Sir William Hamilton and his heirs the right to 'make and provide Quays, Docks, Piers and other erections and to establish a Market'. A group of Nantucket whalers settled there, attempting to make a living in the area after the American War of Independence. To this day parts of Milford have the clapboard look and clean lines of Nantucket architecture. Lord Nelson visited Milford in 1802 with the Hamiltons and celebrated the anniversary of the Battle of the Nile in the New Inn. Elizabeth Rotch, who was at the dinner, noticed that Lady Hamilton cut up Nelson's meat for him. The locals were pleased when Lord Nelson made a speech in which he declared that Milford and Trincomalee in Ceylon were the best two harbours he had seen in the world.

Milford Haven, though, is a great port that never was. In the middle of the nineteenth century, ambitious plans were drawn up to make Milford a rival to Liverpool and Southampton. The Milford Docks Company was formed and its aim was to attract transatlantic trade. In the 1850s, F. Wehnert drew what the docks and town of Milford might look like if the engineer James Thomson's plans were implemented. The drawings show a grand design – huge port buildings as regal as Versailles, formal gardens and relaxed merchants promenading along porticoes. The whole development had an air of prosperity, rationality and utility – except that it was nothing more than what a local historian has called 'another Milford hallucination'. Indeed, the first boat into the newly built docks in 1888 was a fishing vessel called *Sybil*, and a fishing port is what Milford became, until, in the 1960s, the oil refinery attracted tankers into the deep waters of the Haven.

Milford Haven is still a town with big ideas. When we were there, the man in the hardware store was also the undertaker. The shop was shut when he was officiating at funerals and, on such days, between burials, he would sell you a can of silicone wearing a full morning suit. The marina cleaner drove a Jaguar with a personalised number plate, and there's a member of the library who crosses out all the rude words in the books he or she reads. One of the men who worked in the marina told us that he had found a website where you could order a full Viking funeral. For extra payment, you could hire twenty Viking maidens to bare their breasts to mark your departure from this earth. This was definitely his preferred option. That would be forty breasts in all to see you on your way.

The volunteers in the Milford Museum were in a jocose mood the day I visited.

'I'm insulting everybody,' said the lady at the admissions

desk, amid gales of laughter. 'Would you like an old-aged pensioner?'

I said I already had one on the boat, but her offer was genuine, and I was given a guided tour around the museum by a very small old man. My pensioner showed me the mammoth's tusk that had been discovered when the council was building the new bridge. Then I encountered a speaking model of General Hamilton, but he didn't divulge what I really wanted to know: details of his famous *ménage à trois* with Lord Nelson. After the fisheries section was a simulated storm consisting of a ship's railing, some painted storm clouds on the ceiling, a bit of netting and the sound of a howling wind.

Perhaps the most interesting exhibit in the museum is a picture of a giant squid caught in the nets of one of the Milford trawlers in 1911 (see Figure 15). The photograph shows the body of the squid laid out on the dock, surrounded by men, all of them wearing hats. The squid is huge, but strangely flattened, due to its struggles with the net that caught it. The sign goes on to tell you what happened to this Holy Grail of deep-sea oceanography:

> Unfortunately it was mistaken locally for an octopus, and sent to the fish guano works for destruction. This was a great loss to science, as the probabilities may be about 1,000,000 to 1 against another specimen being thus obtained.

If I'd mistaken a giant squid for an octopus and thrown it away I might be tempted to hide the fact rather than boast about it. But Milford has a very attractive honesty about its own limitations. As part of the millennium celebrations, it was proposed that a Preseli stone be hauled from

15   The Milford Haven Giant Squid

Pembrokeshire to Stonehenge, replicating the original journey of the monoliths by sea from South Wales to Wiltshire.
A controversial grant of £100,000 was awarded to the project.
After many difficulties, the stone was hauled by volunteers
to the water and loaded between two large wooden rafts. As
the stone was being transported like this, it came loose and
sank into the Haven, from which it had to be rescued by
divers. The boulder eventually reached the car park of the
Milford Haven docks where it was abandoned, thus proving
definitively modern man's inferiority to his prehistoric fore-
bears. Only in Milford, however, with its endearing lack of
shame about failure, would such a defeat be marked by a
plaque. I liked the place better every time I passed that uncooperative millennium stone.

Any sailor worth his or her salt encounters sirens on a voyage. The name derives from a Greek root, meaning 'to bind or attach' and these mythological creatures traditionally possessed a bird's body with a woman's head. Odysseus forced his men to fill their ears with wax to prevent them from hearing the sirens' song which he himself was determined to witness. Romantic pictures of sirens concentrate more on the flowing locks and naked breasts involved in the spectacle. Sirens, basically, are anything that seeks to stop your journey, knots in which you become tied against your will and better judgement. The first siren we met was called Woo Sung.

We heard about Woo Sung by accident. It was a captain's house that had been built overlooking the Haven, with spectacular views out to the Atlantic through the Heads. The house had a ship's figurehead on the stairs and was for sale.

16   Odysseus and the Sirens

The story went that a certain Captain Griffiths – who was reputed to have rounded the Horn thirty-four times, and who had sailed on the *Narcissus* just before the novelist Joseph Conrad joined her at Cardiff – went away to sea, leaving Mrs Griffiths in charge of building a bungalow for them just outside Milford. When he came back, he found that she had constructed a far more imposing home than he had planned. It was said that the house was named Woo Sung after a settlement at the mouth of the Yangtze River, which the captain and his wife had spent days trying to reach after having been dismasted during a particularly bad storm in the East China Sea. They had sworn that, if ever they got home to Pembrokeshire, they would name their new house after the place they had wanted so much to see. This was the same Woo Sung to which the frigate HMS *Amethyst* escaped, having been held hostage by Chinese Communists in April 1949. After the incident, the *Amethyst* sent the now-famous telegram: 'Have rejoined the Fleet south of Woo Sung. No damage or casualties. God save the King.' Now this elusive, exotic entrance to an oriental port was a feature of the Welsh coastline, a home built out of great peril.

Leighton and I were instantly obsessed. We told ourselves that it was a once-in-a-lifetime house and that we would regret it for ever if we didn't buy it. We did our sums, agonised and made an offer. That was refused, so we bid £10,000 more.

Then, suddenly, we came to our senses. What were we doing? We'd only just managed to free ourselves from our house in Cardiff in order to have time for the voyage. Why on earth would we want to risk not going for another property?

'It's a test,' declared Leighton, 'to see how much we want to do the voyage. If we buy the house, we'll never go.'

The truth was that we were frightened. It seemed easier to buy a house with a figurehead and a view of shipping than it was to be *on* one of the boats passing in front of Woo Sung. It would be so much more comfortable to look at the sea from a centrally heated house than to get cold and seasick. Woo Sung would be a beautiful home for someone, but for us it was a siren, an anaesthetic against the pain of being afraid, as we changed a plan into a real journey. Had we bought the house, we would have been purchasing an idea of the sea, and losing our chance to go sailing in reality. Every time we looked out of the haven at the ocean through the telescope in Woo Sung's bedroom, we would have been reminded of the voyage we didn't dare do. A dream house would have become a nightmare.

The next day I had my hair cropped short, as if I were cutting another mooring line that tied me to our old life. The day after that, we left Milford Haven.

As usual, I was busy stowing things down below when Leighton called.

'Are you ready?' he shouted.

'No,' I replied, 'but what the hell!'

As we left the marina, our friends sounded sirens and hooters, waved from the bows of their boats and their dogs barked at all the fuss. Outside the dock, the Haven looked gorgeous. The fields had their silage hair combed and tied into shiny black bales. The tankers at anchor down in Dale all had their sterns turned to us in a ritual of respect. *Sea Gem*, another Nicholson 35 we knew, passed us and dipped her red ensign,

17 *Jameeleh's* Atlantic Voyage

and we returned the compliment with the red dragon. Our leaving felt very heroic.

At the Heads the sea was showing her petticoats. Just outside the entrance to Milford Haven there is a body of water so turbulent that it's called the Vomit. The seas around headlands, where two or more bodies of water meet, are always confusing, but add to this tidal streams and local currents and, just north of St Anne's Head, you have an area known as Five Tides. You have only to put the bows of your boat out between the Heads and anybody prone to seasickness feels instant nausea. I think of it as the revolving door that lets you out of Milford Haven's sheltered water into the open sea, or a turbulent junction that seems to ask you, 'Are you really sure that you want to leave? It could be rough out there. Don't expect me to make it easy, I don't want you to go.' Nausea is the price you have to pay to leave sheltered, familiar waters and exit into the glittering ocean beyond.

Sure enough, I soon began to feel sick, but took a homeopathic remedy that steadied me. In silence we stared astern as the land dropped away behind us. We were aiming for Bayona in Galicia, north-western Spain, which would take us five days, our longest voyage so far.

We looked around us. Conditions were ideal. A smart north-westerly was allowing us to sail in the right direction, away from the west coast of Britain and France. The sea was slight and, as the sun sank lower in the sky, appeared flecked golden, rose and baby blue. We had done plenty of night sails before, but none this far from land. We looked at one another briefly and then away again, towards Pembrokeshire. I had started to feel extremely cold and much more nauseous. Everything was going well and we should have been ecstatic, but we had been hit by a growing feeling of dread.

'This can only get worse,' said Leighton.

By now we were in the grip of a morbid anxiety. Things were going *too* well. Even the clouds of the beautiful sunset started to look threatening. We felt more and more uneasy. I was so cold that I could no longer feel my feet.

'I think we should turn back,' said Leighton, and I agreed.

We were now convinced that we couldn't cope with a blow, that we just weren't ready. After all, how much actual sailing had we done? We'd only come down the Bristol Channel and done a short trip to Ireland. If we felt so uncomfortable in optimum conditions, how on earth were we going to cope with problems when they developed?

As we sailed back into Milford Haven, dolphins swam in our bow wave. Neither of us quite understood what had happened. We're not cowards, but we had become spooked. Suddenly our new autohelm began to misbehave, swinging the boat's head by ninety degrees at a time, instead of steering a good straight course. Hilda was having a nervous break-down. Paradoxically, this made us feel much better, as it gave us an excuse for abandoning the attempt. But we both knew that we'd decided to return well before the autohelm started to wander. We vowed that we'd tell nobody the real reason why we'd turned back. We'd faced our first test and had failed, but the relief at getting in from all that inhuman beauty on the sea was immense.

It was only as we came closer to the dock that we realised what we had done. A tiny motor boat was coming towards us and Leighton and I had a difference of opinion about which way we should go to avoid it. As it turned out, we were both talking about different boats, but the blazing row that ensued brought us both to the end of our tether. I stood sobbing in the cockpit. I felt like a fool. We'd worked so hard to make this dream possible and we just weren't up to it. We weren't even having a good time. Leighton went on to criticise something I did and I ended up screaming, 'That's right, the bloody autopilot's more use than me. Perhaps you should get rid of me and carry on with Hilda. I hope you'll be very happy together.'

Leighton came up behind me and touched my back until the storm of crying passed. 'I need you more than breath,' he said.

The second siren we met in Milford was fat and called Graham.

We had met Graham in Milford marina and he had fitted the autohelm that had now begun to behave psychotically. He seemed to know a lot about boats, but his story was a little too good to be true. He had worked as a marine engineer but had, unusually, moved from the engine room to become captain. He said he'd been the youngest skipper ever to have sailed with P&O. Why is it that daydreamers are always skippers, never cooks or second mates? More than that, Graham told us that he was soon to be a guest skipper on *Shamrock*, one of the most famous yachts in the world. Why *Shamrock*'s millionaire owner should want a large, bald and scruffy fantasist on board his pristine boat wasn't clear, but it made sense to Graham.

Although we didn't swallow many of Graham's stories, we had no reason not to believe that he was a Yachtmaster and qualified skipper. When we returned to Milford, he spent two days retuning the autohelm he had fitted and persuading us that we had experienced problems with Hilda because we were inexperienced sailors, and not because the equipment itself was faulty. He told us that once we learned to balance the sails properly, Hilda would do her job. He also offered to skipper the boat to Spain. Our confidence had been knocked by our unexpected return to Milford, so we were immensely relieved and accepted his offer eagerly.

By now it was early September and we had to wait for favourable winds again. We met a couple in the marina who were selling their boat – a beautiful Tradewinds sloop, a very good cruising boat – which the husband had spent eleven and a half years building. Now that the yacht was finished, the couple had realised they didn't really want to do the long-distance sailing for which it was suitable. The wife now fancied flotilla sailing in hot climates, so they were selling the boat and getting rid of a false dream. This seemed to us unutterably sad. We told ourselves that we weren't ready to give up.

And so it was that we found ourselves sailing down the Haven with Graham. We waved at Woo Sung as we passed, delighted that we hadn't been caught by that particular siren, not knowing that we had another, more formidable one on board.

In a sailing boat, you do not travel along the surface of the sea but rather on the winds that blow above it. The wind is your road, and if that disappears or changes direction, you have to go with it.

Imagine you are in a car wanting to travel from Manchester

to Falmouth. Suddenly, because of strong winds, the route is closed for three days and you have to spend the time huddled in a motorway service station with other bored travellers. Then comes the news that the wind – and therefore the road – has shifted and that, instead of going south, you have to travel south-west into Wales and wait there for another road to appear.

We were aiming for Spain but ended up in the Scillies. The north-westerly wind we began travelling along died in the middle of the night, leaving *Jameeleh* wallowing in a big sea.

With a third person present, Leighton and I had stopped our usual bickering. Graham had warned me before we set off that I would need to take care of myself, and that they would force me to drink water if I were seasick, to avoid the problems of dehydration. In the event, by taking half the usual dose of medication and making sure I kept warm, I managed not to throw up at all. Graham had told me of his secret weapon against seasickness: a sticking plaster across the belly button. Ridiculous, I know, but his confidence in the fact that I would no longer be sick seemed to work. Not only was I able to stand my watch, from eight until midnight, but I made tea whenever I could and was even able to heat up a casserole down below.

Two days later we left the Scillies in a stiff wind but, just as we were alongside Land's End, it died again. The combination of steep waves and no wind meant that we could not carry on – sailing was impossible and we didn't have enough fuel to get us to Spain. We had no option but to put on the engine and head for Falmouth. We were now going backwards, away from our destination.

Hilda was once more showing her limitations and, in turbulent seas south-west of Cornwall, Leighton and Graham spent hours helming by hand, surfing down huge breakers. I offered to take my turn steering but was told that I wasn't strong enough. Even after we rounded the Lizard into calmer water, they wouldn't let me steer, switching on the temperamental Hilda instead, claiming that she could hold a more accurate course. I was hurt and felt excluded from my own voyage. They had decided, they told me, to go into Falmouth 'for my sake'.

'But I'm fine,' I protested. 'I haven't been sick once.'

The following morning, Leighton and Graham went off to have a cooked breakfast together. When they came back to the boat they dropped a bombshell. Leighton took a deep breath and said, 'It's getting very late in the season, and Graham thinks that, if we want to get the boat to Bayona before winter, you should get off and let us take *Jameeleh* down.'

I continued to wash up and swallowed hard. Graham took over. Nobody was questioning my commitment to the voyage, he continued, but things can go downhill very quickly at sea and, if seasick, I could become a liability.

I was stunned. Leighton, said Graham, needed to learn to calm down when we were leaving port and not to try to do everything. But he moved like a monkey on the deck and his seamanship was excellent. I, on the other hand, said our sailing marital therapist, needed to take care of my seasickness and do more on the boat. Leighton should allow me to make mistakes so that I could learn to handle the boat without us being continually at each other's throats. The weather forecast was bad for the next few days, so Graham would return to Falmouth in a week, and his friend Wayne would go with them on the trip.

I had been made to walk the plank.

I was brave to begin with, thinking that I should put the

needs of the boat before my own and do whatever was best for safety. Then I was devastated. I was beginning to regret packing up our old life. What was the point of all that effort and upheaval if I wasn't allowed to sail on the boat? If Leighton and I weren't even together?

When, finally, we rowed about this decision that had been taken without me, a defensive Leighton made things even worse by telling me that I was, in fact, 'fucking useless' on the boat. He had never spoken to me like that before, so I believed him.

That night, barely speaking, we walked out late to the Point above Falmouth. It was dark, but we looked out anyway.

Sirens make you feel that All Will Be Well when reality is too frightening to face. They seem to offer real solutions to a problem, but they actually promote a flight from reason. As the deadline for departure approached, Graham became harder to reach on the phone. He told us the weather wasn't right for leaving when we could see other sailors departing perfectly safely. On test runs in the River Fal, it had become clear that Hilda still had severe directional problems. Graham had told us that she was fluky because we didn't know how to set the sails correctly, but she was incapable of keeping a straight course and would often meander wildly from side to side even when the canvas was balanced. Now we had the confidence to see that the problem wasn't with us, but with the unit.

We sent the head of the autohelm back to Graham, but he wasn't able or willing to put things right. As the full extent of his deceptions became clear, we felt sick. By coincidence, Leighton saw some charts addressed to *Shamrock* in a shop. Far from being in New England, as Graham had claimed when he'd told us that he was going to skipper her later in the season, she was in Australia, happily sailing the Pacific. Normally we would not have made ourselves vulnerable to such a person, but, in this new sailing world, we clearly needed to be more careful.

While Leighton was making some further adjustments to the rigging of the boat, I went to Cardiff to clear up a last few matters of business. On the train back to Falmouth, I sat opposite a lady who put all our difficulties in perspective. She and her husband had just sold their thirty-seven-foot Taiwanese boat, thereby giving up on their dream of sailing round the world. Family circumstances had changed and a daughter needed support as the result of a divorce. The lady was heartbroken but wished us well. As the conversation went on, I asked if her husband also turned into a raging monster on board. She agreed that men often became nasty skippers – it was a panic reaction to the unknown. How did she cope with that? I asked.

'I just tell myself he doesn't mean it. He loves me really.'

I vowed, from then on, to put our fear of going to sea where it belonged. Our discomfort and resulting anger could be used as a mechanism to give us energy, to drive us on. Terror belongs in the engine of a boat and not at the helm, where we'd been storing it and a load of trouble for ourselves. All I knew was that I was willing to do anything to make the voyage work, however much I had to change my attitude. I was willing to let go of deadlines, absolutes, old self-images and vanities – anything that would enable me to undertake this voyage happily with Leighton.

That night, Leighton and I began discussing our options. We were sick and tired of waiting. Clearly, we weren't ready to attempt the long voyage to Bayona alone or we would have done it, but we were perfectly capable of sailing for thirty-six hours together. Perhaps we didn't need Graham after all. Why didn't we cross the Channel, hop down the Atlantic coast of France in manageable legs and then make a shorter crossing of the Bay of Biscay? That would mean three, instead of five days at sea. If I didn't take the seasickness medication I wouldn't be so drowsy, and so would be able to help Leighton more. This would allow us to create our own luck again and not be dependent on other people. We had taken our voyage back into our own hands and, for the first time in weeks, we felt like ourselves.

What madness had allowed us to forget that there was no point to this voyage unless we did it together, even with all our failings and weaknesses? With his plan for getting rid of me, Graham had come between us for a while. We speculated that he himself had been scared of the voyage to Bayona, had projected that fear on to me, to draw attention away from himself. We were partly to blame, of course, because we had placed a major part of the responsibility for our voyage in someone else's hands, knowing him to be, let's say, imaginative. Our nervousness had made us give up on our own instincts, because we wanted to be nursemaided through this overwhelming experience. Sirens make you forget yourself for a while, but they only serve, in the end, to make your way all the clearer.

The following day we left Falmouth, ecstatic that we had freed ourselves from a trap of our own making. We were just level with the Lizard when, with a huge crack, the block holding the main sheet to the traveller parted. The boom flew out to one side, breaking the gooseneck, which fixes it to the mast. Only the halyard and the sailbag were keeping the boom and mainsail attached to the boat.

Leighton and I were magnificent. I was on the helm and, without being told, put on the engine and kept the boat pointed in a direction that prevented the sail from filling with wind while Leighton hauled in the boom and lashed it to the deck. Then we turned round and headed back into Falmouth. We radioed the coastguards, whom we'd informed of our departure, to let them know what had happened. The officer on duty congratulated us on dealing with the crisis, and said that we'd done well not to need the lifeboat in that situation. We even felt secretly pleased that we'd suffered a proper sailing injury.

'You'd better give up,' said my mother when I phoned her, thus ensuring that I battled on. (Some mothers never learn.) We were downcast, but proud of our own calmness in a crisis. We hired a rigger to repair the gooseneck and the shackle and began waiting, yet again, for good Channel-crossing weather.

I had been practising Zen meditation for a number of years but, on the boat, I found it impossible to find a comfortable corner to do my usual sitting. The boat wouldn't stop moving, which made sitting in a half-lotus position very wobbly. In desperation, I asked a friend how I could possibly carry out my practice under such circumstances.

'Make the boat your practice,' he replied.

This made a good deal of sense. Sailing *Jameeleh* had stripped us of our usual social defences and had pushed us harder than any Zen master. Under the pressure of the unknown, our habits of mind had become gallingly obvious: Leighton would lash out at me, and I would crumble in a resentful heap of generalised guilt. Using the boat as my practice could only mean sailing through such choppy waters with the maximum amount of awareness. Not only was this good seamanship in a practical sense but it would also allow us to learn from what was happening. For example, I was starting to hate sailing, but by observing myself I noticed that this was not because I wanted to give it up but because I wanted to be good at it. Part of my fury was frustration at not being as skilled as I would have liked. This felt like a desire to give up but was, in fact, proof of the opposite, a growing commitment to continuing.

We dismissed Graham from our minds and arranged for a local Raymarine dealer to reset the autohelm unit, then we prepared to leave the UK once again. One morning, I met a Royal Navy commander as I was coming back from the showers. A marina gate that was usually open had jammed shut and the commander and I helped each other to scale a fence, handing over our towels and sponge bags. I invited him back to see our boat, as he was an admirer of the Nicholson 35. I asked him how he had been trained in the navy to cope with fear at sea. He said in clipped, confident tones, 'Be cool, calm, collected. Understand what you're doing and you will be.'

That night, I dreamt that I was kissing Hornblower. It was Hornblower played by Ioan Gruffudd, not Gregory Peck, and he was dressed in full ceremonial uniform. He was a little naive but told me he felt terribly lucky to be kissing me.

I finally felt that we knew where we were going. Relying on ourselves, we were once again in the realm of reality. Now, rather than using a road atlas to navigate a boat, we were steering by a proper nautical chart.

Shortly afterwards, we left for the fifth time and we were finally allowed through. We crossed the Channel at night, and I took the watch from two o'clock until five. I could see a succession of large lit-up cargo ships leaving the Channel. I watched their moving navigation lights like a hawk, constructing the story of their voyage. On radar each ship looked like a steam iron. Leighton was on watch at dawn and woke me when he saw the lighthouse at the entrance to the Chenal du Four into Brest.

I took the boat in and tied her to the visitors' pontoon. A white-haired gentleman bowed formally and welcomed us to Brittany. We told him we'd just completed our first Channel crossing. In fact, we'd crossed more than just the Channel; we'd navigated some formidable marital shoals in order to sail on together. The first leg of the voyage had been very demanding in totally unexpected ways. We felt sure that the worst must now be over and that we had some nice easy sailing ahead.

CHAPTER FOUR

Captain Bastard

'If you ever speak to me like that again, I'll drop what I'm doing and fall to the deck like a collie dog and then you'll be sorry,' I screamed at Leighton as we motored down the Bay of Brest, heading south for Douarnenez.

After our triumphant arrival in Brittany we had celebrated with a meal in a crêperie. As we went to sleep, I heard a drip in the boat and we realised that we hadn't tightened the knob on the stern gland of the engine, to prevent water coming in through the propeller shaft. Leighton went mad, as if the omission were my fault because I'd reminded us of it.

He was back to his normal boyish self the following morning, but that didn't last. The problem was that we had to do a tricky backward manoeuvre to get out of the marina, never easy in a Nicholson 35. Leighton had little confidence in me and shouted so many instructions that he put me off completely. I panicked and he had to come to the helm to take over. Then he yelled and yelled at me as we left the harbour. I admitted that I'd cocked up the move, but tried to tell him firmly that even if I'd done something wrong, he was not to scream.

Hornblower would never have spoken to his crew like that.

Admittedly, he would have had to use the lash on me, but I felt sure that he would not have lost control of his temper as he did it. C.S. Forester's portrayal of the role of captain in the Royal Navy is almost chivalric:

> To be master of the countless details of managing a wooden sailing ship; not only to be able to handle her under sail, but to be conversant with all the petty but important trifles regarding cordage and cables, pumps and salt pork, dry rot and the Articles of War; that was what was necessary. But he knew now of other qualities equally necessary; a bold and yet thoughtful initiative, moral as well as physical courage, tactful handling both of superiors and subordinates, ingenuity and quickness of thought. A fighting navy needed to fight, and needed fighting men to lead it.

I had become addicted to the Hornblower novels because of my father's devotion to them and because of the ideal of seamanship that they portrayed. Horatio Hornblower *did* have a few weaknesses: he was tone deaf, didn't appreciate music, hated climbing the futtock shrouds (but did it anyway) and had a tendency to a pot belly. On the other hand, he was a man of few words, took a sea-water shower every day and possessed a knack for seeing what action might be required in any given situation. He once saved a whole ship by calmly snuffing out the fuse of a bomb that had been thrown on board. His capacity for strategic thinking was outstanding, and his cool assessment of risk led him to take bold maritime actions that nobody else would have thought possible.

In my mind the figures of Hornblower and my father

became subtly mixed. This was not a question of physical exploits but of temperament. When my mother and I rowed at home – usually a tempestuous event – my father would always try to steer us all on a course for calmer waters. A woman should always beware of ideals passed on to her by her father, lest every other man fail by those exacting standards. Hornblower was, after all, fictional. I was fascinated to learn that the Hornblower books, with their celebration of the British fighting man, were written by an author who had nearly been crippled by atherosclerosis, a gradual narrowing of the arteries in the legs. In 1943, it was feared that Forester would have to have both limbs amputated to prevent gangrene. Fortunately, the disease slowed and this was never necessary. According to his son John, Forester was himself very far from the ideal, being an authoritarian father who lied and who was also promiscuous. One time his wife came back from a trip to the country to find C.S. infested with pubic lice. This was reflected in the story of Hornblower's dalliance with a Russian countess in *The Commodore*. Forester, however, remarked that Hornblower had saved his sanity. His son wrote that Hornblower 'was Forester as Forester hoped that he had the courage to be'. Now that we were sailing I didn't always find Hornblower books to be cheerful reading, because they constantly reminded me of how short we both fell of the naval ideals of seamanship. Sometimes I felt that Hornblower was designed to make everybody else look and feel bad.

Leighton had no need to know about the preservation of salt pork, but the demands made on sailing skippers today are still considerable. I asked Ronald Perkins, whom we had met in Milford Haven, and who had built and sailed his own boat, *Weir*, from Australia to Britain, what made a good captain. He gave me a well-considered and full definition, written in beautiful copperplate handwriting:

> An owner-master should be firm and just, resolute and untiring himself, quick to check faults and abuse of privileges, always ready to encourage zeal and never discouraging a man or woman's suggestions, if made in good faith and in the general interest, even if personally he disagrees.

Ronald observed that crews become noticeably more discontented when becalmed, but continued,

> this is where the owner can do much to allay the worst effects, by holding aloof from all argument, by being more incisive than usual and by a display of unfailing tact and good temper himself. This is not an easy task, but is a sure way of keeping a 'happy ship'.

Sailing together on a small vessel is like living in a particle accelerator designed to show up the most hidden faults of your character, traits that are easy to disguise in comfortable conditions on shore. At sea I became more helpless than usual, nervous of doing things incorrectly. I would therefore tend to leave practical things to Leighton, not out of laziness but because I wasn't dextrous or confident enough to make them stick. Leighton, however, under the pressure of keeping us and the boat safe, turned into a man I didn't recognise.

In Falmouth, we had decided to carry extra fuel on board *Jameeleh*'s decks, because the duty on diesel in Europe made it much more expensive to buy. I had scrounged some old fuel cans from the council yard by the marina, not thinking that they might leak. This they did, copiously, as we crossed the Channel, spoiling the beautiful teak decks that Leighton had worked so hard to clean and seal. In Brittany, Leighton surveyed the damage to the decks and blamed me – as if carrying the fuel hadn't been a joint decision. In a book by Peter Noble and Ros Hogbin on the temperament of sailors, I found a passage that I felt described what I was seeing:

> From time to time a 'Captain Bligh syndrome' can be observed in the skippers of small yachts. This is when a normally reasonable and courteous individual, usually a middle-aged man, assumes command of a pleasure boat only to become domineering, over-critical and sometimes foul-mouthed . . . This apparent 'change of character' is, in reality, a reaction to stress and anxiety.

There is a sailing school in North America that specialises in teaching women. I would like very much to have been a student there because their slogan, instantly understood by sailing women worldwide, is simply: 'Nobody yells.'

I couldn't fault Leighton for being willing to take responsibility for us on the boat, but there was something about the way in which he was doing it that wasn't right. Rather than sharing the load with me, he did more than he needed to. He was overprotective – a throwback, perhaps, to when I wasn't well – but couldn't carry the burden of being skipper and doing everything all on his own. Stress made him lash out at the one person he should be keeping on his side and there was nothing I could do about it.

18   What happens to men on boats

As *Jameeleh* motored out of Brest in drizzle, I felt more like ballast in an empty boat than valuable cargo. We passed a bulk carrier on its way to discharge in the docks. Brittany was the first place abroad to which Cardiff coal was exported, when it began to be used by sugar refiners in Nantes. They were impressed with the coal's low smoke and high steam-generating qualities and soon the fuel began to interest the French naval authorities, who decided to test Welsh coal on a voyage from Nantes to Cádiz. Their firemen, unfamiliar with coal of such quality, ignored warnings against stoking the boilers too often. The resulting blaze burned through the bottom of the ship's furnace while they were at sea. It may have ruined one boiler, but that fire convinced the French Navy that a little bit of Welsh coal goes a long way. They began using it in their ships, and the British Admiralty later followed suit.

Like any source of energy, however, coal could be a danger as well as an asset. In the 1850s the new cargo was still not fully understood, especially the need for ventilation. In October 1856 an explosion on board the Prussian barque *Frederick Ritzhoff*, moored in Cardiff's West Dock, killed six members of crew and injured eleven others. A book published in the 1940s and written by Captain R.E. Thomas emphasises that 'the carriage of coal is attended with risk both of fire and explosion, the loss of many lives and fine vessels being due to these causes'. Spontaneous combustion was one hazard but explosions happened because 'coal emits an inflammable gas (marsh gas) particularly immediately after loading and when newly worked or freshly broken, which gas, when mixed with a certain proportion of air, will quickly explode if brought into contact with a spark or light'.

Leighton and I certainly seemed to be carrying an inflammable cargo on board *Jameeleh*, with our temperaments frequently mixing into a volatile gas. I couldn't understand what was happening to us; we had always got on so easily before. One of the greatest strengths of our marriage had been that, as well as being in love, we actually liked each other. This is more rare than you might think. It's relatively easy to be infatuated, but to like someone deeply, to approve of them, and to continue to do so for a long time, is by no means common.

Leighton had, for reasons I couldn't fathom, turned into an angry man whom I didn't even like. But I did understand one thing: if we continued in this way we were in danger of experiencing a marital explosion that would put a premature end to the voyage.

The rest of the day's sailing from Brest to Douarnenez was largely uneventful, except for my encounter with the French SAS.

It was a rainy day, and the Atlantic was performing a dance of the seven veils from the west. We were crossing Douarnenez Bay on a heading of 114 degrees. Rain had dampened down the seas, changing the outlines of the waves into rolling grassy hills. Hilda the Autohelm was being uncharacteristically stable and Leighton was down below. I had taken shelter from the rain under the spray hood when suddenly I heard a voice calling.

I looked over the gunwale and there, completely unexpectedly, were two men dressed in black alongside us in a RIB. Both were young and fit and looked as if they were about to deliver a box of Cadbury's Milk Tray. They were shouting something, but I couldn't hear, so they doubled back and swooped even closer to the boat.

'You must go south,' they said in French, 'there is an exercise.'

I was rapt by these shiny, intent and fast-moving men, but I suddenly became suspicious. They hadn't told me who they were, so why should we change our course, just because some unidentified men told me to do so? After all, they could have been drug runners or anybody.

I drew myself up to my full British height and asked, marmishly, '*Et qui êtes vous?*'

They never did tell me who they were. By the time Leighton came up from below, the RIB and the men had long since disappeared.

'I've just been talking to the French SAS,' I said casually. 'I think we'd better alter our course.'

Sure enough, quarter of an hour later, a Hercules transport plane flew over and deposited a number of parachuted men on to a prearranged target, just where we had been heading. We speculated that there might also have been a submarine in the area.

We had another blazing row as we docked in Douarnenez. Coming into a strange harbour always provokes a crisis of seeing, as you move from making passage into pilotage. *The Admiralty Manual of Navigation* defines navigation as 'the science of finding a ship's position, and the art of conducting her safely from place to place'. Pilotage, however, 'is the art of conducting a ship in the neighbourhood of dangers, such as rocks and shoals, and in narrow waters. This necessitates a knowledge of charts, *Sailing Directions* and other publications, and also of artificial aids to navigation such as buoys, lights, fog signals and radio aids.'

As the water becomes progressively shallower under the keel and even before you can see the marina entrance, you have to point the boat at the land. If the port is to give any kind of shelter from the sea, its entrance will be far from obvious. You have a general bearing but, as you head in, you feel as though you're driving headlong into a brick wall. Fortunately, everything happens slowly in a boat, in real time, not like the swoop of an aeroplane on to a runway or the rush of a motorway slip road into the centre of a town. You think you're close to land and then, as the detail grows, you realise that you weren't close at all a quarter of an hour ago. The solid mass of a town resolves into individual buildings. There's a church and a prominent row of shops, a boatyard and, yes, there's the end of the sea wall, what might be a harbour master's office, and we can see a group of masts like the stored spears of a theatrical production; and now we're close, we can see the individual stones in the quay wall, so we must be in.

As I eased the boat in alongside the visitors' pontoon, Leighton kept distracting me with screamed instructions: 'Bow thruster! Bow thruster!' and then, 'Stop her!' after I had done just that. He had an accident while siphoning the remaining diesel from the leaking oil drums into the main tank, which meant diesel went everywhere in the cockpit. This was my fault, he raged, for having had such an impractical idea as extra fuel cans. I looked on, feeling desperately sad.

Until now, Leighton and I had been sailing in wide emotional waters, with only the usual hazards on which our marital boat could be shipwrecked. By undertaking this voyage, however, we had placed ourselves in busy psychological shipping lanes. We were going to need new methods of navigation, alternative ways of seeing our way, if we were to get into port safely.

In sailing down the western coast of Europe, from Wales to Brittany, Leighton and I were following a major trade route in the early history of the region. When travel on land was severely constrained by dense forests, the sea looked like an open motorway to early traders, missionaries and migrants. Because winds and currents have not changed substantially since then we had no choice but to follow the courses dictated by them. As Felipe Fernández-Armesto had written:

> Strictly speaking, oceans do not really exist: they are constructs of the mind, figments of the cartographer's imagination, landlubbers' ways of dividing up maritime space according to the lie of the land. What matters to seafarers . . . is not the definition on the map but the reality of wind and current. It is the wind and current that unify bodies of water, not the land masses or islands round about.

There are a limited number of ways of getting from A to B in the fastest time possible, using the prevailing conditions. This is why the shipping lanes are always crowded, no matter how large the sea.

On the Celtic fringes of Europe, there was a tradition of seafaring holy men, ranging from bishops to saints or pilgrims, who wandered to remote areas looking for lonely places in which to devote their lives to prayer. In the spiritual landscape, these men and women would have been the earliest lighthouses. This might even have worked practically. Hermitages would have been situated on the most beautiful and dangerous headlands, where a dwelling would have provided a warning light to mariners. In their leather coracles, the Celtic saints wandered as far as Iceland and, very probably, America. I think if I'd been sailing in those tiny, tough, but insubstantial vessels, I would have become very religious as well.

In order to have a break from the tense atmosphere on the boat, I took myself off to the Maritime Museum in Douarnenez, where an exhibition showed the reconstruction of an early Celtic voyage. One of the panels recounted the story of St Efflam who sailed to Brittany on a stone. Such stories are so widespread along the Atlantic coast of Europe, from Ireland to Portugal, that they must have been a mythological way of describing a common experience. But how could anybody sail a stone? Were the early voyagers such good seamen that they could even float a boulder? The millennium stone in Milford Haven had made fools of its modern curators by showing how difficult even shifting a would-be menhir can be. The museum in Douarnenez pointed out that there was a connection between the legend of St Efflam and the cult of stone circles in Brittany. Might such accounts mean that no vessel was impossible to sail if you were acting in accordance with the will of God? If mountains can move, then crags can float and carry passengers.

Enda was said to have sailed to the Irish Aran islands in a stone boat. Cartographer and artist Tim Robinson identified this moment as the overlap between a mythological way of describing a society's experience and the Christian, historical model: 'St Enda's boat is the coming of history to Aran, symbolically its foundation stone.' At the same time, Enda's stone boat, writes Robinson, 'is headed for deeper harbours in the mind'. We had already discovered that seeing things accurately at sea can be difficult. I dismissed the legend of saints sailing stones as Celtic fancifulness.

Before the night was out, however, Leighton and I had seen a stone boat of our own.

We decided to sail round the Cap du Raz during the night, so that we arrived in the resort of Bénodet at dawn, thus avoiding the necessity of entering a strange harbour in the dark. We read the tides correctly and passed the notoriously turbulent cape without difficulty. However, once we were round the corner, we found ourselves in waters that were being heavily fished. Our thirty-five-foot yacht felt like an invisible particle in the subatomic night.

We were surrounded by the moving lights of fishing trawlers, and in the dark it was difficult to tell what kind of fishing was going on. Each trawler might be hauling in nets from behind it, laying them in a circular pattern or dredging. The most frightening of the fishing constellations were the purse-seiners, two boats working a net hung between them. The movement of these boats was swift and unpredictable. You would think that they were settled on a certain course when suddenly they would swing their rotating searchlights and swirl predatorily towards us, as if engaged in a demented tango. The radio channels were full of the trawlers calling up vessels by their positions and speed. I answered in my best French, but the calling vessels never identified who they were. The waters were so busy that, rather than taking our turn at watches, we both stayed uneasily on deck.

Then several things happened at once. We had been watching the circling trawlers on the radar when I spotted what I thought was a large unlit vessel on our port side. By now our nerves were frayed by constant avoidance of the fishing fleet around us and we complained loudly to one another about bloody French trawlers fishing illegally and not showing navigation lights. We both stared in horror as a large black boat shape loomed towards us, still dark. It was impossible to tell how near the boat was, as we couldn't guess its size. And then the penny dropped: forget fishing boats, that was a rock. No wonder it didn't respond to a radio call. We had come almost within hailing distance of a Breton rock. In my passage planning I had brought us in too close to the notorious Breton coast, famed worldwide for its vicious skerries. I called myself seven types of fool for having cut things so fine.

We changed course rapidly and Leighton went below to check our position. While he was there, the world suddenly disappeared.

'Fog!' I shouted.

I remembered only then that the Breton coast is also renowned for its fog. The water around us became strangely intimate. Coastline and fishing fleet were now invisible. Our world shrank to the loom of our navigation lights in a moist new medium – neither air nor sea but a stifling cloud of something in between.

Fog is a sailor's worst nightmare. It is especially hated because it leaves a crew utterly helpless. If you can't see where you're going then you can't know what to do to save yourself. In the 1955 *Admiralty Manual of Navigation*, the gravity of fog for the sailor calls forth an uncharacteristic outburst of feeling. When inward bound and caught by fog, the Admiralty asks: 'What should be in the Captain's mind as he approaches the land? We have no hesitation in replying: "I shall not grope or blunder in to narrow waters or near danger without adequate precaution."'

Here we were, too close in to a rocky coast, in the middle of a fishing fleet and completely surrounded by fog. I knew exactly how we were going to die. I felt sure that, at any moment, a trawler would come charging out of the fog and mow us down, leaving no trace of us except for a couple of floating fenders. I told myself to stay calm but heard myself panting loudly, as though my body were an animal with a mind of its own.

There is an established procedure for travelling by boat in fog or thick weather, with a number of tried and tested things you can do to help yourself. These are listed in the *Admiralty Manual of Navigation* and have changed little over the years:

On Entering Fog

1. Reduce to moderate speed.
2. Station lookouts. A good plan is to have two lookouts on the forecastle and two at the masthead, each with his own sector . . . Forecastle lookouts should be taught to indicate direction by pointing with the outstretched arm.
3. If in soundings, start the sounding machine.
4. In the vicinity of land, have an anchor ready for letting go.
5. Order silence on deck.
6. Close watertight doors . . .
7. Start the prescribed fog signal.
8. Warn the engine-room.

9. Decide if it is necessary to connect extra boilers.
10. Memorize the characteristics of air and submarine fog signals which may be heard. Remember that sound signals on some buoys are operated by wave motion and are thus unreliable.
11. Make sure that the siren is not synchronizing with those of other ships, or with shore fog signals . . .
12. Listen for radio beacons . . .
13. Start operating radar.
14. If in any doubt, put the ship at once on a safe course, parallel to or away from the coast.

The first thing Leighton did was have a pee. I was terribly impressed by his calmness in such a dire situation. I, as it happened, also wanted to relieve myself at that point (it was around two o'clock in the morning) but as I was on the helm I couldn't move. I slowed the boat down and concentrated on listening. Leighton then calmly went about preparing the boat. First, he insisted that we both wear our life jackets (but not our safety harnesses, lest the boat should go down quickly with us tied to her). Then he brought out the fog-horns and rigged up the searchlight. He then prepared the anchor, so that we could stay in shallow water until visibility returned.

Leighton had been in thick weather before on large ships and told me that sometimes lookouts were posted up the mast to enable sailors to see over the fog. At such times you could see stars above and the masts of other vessels like submarines' periscopes in the ocean of moist air. Leighton rigged a ladder up the mast so that he could climb it if this way of navigating became necessary. Because we could see nothing and were off a rocky coast, our best bet was to motor from buoy to buoy. We could use radar and the GPS to help us. That way we should be able to avoid all hazards and find our way into Bénodet.

Our first priority was to know where we were. We could see the exact position of the boat in relation to land on our GPS plotter. We had a pilotage book and I had insisted that we carry an up-to-date chart of the coast. Leighton had argued that the plotter would be adequate but that night we found that there were some buoys marked on the chart that did not appear on the plotter. Ever since then we've always carried both.

It was a busy night. I stayed on the helm while Leighton plotted our course. My Zen teacher had once told me to meditate as if my life depended on it. Now I was helming with the deep concentration you can summon only when you think your life is at risk. Normally it's only possible to steer well for two hours at a time. I did six hours straight. At the end of that period I still hadn't peed, but nothing was going to stop me from keeping the boat dead on course.

Leighton was admirable, methodical and measured. We found the first buoy at around 3 a.m. and knew then that we would be able to make our way in, even if all our electronics failed. The buoy's sound signal was activated by wave motion and we heard the mark sighing on the swell before we saw it. The moaning of lonely buoys at sea is eerie, like a person forever calling out to others who will never be able to help. The fog had hung the fibres of my woollen hat with diamonds. Dawn arrived creating white-out, and, as we came closer to Bénodet, we passed small boats with one or two fishermen pulling up lobster pots, or simply holding rods and staring at the fog. Behind them there was no horizon, so they seemed hung on a screen while sea, sky and light were in a state of suspended animation. There was little to hear except the squealing of a solitary swallow feeding in the pearly sky and the gurgle of *Jameeleh*'s bow wave through the water's silk. Finally, we found the fairway into Bénodet and tied up at the marina.

The only thing Leighton had forgotten to do in his fog drill was to tell me that we weren't about to die. I had spent six hours thinking that we had only minutes to live. I'm an alcoholic who hasn't drunk for fifteen years and yet, faced with extinction, I started to crave a cup of French coffee. I was surprised that it wasn't brandy that I wanted out there, but something to make me wake up even more. As it was, I never bothered with the coffee either, but spent a very long time in the loo.

After I'd relieved myself, Leighton and I looked at one another over breakfast. I was surprised by the well of calm from which we'd both drawn in a crisis. It was as if we'd left the surface chop of our bickering and entered a different medium, in which we could concentrate and keep ourselves safe. Perhaps we had begun to make our way by a kind of sight that was totally new to us both – and by that I don't mean radar.

CHAPTER FIVE

Through the Depression Factory

> Transient episodes of anxiety, sadness, or elation
> are part of normal experience and actually serve a
> dynamic purpose in the development and main-
> tenance of human social order. The emotions are
> not aberrations of mind but barometers of experi-
> ence that have been essential to our successful
> evolution. Seeking ways to blot out variation in
> mood is equivalent to the ancient mariner throw-
> ing away his sextant, or the airline pilot ignoring
> his navigational devices.
>
> Peter C. Whybrow, *A Mood Apart*

After all our difficulties in seeing our way, next morning the
sun came out in Bénodet. Coming back from the showers I
could see silver ripples playing on *Jameeleh*'s hull. The
shimmer made the boat appear transparent. The whole world
had become see-through: the out-of-season resort where
Marcel Proust came for his holidays, men fishing in the
marina, the craftsmen varnishing a wooden boat next to us,
and Leighton on deck, rearranging the ropes. Each element
looked as delicate as tracing-paper impressions, all layered
on top of each other and copied in silver and light, shining
like treasures but as insubstantial as nothing at all.

Our next day's sail, from Bénodet to Lorient, was stunning. It was late autumn by now, and I could smell woodsmoke coming off the land, a sweet blackberry aroma. It was warm enough to shed our heavy sailing clothes, and I cavorted on deck in a T-shirt and knickers and then even less. Leighton played with fishing lines over the stern of the boat but caught nothing, not even the Day-Glo orange jellyfish that moved like pouffes just beneath the surface of the water. Several times I was startled by what I thought was a dark reef under the boat, as if we had sailed into sudden shallows. I laughed when I realised that it was cast by *Jameeleh*'s own sail and that I had literally been frightened by our own shadow. Metaphorically, this was to happen to us time and again on our voyage, during which the most formidable hazards we were to face were internal and emotional, all the more dangerous because they were never marked on the Admiralty charts.

Another danger invisible on nautical charts is a force of awesome energy. The weather that sweeps across the North Atlantic, and which is dominated by low-pressure systems, has more of an effect on sailing than almost any other physical phenomenon. Not given to exaggeration, the Hydrographer of the Navy described these depressions in *Ocean Passages for the World* as follows: 'Of immense power, they cover great areas of the oceans with uninterrupted winds of long duration, and build up extensive areas of high seas and heavy swell. They are an important factor in deciding the route of a passage.'

Depressions – of the clinical kind – had already acted as a kind of guide in my life. We would not have undertaken this journey had it not been for a terrible low, whose internal pain forced me to reassess where I was going in life and to change direction. The next stage of our voyage, however, was to be dominated by the need to navigate around storm systems of vast scope and vigour, and which regularly kill sailors in the Bay of Biscay.

A depression on a weather map looks like a whorl in a tree. The closer together the isobar lines of the system, the deeper the low and the stronger the winds will be. The key to the whole system is the difference between temperatures at various points on the globe. When cold air meets a section of warm, the cold forces the warmer air to climb up along its back. The first sign from the ground of a coming depression is the sight of the warm air, which has been forced up the wedge of colder atmosphere (as on an escalator), condensing into high cirrus clouds. These are the faint wispy clouds up in the jet stream. They look as if someone has smudged wet white paint. We see this when the centre of the low is still up to a thousand miles away. As the depression comes closer, the cloud gradually lowers and, as the warm front itself arrives, rain falls. Later, more squalls happen as the cold front follows behind.

The notoriously temperamental UK climate occurs because of the way in which these cold and warm bodies of air repeatedly interpenetrate each other. Cold air French kisses the warm, which loses its identity for it, rain washes the atmosphere clear, and the rotating air knots together, copulating and mounting endlessly, producing offspring of showers and gales. Each frontal system comes over the UK like a temporary country in its own right, whose progress has international repercussions for clothes lines, gardens, sports fixtures and

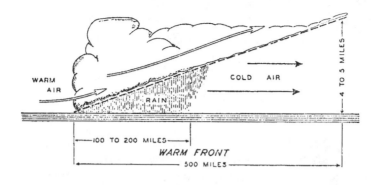

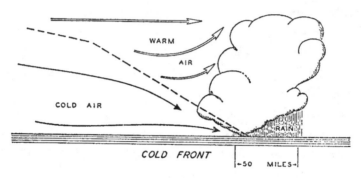

19   Section through warm front and cold front

people's spirits. Such changeability is neutral, neither good nor bad in itself, because the same energies that deliver foul weather also bring the fair. This is sexiness on a continental scale.

The phenomena of warm and cold fronts were first described by Norwegian scientists during the First World War. As they developed their theory the scientists used military metaphors drawn from the Battle of the River Marne, where there had been stalemate at the front in 1914. On weather charts, cold fronts and warm fronts look like sets of bunting being blown in from a street party out in the Atlantic. The cold fronts are shown by blue triangles, or Jean Paul Gaultier bras (frozen nipples is how I always remembered it for RYA exams), and warm fronts by red blancmanges in a line (silicone breasts in sunny St-Tropez). When rain comes as a result of these fronts interacting, it looks, on television weather maps, as though Britain is being invaded by hair. Bad storms mean a lot of hair coming in from the sea today. Some days Britain is covered in a feral pelt of rain, giving new meaning to the concept of a Bad Hair Day.

The whole North Atlantic could be described as a gigantic depression factory. The main feature of this climatic system is the endless succession of depressions moving from west to east, part of a conveyor belt stretching from Newfoundland and well into Continental Europe. The Azores High prevents these lows from hitting the Iberian peninsula, herding the rain-loaded clouds further north-east. The British Isles and the north-western corner of Europe as far south as Cape Finisterre lie just where the Atlantic depressions arrive, fully formed, off the oceanic assembly line. A rainfall map of Europe shows how the north-western part of the Continent catches the rainfall as moisture-laden winds from the Atlantic hit land, rise, condense and then begin to rain. These conditions are the atmospheric rock formations that define our weather landscape. If Atlantic depressions could be harvested and sold, nations like Wales would be wealthy.

I've heard it suggested that the depressions advancing towards us from across the Atlantic week by week are not, in reality, a parade of individual fronts, but the same front reforming time and again. Each occurrence of the low produces different weather nuances, but is the result of a fundamentally identical play of forces. The same can be said of clinical depression – early experiences leave scars that remain as weaknesses in our psychological make-up. Whatever the pressure that triggers a new episode, the tendency is to reactivate these old emotional configurations, giving the patient the familiar feeling of 'Oh no, not this again'. The individual drops of rain may be new, but the pattern in which they fall is distressingly familiar.

I once heard a train announcement on Llanelli railway station, informing passengers of a change of platform. The official voice declared: 'Passengers over b'there come over by 'ere, and passengers over by 'ere, go over b'there.' Everybody understood these instructions perfectly. Ports are paradoxical places in that they are simultaneously 'by 'ere' and 'b'there': they exist as geographical locations in their own right, but also as connections with any number of distant ports. Lorient was the port of the French East India Company during the eighteenth century. It is simultaneously a traditional Breton town and the embodiment of a civic life based entirely on trading in exotic goods. In Brittany there's no need to sail to India in order to reach the Far East; the Orient (l'Orient/ Lorient) is already there.

The economic importance of Lorient is clear as you approach from the sea. The port is well fortified, with all shipping having to enter by a very narrow channel, overlooked by gun emplacements. We decided to berth in the marina at the centre of town, and so passed the notorious U-boat pens outside the city. These huge concrete structures sheltered the German U-boats that harried Allied shipping in the Atlantic during the Second World War. Even today the deep purposefulness of those massive concrete structures has a sinister look and we shivered as we passed. We motored round a group of laid-up warships. Cormorants perched on what was left of their aerials, no doubt broadcasting news of the evening's fishing across the bay.

We might have reached the European Orient, but it was already early October and we were desperate not to spend the winter in the rainy, cyclone-prone north-west of Europe. We would need to be well south of Cape Finisterre in Spain if we were to have a chance of better weather, but in order to reach there, we would have to cross the infamous Bay of Biscay. We had coasted as far south as we dared and were afraid that the prevailing westerly winds would blow us ashore, leaving us unable to push our way out of southern France. This is known as becoming 'embayed'. We wanted to head for southern Portugal but to do this we faced three or four days at sea. I had been living in the depression factory – internal and external – for a very long time, and we were keen to see if we could move beyond it.

In sailing circles it is considered wise to cross Biscay ideally by the end of August and certainly before the equinoctial gales of autumn. The equinox in the middle of September had already passed and no gales had arrived, but it was only a matter of time. These regular gales can make an already dangerous stretch of water lethal. Not only is the Bay of Biscay the delivery end of the Atlantic depression factory, it also receives the full brunt of the Atlantic swell. Waves produced thousands of miles out in the ocean are free to build without any obstacle in their path until they hit the west coast of Europe. In deep water this matters little, but when the energy of this swell is pushed upwards against a shelving seabed, these breaking Atlantic rollers can produce mountainous seas. Yachts are regularly reported lost in Biscay. Once we were out in the middle of the bay, we would be two hundred miles from land. If we encountered bad weather then, there would be no friendly coastguard to call and nowhere to run.

There was, however, a good side to being in the depression factory. It meant that we could use the winds generated by its climatic turbulence to travel south. There was little danger of being becalmed. In fact, autumn sees the start of many of the big professional sailing races for this reason. At Lorient marina we were moored next to the French skipper Luc Coquelin, who was preparing his boat for the forthcoming Route du Rhum, from Brittany to Guadeloupe in the Caribbean, a race in which Britain's Ellen MacArthur was also competing. Luc and the other racers were hoping for big winds and we, as novices, wanted to be well south before these autumn gales arrived.

We knew that the window of good weather we were enjoying after the fog would soon close, but we were frightened to face Biscay on our own. We dwelt in an in-between place of terrible indecision, imagining everything that could go wrong at sea, but unable to feel comfortable in port. I've heard this described as the Dentist's Chair stage of going to sea. You know you've got to do it, but you'd do anything to avoid submitting to the injection and the drill.

We talked to everybody we knew in the port, asking their advice about local conditions. The more we thought about going, the more impossible it seemed. I asked a professional French skipper of many years' experience: 'The sea is totally unreasonable. We are not reasonable creatures either, so how on earth can we be expected to cope at sea?'

'I don't know,' he said carefully. He paused for another moment. 'I just go.'

'Look,' shouted Leighton when I urged throwing caution to the wind, 'you have no idea what the sea can be like. I've been out there in bad weather, I *know* what the sea can do.'

'If we don't go now, we'll be stuck in Brittany for the winter,' I replied grimly, feeling that my ignorance might, for once, be an advantage.

Lorient suddenly became unbearable. We were moored near a building site and the sound of pile-drivers reached a crescendo and seemed to come right into the boat, juddering against our nerves. Here was the dentist's drill without anaesthetic. Late-summer flies found a warm refuge in *Jameeleh*'s saloon, driving me wild. I chased after them trying, and failing, to swat them with a tea towel.

'I can't stand it, Leighton,' I screamed. 'Nothing could be worse than this. We won't be able to live with ourselves if we chicken out. Whatever happens, let's face it. We *have* to leave.'

Once we'd decided, the overwhelming sense of purposelessness disappeared and we were left with sheer terror, which I much preferred.

We sailed on the afternoon tide, leaving the jackhammers behind. The bluebottles came with us in the boat, but once we were out at sea I didn't have the heart to shoo them out of the cabin. In the end, I was grateful to those Lorient flies because they had given us the final impetus we needed to depart. Now Leighton, some Breton bluebottles and I were going out to face the worst together.

In silence we watched as the buoys marking Les Errants flashed, calling out warnings about yet more rocks. By dusk we had left them behind and were out in the infamous Bay of Biscay.

During our complicated manoeuvres to leave the British coast, I had done a good deal of research into seasickness. For us this wasn't an academic exercise but an urgent matter of safety, as we were short-handed on *Jameeleh*. Leighton was gallingly immune to seasickness. From time to time, in rough seas, he would claim to be feeling 'a bit off', just to keep me company, but I never believed him.

I wonder if this doesn't provide a clue as to the adaptive role of seasickness in mariners. Seasickness is caused by a neural mismatch between the information given to the body about its movements by the eye and that conveyed through the organs of balance in the inner ear. When these two sets of information conflict, the result is nausea. Looking at the steady horizon synchronises them again, but it's difficult to explain why seasickness happens in the first place. For it to have been preserved by evolution it must have some useful function. It certainly upstages fear, making sailors concentrate on something else. In *The Navy 1939 to the Present Day*, the most powerful testimony I've ever read about the misery of seasickness was given by a Corporal Joe Humphrey in his account of landing on Sicily during the Second World War: 'Every Marine Commando was feeling so sick, I don't think we could have cared if the whole German army was waiting for us on the beaches.'

Perhaps the malaise is a way of stopping you from confusing your organs of balance further still, by ensuring you feel so sick that you're unlikely to move any more than is strictly necessary on a boat. Nausea during pregnancy might work in this way, ensuring that expectant mothers eat only the plainest, least risky food for their unborn babies. Interestingly, women have been shown to be 70 per cent more susceptible to seasickness than men, and the effect is, unhappily,

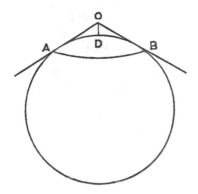

The Visible Horizon

is that circle on the surface of the earth which marks the extent or limit of an observer's view at sea.

O represents an observer's eye, the line O D the height of the observer's eye above the level of the sea, the circle A B the visible horizon.

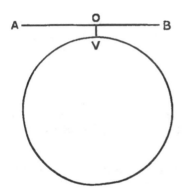

The Sensible Horizon

is that plane at the observer's eye at right angles to the vertical or plumb-line.

O represents the observer's eye, O V the vertical or plumb-line, A O B the sensible horizon.

20   Definitions of horizon

exacerbated by menstruation. The whole thing reminded me of depression, in which two views of the self no longer compute, requiring a period of withdrawal, during which a new internal horizon can be drawn.

I had already experimented with conventional seasickness medication and found the drowsiness they produce a serious drawback. My cousin, who's an astronaut, suffers from space sickness, so I asked him how he deals with the problem. Vomit in orbit must be a real drag. He emailed me that he took one Dramamine-based medication along with another

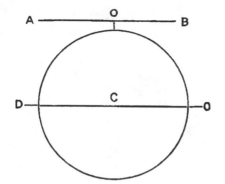

The Rational Horizon

is a plane through the earth's centre parallel to the sensible horizon.

O represents the observer, the plane A O B is the sensible horizon, C the centre of the earth, the plane D C O the rational horizon.

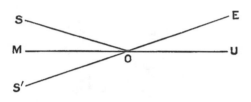

The Artificial Horizon

is a horizontal reflecting surface, the plane of whose surface is parallel to the rational horizon, the best being a tray of mercury at rest. It is used for taking altitudes on shore.

M U represents the surface of the mercury at rest, E the observer's eye, S the object, S' the object's reflection, S O S' twice the observed altitude.

to counteract the sleepiness. That combination made it virtually impossible to feel sick.

Several remedies short-cut the information being taken in by the eyes. It was alleged that Lord Nelson, who was famously prone to seasickness, suffered less from the malaise after he had damaged the sight in one eye. If it were that simple, an eyepatch would be a common remedy for seasickness. I read that Nelson injured his right eye but that he wore a patch over his left, which was sensitive to strong light, so I'm still confused about which eye the seasickness patch should cover. I have heard also about a pair of glasses whose lenses are half filled with tinted blue water, thus creating an artificial horizon on which the sailor can concentrate, even when he or she goes below, out of sight of the actual horizon.

I have discovered the curious fact that it's impossible to have hiccups and to feel seasick at the same time, maybe because each individual hiccup provides a temporal and spatial point of reference for the body, a radar blip in an ocean of nausea. This is my unique contribution to the science of seasickness.

I tried eating, sucking or chewing any number of things to prevent nausea. Root and crystallised ginger were recommended, but did nothing for me. On D-Day, British soldiers were given chewing gum to help them with sickness as they crossed the Channel, but survivors complained later that it didn't work. Someone once told me that marmalade was used by Mary Queen of Scots as an anti-seasickness medicine when she sailed from France to Scotland. Nantucket whalers made the nauseous swallow a piece of pork fat tied to a string, which was then pulled back up. If this didn't work, the process was repeated. I heard a similarly surreal cure involving pork fat and jam from a mariner who had sailed from Cardiff. As sure-fire ways of getting the vomiting over with, both options were winners but I wasn't about to try them. At sea I prefer to postpone being sick for as long as possible, thus avoiding the additional problems of dehydration. I have a different policy for sickness caused by excess alcohol, however, believing that the sooner you vomit the sooner you can drink some more, but that's another story. And I doubt if pig fat tied to a string will catch on with the nation's drinkers.

Through trial and error I have gradually developed a system for managing my nausea. The most important element for me is a homeopathic remedy, *tabacum*. Homeopaths very sensibly distinguish three types of motion sickness, each with its own solution. *Tabacum*, based on the tobacco plant, addresses the type of nausea where you get cold and need to be out in the fresh air. *Cocculus indicus* treats nausea with more vertigo in it, and *petroleum* treats sickness in vehicles using petrol. The great advantage of these tiny pills is that they act instantly and don't make me drowsy. Some days, however, they are much less effective than others for reasons I can never work out.

Two further necessities in prophylaxis are to keep warm at all costs, and to keep eating and drinking to prevent dehydration. Another golden rule is never to go below if you can possibly help it, as it results in instant nausea. This leaves one with a dilemma about toilet matters. For a woman, peeing over the side of a moving boat is not only uncomfortable but dangerous (believe me, I've tried it). The best and most cost-effective anti-seasickness device I ever bought was a small painter's bucket so that I could relieve myself discreetly on deck and throw the contents over the side. This needs to be done downwind. I once seriously lost favour with Leighton when he was unexpectedly covered in warm yellow spray. He loves me, but not that much.

The last secret weapon I learned to prepare before leaving port was a plastic bag full of crackers, bread sticks, mints, boiled sweets, dried fruit and homeopathic remedies.

The plastic bag itself came in very handy as a last resort.

Of course, the traditional and infallible remedy for seasickness is the acquisition of sea legs simply by spending time on a boat. To begin with, Biscay treated us gently, with light winds and smooth seas. I went to bed as we cleared land, fully expecting to be called to stand my watch in four hours' time, but Leighton was so anxious about the crossing that he couldn't relax, so he let me sleep longer. In fact, he didn't sleep at all the first night, even when I came up to take my turn.

During the first hours of the voyage, I lay in the cabin, wedged into the bunk, and was soothed to sleep by the silken shoosh-shoosh of water parting around the hull. Gradually, however, the wind increased and I found being below unexpectedly noisy. We were still close to land, so the seas were short and choppy. From inside the boat the water didn't sound liquid at all, but as if we were travelling along a rocky road pitted with potholes. We had left Lorient in a light south-easterly, which was forecast to veer north-easterly later that night. All the sailing literature tells you that it's viable to cross Biscay on anything but a south-westerly wind, as that will end up pushing you back towards land and may make exiting the bay impossible. Any wind with 'south' in it is not recommended. As the night went on, the wind refused to turn as predicted, and grew even stronger. By dawn it sounded to me as if we were speeding over a road studded with nuts and bolts, megalithic stones, and the odd refrigerator thrown in for good measure.

When I got up, Leighton, who was concerned that the wind hadn't yet turned, persuaded me to call a passing tanker to see if they'd received a weather forecast. By now we were out of sight of land and therefore couldn't receive the forecasts on our VHF radio, which operates by line of sight. We'd heard many stories about modern tankers neglecting to keep a listening watch on Channel 16, as always used to be the case, but we were delighted when we received an answer to our request. The weather forecast continued to be good, so we had no excuse to turn back.

During that day, the seas and wind continued to increase

in force. Everything not tied down on the boat took on a life of its own, as if we were weightless in space. Except that these objects were heavy and wanted to attack us. Making a cup of tea became a dangerous activity, as the kettle kept jumping up, trying to scald me. Loose knives hurtled towards me with malicious intent. Clothes became very uncooperative and difficult to put on. In the growing swell from the south-west, I suddenly remembered what it was like to be a very young child, unable to handle the world. Then and now, I would hit myself against objects, lose my balance and fall over. When I was eating or drinking I could no longer count on liquid reaching my mouth safely, and I spilt apple juice all down the inside of my clothes. In fact, in a thermal sailing suit under waterproof salopettes and overcoat, I felt as though I were an infant again, padded and clumsy. And going to the toilet, with so many layers to shed, was a nightmare. We both looked and moved like Teletubbies. I was exhausted just by trying to stand upright as the seas around us became increasingly demented.

And then the barometer began to drop. It was dusk on the second evening and Leighton had just declared that we were two hundred miles from land in any direction. We both

21   Sectional view of a squall

checked the barometer and the barograph in the saloon, and watched in dismay as they plummeted together, a sure sign of an imminent blow. We looked at one another in dread and then went up to the cockpit, trying to read the sky above us for more information. It was as if we were in some horrible virtual classroom and were being shown, in living cyclorama, the classic Features of an Approaching Depression. Our hearts sank as we watched a huge bank of cloud work itself up across the sky in a wedge. We could see lightning in the distance, and that cloud over there could be another squall ahead. We could read our fortune in the south-westerly sky, and the immediate future certainly looked colourful.

High pressure means opposite things emotionally and meteorologically. A high-pressure system is an area of weather that is stable, with little wind, and is slow to change. This is only a problem for yachts if they become becalmed. A low-pressure system, or depression, is the opposite. Low atmospheric pressure in an area means that air rises and winds blow in from other parts of the ocean. The lower the atmospheric pressure, the faster winds come in to fill the space. A low means high stress for sailors.

As it became dark, Leighton prepared the boat for the onslaught. He went all round the deck checking that everything was battened down tightly. He exchanged the genoa sail at the front for a storm sail and put two reefs in the mainsail, to reduce the area of canvas exposed to the wind, making it less likely that the boat would be knocked over in a sudden gust. We made sure we both had something to eat while we could. Then we sat in the growing gloom of the cockpit, waiting for the blow.

'Oh God, now we're for it,' groaned Leighton. 'This could get very rough.'

I said nothing. He continued, apprehension making him unable to relax. 'I knew we shouldn't have come. We should have stayed in port. Much better to be in there wishing we were at sea than out here, wishing we were in.'

If there is one big similarly between atmospheric depressions and the emotional kind, it's the way in which an unstable centre sucks in bad weather from elsewhere. Once a patient becomes depressed about a life crisis, that vacuum tends to pull in bad memories from the past, previous experiences of despair and defeat. As they're drawn in, negativity generates its own momentum, and it's difficult to remember that the real crisis is in the present and has little to do with that past history to which you now feel so vulnerable.

On the boat, waiting for the storm, we could see this process being enacted physically, above us. From the west the depression brought in a spectacular parade of clouds lit up against a green sky. In the clouds I could see clowns and cowboys, trolls and birds of paradise. I watched huge grotesque profiles of dwarfs and princesses. Groucho Marx was there and a couple of Barbie dolls. If this was my subconscious looking at the Rorschach blots of clouds, then I was in trouble. I saw Punch and Judy, the busts of Roman emperors, elephants, parrots, sea horses, moose, bison, all in a glorious, vulgar Mardi Gras parade. I had never witnessed such an atmospheric carnival before, nor had I expected a depression to be an event of such joyful energy.

Observing the sea casually staging such staggering effects without even needing an audience, I suddenly understood that turbulence is a constant. It made little sense, out here, to be afraid of tumult. The trick was to know how to deal with it, to have a good emotional boat. Part of that meant fully understanding how fluid the world really is, even though it looks fixed, and to know where you are in that process of flux. A giant poodle cloud morphed into a gargoyle and then into a witch. By now the wind was blowing force six and gusting seven. As the cloud drew closer I braced myself at the helm for the inevitable blast of wind and accompanying rain. Depressions have a rhythm of their own and I was starting to move to this one's music.

Several hours had passed and, although the weather was becoming ever more lively, the savage storm we had feared did not materialise. The barometer began to rise again and Leighton decided that he had to get some sleep, so I stood watch. Even though we were far from land, I could still see the navigation lights of large cargo ships. A port light in the distance, I decided, was a ship on its way into La Rochelle from the Atlantic.

The sea at night is a terrible place for hallucinations. At one point I became convinced that I could see a long scaffolding structure, studded with red lights. I was sure to begin with that this was miles away, but then suddenly feared that the immense structure was bearing down on us. The radar showed nothing but I had to believe my own eyes. In a panic I called Leighton. He had told me not to hesitate to ask for help if I was unsure about anything. He knew from experience how easy it is to see strange things in the dark. When he was in the merchant navy and had to stand watch at night, it wasn't uncommon to hear of sailors mistaking stars for hazards. He himself was once ridiculed for reporting an aeroplane when he was half asleep. On this occasion Leighton could see straight away that there was nothing to concern us, that I was making a story out of nothing. Grumbling, he went back down below, staggering with fatigue.

Our third morning at sea felt entirely different. We could feel that we were further south, because we were sailing in strong sunlight. When he was drenched by waves crashing on to the deck, Leighton noticed that the sea had become warmer. The waves were still large but the colour of the sea had changed from the navy of the Breton coast to a deep turquoise. We estimated that the waves were six metres high by now (the size of a house), and hitting us on the beam, rolling us from side to side. At breakfast I no longer needed to force myself to eat: I was actually hungry. I wedged myself into a corner of the cockpit and wolfed down my muesli, grinning broadly at the breakers we had left behind. Being at sea without feeling sick was an entirely different experience. The motion stopped being a torture and became enjoyable. I had gained the fabled sea legs at last. Perhaps I could live in chaos, after all.

I was startled a short time later, when I caught a quick motion out of the corner of my eye and saw a small bird perched on the gunwale of the boat. It was tiny, with green feathers and delicate thin legs. Bold Cleopatra-kohl lines were drawn from the corners of its eyes. I was astonished when it jumped even closer to me and landed on the wheel, which was being driven remotely by Hilda the Autohelm. The bird – probably a wood warbler or chiffchaff – was panting, clearly exhausted. Every gust of wind blew deep into its feathers, parting them to show their earth colours. It was strangely moving to meet a creature even more frail than us out in these mountainous, working seas, as unprotected as a human heart beating in a world of violence. I put out some crumbs for the warbler, but they blew away in the strong wind. Shortly afterwards the bird took off over the immense sea-scape around us. That night I dreamt that the bird had

22   No longer seasick

hopped into the cabin to stay with us, and I was pleased, as long as he promised not to shit everywhere.

Later that morning I even went below to make food and look at the plotter. Before, all I'd been able to manage was a purposeful dash for the bunk, trying to get horizontal before the dreadful nausea hit. I even managed to use the head, but found the motion of the boat had made this a most uncomfortable sensation. The water in the pan sloshed as the boat moved, wetting my bottom with an unspeakable mixture of liquids and solids. Leighton confided that it was even worse for him sitting down, as he had to try to hold his bagpipe equipment out of the turbulent toilet water. No wonder sailors get constipated at sea.

By now we were keeping regular four-hour watches, taking turns to sleep. One of the reasons the sea holds such fascination is that it's a blank canvas on to which you can project personal preoccupations. The sea is all things to all men. I should have been bored but I found myself absorbed in watching the light changing on clouds and water. Sailors have described how looking deeply into the chaos of the boat's wake draws the mind out from the body and leaves you empty in the middle of constant change. As I looked out of the cockpit at the sea and sky, I found all manner of memories coming back to me from my subconscious. Tiny incidents from my childhood hit me with remarkable vividness. I remembered how Mrs Jones, our primary school teacher, used to keep a pot of honey in her cupboard and give us a spoonful when we had a cough, and how I used to pretend to have a sore throat to have more sweetness. I thought gratefully of a stranger in Tel Aviv who had brought me a glass of water after I'd been sick on a bus, only to disappear immediately. The clarity of these recollections was astonish-

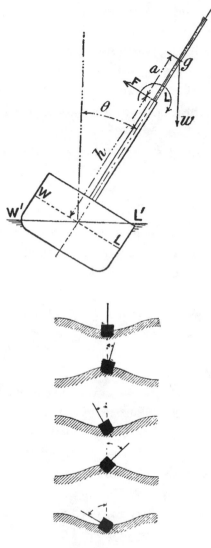

23   The rolling of ships

ing, and they gave me great pleasure, as if the riches of a whole life were being let out of the safe just for a moment, to glint on the velvet of the sea. The clouds brought in by the depression held little meaning other than as indications of meteorological fluctuation, but the state of mind they conjured up in me was dynamic with personal significance.

At one point I spotted a lobster-pot marker that had clearly drifted a long way from land. Normally, we would take great pains to avoid these floats, as they indicate nets in which our propeller could become caught. I imagined that this free-floating flag marked a mystical meeting point for fishermen in the deep waters of Biscay. After passing it, I felt we were halfway across.

So time went on. We ate, we slept, we looked at the sea. By now the waves were even steeper. We were sailing down ridges that hid us completely in their troughs. When we were on top of the waves, we could see all around us, but when we were down, we could see nothing but water above. We could have been close to a fishing boat but, if we'd been rising and falling in sync with one another, we would never have sighted it. In a flat sea, nothing is hidden from you; a tanker is clear from miles away. Rough seas make travelling a private matter, hidden in deep troughs of thought, like pain.

The motion of the boat was now so violent that, when I woke, I found myself groaning and thinking, 'Oh no, this isn't still going on, is it?' That night, when I was called for my watch, I was so afraid that I cried. I was shaking as I pulled on my waterproofs, but didn't tell Leighton because he was so exhausted that he needed all the sleep I could give him. There was one advantage to keeping watch at night: I couldn't see the enormous waves as they raced towards us, and that was a mercy.

By now, we were both beginning to suffer from aural hallucinations. In the middle of the third night I was down below in the bunk when I heard Leighton chatting to a posh

Englishwoman with a Radio 4 voice. I wasn't surprised by the conversation, but was full of admiration for the skill of the person who'd manoeuvred another boat close enough for the Radio 4 woman to come on board *Jameeleh*. Of course, there was no visitor and no other boat. The following afternoon, I swore I heard a very loud commentary on a horse race, broadcast with the hysterical excitement of Saturday-afternoon sports coverage. Leighton confessed that the scuppers, which let water drain out of the cockpit, were talking to him. They didn't have much to say, only 'Simon', but that was disturbing enough. I heard Hilda speak as well, something about 'mothering' in the screech of the autohelm.

It was during the afternoon of our third day at sea that we faced our biggest crisis so far. Leighton had been plotting our position conscientiously on a chart, and this had shown that we were, despite all our efforts, being pushed east into the Bay of Biscay. We had originally been heading for Bayona, south of Cape Finisterre. Because the wind was now from the south-west, we couldn't sail directly into it. We could tack out into the Atlantic, but this would send us north-west, away from our destination, and add a long time to our passage. Our weather window was tight as it was, so we couldn't afford the extra time for this course of action. The opposite tack would set us deep into Biscay. The seas were becoming mountainous, the wind was dying and we were being pushed by a huge force towards the dangerous coast of northern Spain.

Three days and nights of hardly sleeping had taken their toll on Leighton. When he realised what was happening, he exploded with rage and frustration. He said he was exhausted because I was so useless with the sails, and that we were now in real trouble. 'I should never have let you push me into coming, I knew it would turn out badly,' he ranted.

'Now is not the time to talk about this,' I replied coldly. I was stunned by this volte-face. 'If you thought we shouldn't have come, you should have said so at the time. You can't keep quiet when the decision is being made and then say "I told you so" when things go wrong.'

Everything Leighton had said about our current situation was true. I had also been growing increasingly uneasy during the day, but had saved energy by repeating to myself, 'I chose this,' which seemed to help with the fear. He had worked tirelessly to keep us moving safely and well. I could see that Leighton was on his last legs. He told me that even his hair was hurting with fatigue. I was shocked by his misdirection of worry and fear on to me, and very disappointed because it was totally unlike Leighton. In the past, I had seen him accept raw deals from other people time and again, and carry more than his own share of difficult and arduous work cheerfully. I didn't recognise the version of events Leighton was now screaming at me. Had I pushed him to leave against his will? I couldn't have done that to the Leighton I knew, but this was a different person. I couldn't respect anybody who didn't take full responsibility for his own choices. I couldn't even look at him.

After so long out at sea, everything began to happen quickly. By teatime we could see the stunning mountains of Galicia. Leighton sent me off to sleep, but I refused. I'd earned this landfall, and I wanted to see every moment of it. I pulled out all my stops and did everything I could to support him. Leighton decided that the safest bet would be for us to make for La Coruña. When the wind finally died we had enough fuel to motor in, but we were still eight hours away from port. As the light ripened into sunset, I pulled out the charts and pilotage books for La Coruña and plotted our course. Then I heated up a meal of shepherd's pie and peas, so that we had at least eaten before dark. Leighton and I decided where we'd anchor when we arrived, and he prepared the equipment. The swell was now bigger than ever, suggesting that there was heavy weather coming from the south-west, pushing up the seas like a rucked carpet on a dance floor. We hoped sincerely that we would be safely in port before the dancing began. Now we were really racing the weather clock.

As dusk fell we saw the lights prick on along Cabo Ortegal. Against land the swell was even more obvious. One moment we'd be steering by a certain light on the cape, the next a wave would come between us and it, blacking out everything. We were surfing down waves of darkness.

It was a long night coming in. Things looked up when we finally made the powerful Torre de Hércules light outside La Coruña, but we had the swell with us until the very last. Fishing vessels with floodlit decks passed us at speed as we headed for the breakwater. By the time we slipped behind the sea wall I couldn't see straight, nor could I make sense of the lights marking the channels into various parts of the port.

Finally, at 4 a.m., we were anchored. I cooked sausages and scrambled eggs to celebrate our arrival in Spain, and we ate them in the cockpit. I thought I was hallucinating again when I could hear convivial conversations from several directions. As our eyes became used to the gloom, we saw that we were, in fact, surrounded by tiny unlit boats no bigger than coracles, with groups of Spanish men fishing in them.

We had made it safely to Galicia, but I feared that our marriage had been blown into dangerous emotional waters. It was a place we'd never been before.

A few hours later I awoke shivering with shock, fatigue and paranoia. Shortly after, one of the blocks holding the main sheet to the traveller (if you're not a sailor, you don't need to know) crumbled in Leighton's hand. We looked at one another and went pale. We had been sailing all across the bay, and sailing hard, not knowing that, at any second, the boom could have flown loose and hit one of us in the temple. We vowed never to think of ourselves as unlucky again and agreed that, however scary, this crossing was the most awesome thing either of us had done in our lives.

Later that morning we were humbled further. We had crossed Biscay as the door of autumn slammed shut, and on winds that should have made it impossible. In the yacht club, Leighton and I looked at a weather chart for the area. There were gale warnings posted for the whole of Biscay between Iroise in Brittany and Finisterre. La Coruña was surrounded by five separate lows. The equinoctial storms that had been so late had finally arrived with a vengeance.

That night, in port, a gale hit us with brute force like a speeding wall. We had made it through the Bay of Biscay by the skin of our teeth.

CHAPTER SIX

Light over Danger

A good lock has no bar or bolt,
   And yet it cannot be opened.
A good knot does not restrain,
   And yet it cannot be unfastened.

Lao Tzu, *The Tao of Power*

'Everything will be much better once we get past Finisterre,'
said Leighton for the hundredth time. I'd stopped believing
him.

We should have felt ecstatic to be in La Coruña but the
lows surrounding us as we completed our crossing of Biscay
had climbed aboard the boat. Leighton was frustrated with
me for not being a better sailor and felt that, however much
he did to make up for my shortcomings, it wasn't going to
be enough. I felt hurt and furious. My spirits sank, making
Leighton even more nervous. We felt that we had at least
deserved a high.

Now that we were in Galicia, I was determined that I
should continue to practise handling the boat, and so when,
on the second day, we moved *Jameeleh* from outside the old
sailing club in La Coruña to the newly renovated Dársena de
la Marina in the centre of town, I asked Leighton if I could

take her in myself. This was one job that did not require physical strength, only dexterity and good hand-eye co-ordination. Leighton had been unhappy with me at the helm since an incident with our first boat, *Nitro*, when I'd botched an approach to a pontoon and scratched her side. Graham the Siren, however, had done me one great service, for which I was very grateful: he had shamed Leighton into letting me practise my boat handling and had argued, forcefully, that all I needed was experience.

Boat handling is one of the basic skills in seamanship. It looks deceptively easy, like driving a car, but is, in fact, quite different. The main problem is that, if you think of the boat as a car, not only does it have no brakes, but it's embedded in the sea, which is a road that never stops flexing. You can stop a boat by putting the engine into reverse, thus checking her forward motion, but you have no control whatsoever over the tide running beneath you, or a strong wind blowing around you, and these may even be pulling the boat in two different directions. The most you can hope to do is to com-pensate for these forces by reading their effect on the boat and taking them into account as you attempt to slide her into the designated berth. At best, it's like driving on ice.

Many ports will not allow ships to enter unless they use a Port Authority pilot, who has crucial knowledge of local con-ditions. Often, you can see small pilot boats dashing out to approaching ships that have put a companionway down their hull, to enable the pilot to climb on board. When a ship leaves port, the same is done in reverse, with the pilot being picked up by the small vessel once the ship is clear of hazards.

The best description I know of the difficulties of boat hand-ling was written by Captain Rob Lovell in an article on marine pilots. The piece notes that most 'marine incidents' occur within harbour limits or the approaches to a port. The marine pilot 'earns his living working solely within these moments of terror'. Analysis of pilots' urine has shown that levels of adrenalin in their blood are up to seven times higher than in a normal person, which explains why they might have difficulties going to sleep after a night shift. Docking – with its attendant fear of collision – was always a flash point between me and Leighton, so I'd already experienced a few doses of the pilots' adrenalin myself.

Captain Lovell examines why marine pilotage is so demanding. The problems of manoeuvring and docking large commercial vehicles are entirely different in scale from our task of shifting a small yacht, but the principles are identical. Lovell asks you to consider the following:

- The marine pilot is trying to manoeuvre the largest movable man-made objects on earth.
- He drives them down relatively narrower channels than the driver of a road transport truck is required to do.
- It is not uncommon to have an 80,000-tonne displacement vessel powered by as little as 8,000 horse power. This equates to one horse power per 10,000 kg. It's a bit like having to drive a Mack truck and semi trailer powered by a lawnmower engine and then park it in a parking place with a metre clearance each end.
- Now to make it interesting, let's simulate leeway drift [the effect of wind on a ship] by making the truck slide sideways at one km per hour, and the current by making the parking place move along the road. We'll give you two smaller

- side-on lawnmowers to help push the truck sideways into the kerb but, like the truck, they too are slipping and sliding.
- Sounds too easy, doesn't it? Let's add one more dimension: we won't give you any brakes, we'll make you slow the truck down by causing the wheels to spin backwards, and when you do so, you have to let go of the steering wheel, because large ships do not steer when going astern.
- Finally, if you mess it up, we'll throw you in court and make you justify why you should have a job.

The relationship between captain and pilot is potentially problematic. Taking a pilot on board is compulsory in many ports (and certainly in places like the Panama or Suez canals), and although the pilot gives instructions to the crew, the captain never relinquishes his authority over the ship. The legal definition of a pilot is 'any person not belonging to a ship who has the conduct of her'. In his book on maritime law, from which this definition is taken, Christopher Hill goes on to comment: 'That he has exclusive control and conduct of the ship is seldom disputed, but this is very different from having command of the ship.'

During our voyage we met Dietrich, an East German sea captain with many years' experience on merchant vessels. He had been privileged to sail with the German submarine skipper on whom the award-winning television mini-series *Das Boot* was based. Despite his long years of service, Dietrich was still entranced by anything to do with seamanship and the sea, and was determined to continue learning. He told us that, very often, a captain is frightened before going out to sea, and that he himself never sleeps on the night before sailing. (Leighton was the same.) The relationship with the pilot brings this unease into focus, as the captain doesn't know how the officer is going to handle his ship. Some, said Dietrich, like to push the ship by using the engine a good deal, while others will ask for the ship to be singled up (that is, for all the ropes to be cast off until the ship is held only by one rope astern and one for'ard) and then say, 'Now we wait and see what she does.' The pilot then observes the effect of the wind and tide on the ship and acts accordingly. This last method was the one Dietrich favoured, because 'the best manoeuvre is a slow manoeuvre'.

At the root of the problem between captain and pilot at sea is the question of split authority. Hill argues:

> Divided authority has traditionally been the cause of disaster. Conflict would seem to be inevitable. We know how dangerous a car becomes when driven at the same time by husband *and* wife (sitting beside him). One theory of the pilot's role is that he is perhaps the ship's Master's most expert navigational aid; unique because he is a human being not a machine such as a radar set or echo sounder.

Hill doesn't seem to have considered that a wife might actually be driving the car, but that is secondary to his point about the pilot being a skipper's best navigational aid. This definition doesn't allow for the process of learning, nor for the radar set's reaction when it was soundly kicked for not knowing its job.

And so it was that my request to move *Jameeleh* to the new marina failed to inspire much enthusiasm in Leighton. He agreed reluctantly, not wanting to put me in a worse mood than I was in already. I asked him, before we did anything, if we could sit down quietly and talk through the manoeuvre, taking into account what the boat would do, given the weather conditions. I wanted to rehearse the move in my own mind, so that I was clear in which order I would turn the wheel and in which direction, when I should go astern and how I should compensate for the tidal drift in the new basin. Leighton was impatient to be gone.

'Look, either you're taking the boat in or you're not. There's no need for a big discussion. Just get on with it.'

Leighton's view was that, if I was going to be skipper, I should make the decisions. I hadn't really wanted to be skipper, I just wanted to handle the boat, but it seemed there was no intermediate role between captain and crew. I argued that I couldn't decide anything before discussing all the choices. Leighton was scornful.

'You can't take command without taking responsibility,' he growled. 'You're the skipper, *you* decide.'

I didn't say anything, but I thought we sounded like a cliché – masculine authoritarianism versus a more feminine principle of management by consensus.

Of course, it went badly and we ended up having a terrible row. The berth I chose (exercising my authority, as I'd been told to do) was far from straightforward to get into – but then I'd have known that if we'd had a chance to discuss the matter. We berthed the boat, with some difficulty, but during the process Leighton bombarded me with instructions that confused me. I finally saw red when he shouted loudly all over the dock: 'Stop the fucking boat!' If he knew so much about it, I told him, he should do it himself, so he did. The atmosphere on board for the rest of the day was terrible. Even a shopping trip to the glorious fish and fruit market in the centre of La Coruña didn't improve matters.

Looking back, I can see that maritime law's distinction between the roles of skipper and pilot would have been very useful to us at this point, with the captain in overall charge of the safety of the vessel during the manoeuvre, but the pilot delegated to handle the boat as he (or, in this case, she) sees fit. From then on, whenever I wanted to annoy Leighton as we were leaving or entering a port, I would sing a hymn that a friend had taught me:

> Do you want a pilot?
> Signal, then, to Jesus
> Do you want a pilot?
> Bid Him come aboard.
> For He will safely guide
> You 'cross the ocean wide
> Until you reach at last
> The Heaven-ly Har-bour.

In the past, pilots could receive a very raw deal from the crews of the ships they guided into land. According to the *Black Book of the Admiralty*:

> It is established for a custom of the sea that yf a shyp is lost by defaulte of the lodeman [the pilot] the maryners may, if they please, bring the lodeman to the windlass or any other place and cut off his head withoute the mariners being bounde to answer before any judge, because the lodeman has committed high treason against his undertakynge of the pilotage. And this is the judgement.

No harm had come to *Jameeleh*, so I felt that I was being reproached unfairly. When, however, a few days later, we needed to go for fuel in the other marina in town, my confidence was so dented that I mutinied and refused to take the boat. It seemed Leighton could be pilot and skipper at the same time, so there need be no more conflict between us. If I was the skipper's best radar set, then I had switched myself off.

'Don't you think we should go and see the fuel berth in the other marina, do a recce before we take the boat in?' I asked.

'No need. Waste of time,' replied a grumpy Leighton, so I shut up.

I was holding the ropes in the bows as we came into the unfamiliar marina. Leighton had decided that the fuel berth was down past the first pontoon, and was heading towards the quay wall by the club house when we saw a *marinero* running towards us, waving his arms. He screamed at us in Spanish that the water was too shallow for us by the wall and that we would go aground. The fuel berth, it transpired, was on the other side of the pontoon, not at all where Leighton thought he'd seen it.

Leighton jammed the engine into reverse, desperate to start moving astern before we hit bottom. We raced backwards towards a row of moored boats, with *Jameeleh* doing her usual trick of steering erratically as she went astern. Leighton was going too quickly to stop. By some miracle, we slid past most of the boats without hitting any of them but we then caught the transom of one, pulling her swimming ladder askew with a terrible sound of fibreglass on metal. Somehow we got the boat into the right berth for fuel and switched off the engine.

Neither of us spoke.

There is a Tao saying: 'There cannot be blame if a ship meets rocks.' I went over to the boat we had hit and exchanged insurance details with the French crew. I didn't say anything when we filled up with diesel and paid the *marinero*, who shook his head at us. Nor did I say anything when we paid cash for the boat's ladder to be repaired, nor when Leighton had to fill a deep scratch in *Jameeleh*'s hull.

By the end of the day Leighton would have been glad of a reproach, but I was enjoying the occasion so much that he wasn't going to get a peep out of me. I was amiability and restraint itself. My magnanimity was going to be his punishment.

La Coruña, at the north-western tip of Spain, has many historical links with South Wales, to which it has been connected for centuries by the ancient motorway of the sea. Galicia, with its own pre-Roman language, *gallego*, is part of the Celtic family that has intertraded, quarrelled and intermarried over the millennia. I was brought up speaking Welsh and found Galician easier to understand than Spanish. I had often surmised that my father, who is a short Welshman with very dark hair, was of Celtic Iberian stock.

Although South Wales did have its own iron-ore deposits near the coalfield, a richer grade was needed for the Bessemer process to convert iron into steel, so Spanish iron ore was imported into Cardiff from the nineteenth century onwards. During the Spanish civil war, Welsh skippers like Potato Jones, Corncob Jones and the mouthwatering Ham and Egg Jones broke Franco's blockade of the Catalonian ports. Indeed, as late as the 1950s over a dozen vessels were still regularly engaged in the transport of iron ore from La Coruña and Vigo to the steel furnaces of Port Talbot and East Moors in Cardiff.

La Coruña is still importing coal. A neighbour of ours in the marina complained that his boat was covered in coal dust one day, after a ship had discharged her cargo. This reminded me of a story I had heard about my father. When he retired from the Port Health Authority in Cardiff, one of his students recalled the first time he'd accompanied my father on a visit to a ship that was loading coal. In order to get on board the ship from the dockside, a ladder had been placed from quay to deck. My father, an old hand at the process, paused, assessed the situation and then dashed across, running nimbly into the wheelhouse and out of sight, leaving the student alone on the quay. The youngster was less sure of his feet and decided to go across the ladder on his bottom. In the middle of his crossing, however, he heard a loud roar and, before he could react, found himself enveloped in a cloud of coal dust and looking like a Black and White Minstrel.

Because of my father's work as a public health inspector, our family knew more than the general public did about the dirtier side of Cardiff life. When we were children, we used to draw our pictures on scrap deratting forms, certifying that ships arriving at Cardiff had been rid of unwanted passengers. I still have a couple of these cards with pink houses and neon suns drawn in wax crayon over diagrams of 1960s cargo ships. My father would come home with stories about houses so full of cats and dogs that you walked on an eighteen-inch-thick carpet of dried animal excrement in the parlour. (The surprising fact here was that the room didn't smell particularly bad. If you allow dog excrement to dry out long enough, it gives out a musty, slightly sweet aroma. It even used to be imported to the UK from Basra, for use in the dyeing industry and manure works. In *Stowage*, Captain R.E. Thomas recommends that the cargo should be carried on deck 'protected by tarpaulins from rain and spray, as moisture and heat cause it to throw off very offensive smells'. It might have been less malodorous if they'd dried the dogshit in a Cardiff sitting

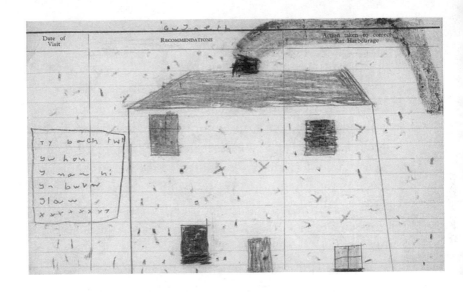

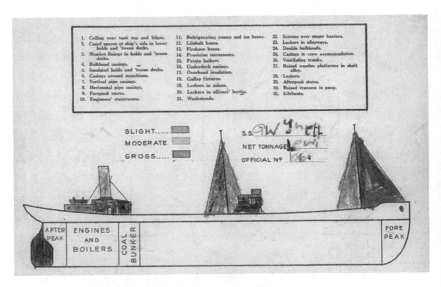

24   Cardiff Port Authority 1960s Rat Harbourage form

room, but I digress.) My father, whose regular work included inspecting restaurant kitchens, never *ever* ate out. He once had to deal with a complaint concerning a tin of peaches, which included part of a severed human finger poached in syrup.

But of all the things that caused my father problems, top of the list, way above complaints about rat sightings and blocked drains, were prawns. If the phone rang at home on a weekend, it was almost guaranteed to be because imported frozen prawns had proved to be unfit for human consumption. My father's job was to take samples to be tested by the public health's laboratory for bacteriological fitness, and then either pass or condemn the cargo. In the 1970s, the market for imported prawns had only just opened up in the UK, and in the early days of prawn farming, the importance of growing the cash crop in water untainted by sewage was not always understood.

I should, therefore, as the daughter of an environmental health officer, have known not to cook half-thawed prawns, but I'd bought a lovely fresh piece of bream in La Coruña's market and wanted to make a seafood sauce from mussels, prawns and tiny scallops, which you could buy frozen from a stall in the market. I thought it would be all right if I cooked the sauce thoroughly, which I did.

It wasn't. The food poisoning hit us twenty-four hours after we'd eaten the delicious meal. I knew it was bad when I started having stomach cramps. I was the first to be sick, having to run up a long pontoon to the Portakabin where the loos were situated. It was another windy night – there was a two-thousand-mile-wide storm out in the Atlantic and we could feel it in La Coruña – and as the boat began to bounce around Leighton also began to feel ill. This was the worst type of sickness, with matter coming from both ends. All I could feel as I was projectile-vomiting over the side of the boat – no time now to make it up to the toilets – was deep shame at having brought this upon us. 'I've killed us,' I thought. 'We've just crossed Biscay and now they're going to find us both dead on the boat, with blue mouths.'

I had thought that seasickness was the pits on a boat, but it's not. Now in the marina, *Jameeleh* was moving around in the swell, snatching at her ropes, which together with the seafood poison created a nausea deep inside us. At that point I wanted to sell the boat – anything to be lying down on something that wasn't moving. I staggered up the pontoon to the loo and had to vomit again into the dock, ignoring the smartly dressed Spaniards wearing beautiful leather shoes and opulent coats, out for their early-evening *paseo*. Between our fights and food poisoning, I had never felt so lost and disorientated.

A few days later, and looking much slimmer, we began to explore La Coruña properly. I needed to submit a book of poems to my publisher, so Leighton agreed that we should stay at the port for two weeks, while I finished the manuscript. The city is famous for its crystal balconies looking out to sea. The climate is notably warmer than the British weather, but very rainy because the Galician coast is the first land in Europe hit by Atlantic lows. Thus La Coruña's squares are filled with palm trees and *datura*, or angels' trumpets. The city's oldest churches are Romanesque, as the port was one of the main landing points for pilgrims wishing to follow the path to Santiago de Compostela to the south.

We had seen La Coruña's most interesting historical feature, however, on the night we had ridden the Biscay swell into the city. I had been struck then by the startling brightness of the main La Coruña light, but had no idea that the Torre de Hércules had been in continuous use since Roman times, making it the oldest working lighthouse in the world. We had been deeply grateful to the tower as we came into La Coruña and decided to make our own pilgrimage to the light.

We were still a little shaky on our legs as we walked to catch the bus out to the *torre*. On our way we paused for a moment to admire the pilot boats moored in the marina basin. Written in bold letters on the side of their vessels was the word *Prácticos* (*Pilots*). These boats were fast, powerful and highly manoeuvrable. All my life my parents had been telling me to stop dreaming and to 'be practical'. (They were on to a loser, really, because dreaming is the most practical way for a poet to live.) Here, though, were the vessels of men who were, above all else, pragmatic and realistic. These mariners could berth a boat on a seashell, deal with bad weather without fear, and steer ships in a slow, measured way, docking them so gently that they never even touched the quay. These were the skills and mental attitudes to which I still aspired.

The relationship between pilots and lighthouses – both of which bring sailors safely into port – is particularly evident in La Coruña. In Britain, Trinity House – originally a society of pilots, established by royal charter under Henry VIII – is today responsible for the lights and navigation marks that guide shipping around the islands. This extension of the society's functions was decreed by an act of Parliament during the reign of Elizabeth I:

> The Trinity-House at Deptford Strond . . . shall and
> may lawfully by vertue of this Act, from time to time,
> hereafter at their wills and pleasures, and at their
> Costs, make, erect and set up such and so many
> Beacons, Marks and Signs for the Sea, in such places
> of the Sea-shores and Up-Lands near the Sea-Coasts,
> or Forelands of the Sea, only for Sea-Marks, as to
> them shall seem most meet, needful and requisite,
> whereby the Dangers may be avoided and escaped,
> and Ships the better come unto their Ports without
> peril.

Sea marks, therefore, are tools in the marine pilot's trade.
When we were still in Cardiff, we used to see the Trinity
House boats maintaining buoys in the Bristol Channel. I'd
always feel emotional about these activities because sailors'
lives depend on the skill of these seamen. If a road sign blows
down you might, at worst, waste some time by going to the
wrong place but you would be unlikely, as a result, to drive
unwittingly off a cliff, under the impression that you were
still going in the right direction. A faulty light or a drifting
buoy at sea could lead you seriously astray and on to rocks.
It was gratitude for avoiding this fate that excited us as we
took the bus out of the centre of La Coruña and on to a
headland jutting a short way into the Bay of Biscay.

As we walked out to the lighthouse on its rocky promontory, we passed large groups of Spanish couples, dressed up
for sightseeing. The ladies had swollen ankles and were wearing their best but most uncomfortable shoes. The group
talked continuously at full Spanish volume, couples calling
to each other like lights.

I was totally unprepared for how the *torre's* handsome

25   La Coruña, *Torre de Hércules*. Engraving by Ruidavets

sandstone tower dominated approaches to La Coruña. The
Torre de Hércules is believed by some people to have been
the first lighthouse ever built. The original version is said to
have been raised on the site by the Phoenicians, the greatest
traders of the ancient world, whose mercantile empire had

been built up from their home on the shores of modern Lebanon. Someone once described them to me as 'the Ferengi of the ancient world' which, for any non-Trekkies, means that they were the biggest wheeler-dealers in the centuries before Christ. The Phoenicians were remarkable sailors and, by the fifth and sixth centuries BC, had circumnavigated Africa. It was said that they were willing to sail at night when no other nation would do so, therefore their interest in lighthouses is hardly surprising. When the tower was renovated in 1791, new inscriptions were revealed in the stone which suggested that a Roman architect called Cayo Sevio Lupo had added to the Phoenician structure in the time of Augustus Ceasar. Another theory derived from the inscriptions suggested that Lupo was a Galician king who dedicated the tower to the god Mars and the hero Hercules. This was the first time on our voyage that I had come across Hercules, but he was to become an important and ubiquitous presence over the coming months.

Inside, the tower's stonework was cool. We admired the extraordinary internal stonemasonry, which had kept the tower up in such an exposed site for so long. As we climbed the stairs, the stonework changed from Roman chunkiness to medieval arches and then to late nineteenth-century practicality. The walls were punctuated with windows, and we felt giddy as our focus on the masonry alternated with dizzying glimpses of sea and sky. At the top we burst out into the roaring wind and contemplated the Biscay swell crashing below on savage rocks.

Danger below, security above. On the rocks lay destruction for a boat, but, directly above it, the light meant safety for maritime traffic. A lighthouse tower is the ultimate in *noli me tangere*: see, but don't come close. Destruction and help are located at exactly the same spot. This is how you get light

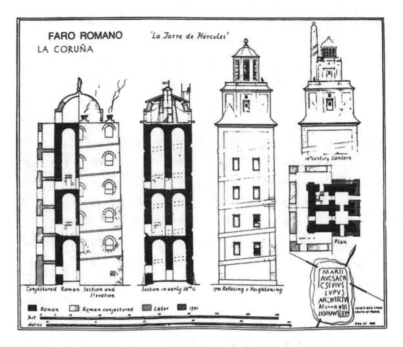

26   Torre de Hércules

from a stone; you pile the masonry as high as possible and let the lamp shine out. This is a place where the aspect you present to the world is the only important thing, where vanity about the state of your light and the kind of distance from which it's visible is a virtue. A lighthouse doesn't need to look out, it only needs to be seen. In the nineteenth century, the poet Jacinto Verdanger compared the tower to the eye of God, always open.

When Leighton first went to sea at fifteen he discovered that he was terrified of heights. When everybody else was asleep at night, he'd leave his bunk and climb as far as he dared up the mast. Little by little he became comfortable with the altitude, going a little further each time, until he reached, and could relax at, the very top. Losing his fear of falling, he became, like Melville's mariner in *Moby Dick*, 'a transparent eyeball' in the crow's nest, seeing the bucking world around him, forgetting himself in the view. Thus, when he was asked, by day, to climb aloft, he was able to do it, holding on to the swaying mast with one arm and doing the maintenance work required with the other. Nobody knew how hard he had worked to gain this seaman's nonchalance about height. Later, after he left the sea, he earned a living working as a rigger in the East Moors steelworks in Cardiff. There he was so at ease on narrow ledges that he could lean out into space, grabbing ropes and beams as they were lifted towards him by crane. By the end he could even doze in the crook of a girder's arms.

At sea, however, Leighton didn't really lose his terror of falling until he learned to trust his own knots. The first time he had doubted the safety of a rope was on his maiden voyage, when the chief mate ordered him to wash the wheel-house windows, which required Leighton to be lowered from a height on a rope with a bowline tied in it. He didn't like the look of the knot and swore he'd never let anybody else rig his equipment again. As he became more experienced in tying knots, he told me, he became more confident that his turns were not going to slip. The rule was that you never trusted your weight to a bosun's chair unless you'd rigged it yourself, like checking your own parachute. Being a bosun, Leighton was particularly qualified in rope and tackle work. This comes in handy to this day. When I took him to meet my aunt and uncle in America before we were married, he passed a very important masculinity test by helping my cousin to retrieve a broken footbridge from a creek, using a cantilever. They still talk about the way Leighton swung that bridge.

It's always a pleasure to watch Leighton tie a knot or do some splicing. He hunches over his work with the abstracted confidence of someone who really knows what he's doing. Early on he taught me the most basic knots – the round turn and two half-hitches and the bowline (pronounced 'bowlin'). This process was made more difficult by the fact that Leighton is left-handed and I'm not, but we got there in the end. The bowline is the knot commonly tied by visualising one end of the rope as a rabbit and making it go round a tree and down a hole. Leighton showed me the seaman's way of throwing a bowline with a flick of one hand, which I've been able to use on a number of gratifying occasions to surprise sailors cynical about women. I suffer, however, from knot amnesia, and still struggle to tie a fender to a stanchion; some days I can't manage it at all. I think I must hold the world record in the length of time it takes not to learn how to tie a clove-hitch.

Ropes were proving to be a problem for us in La Coruña. In the UK, with its large tidal range, we were used to docking in level water behind lock gates. On the Continent, we found, harbours were not usually sealed off from the sea, so the pontoons and boats rose and fell twice daily with the tide. In La Coruña this was like being lifted on an elevator into the centre of town and then dropped down gently again. This openness to the sea meant that our mooring ropes, which had been perfectly adequate in the UK, were now deeply unsatisfactory. They frayed on the cleats to which we tied them and, worse still, made a terrible screeching noise as the

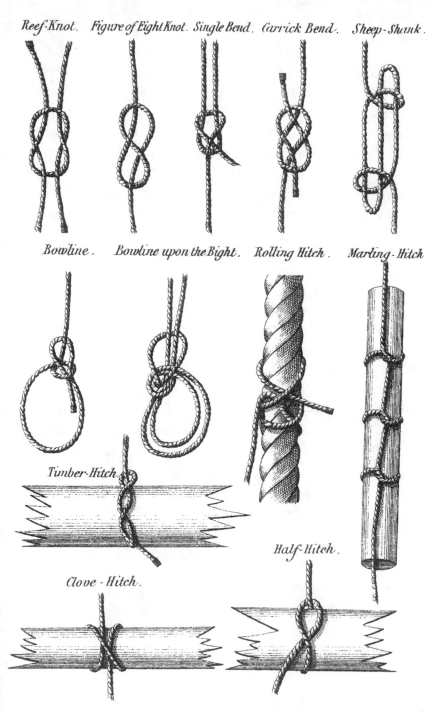

Reef-Knot.   Figure of Eight Knot.   Single Bend.   Carrick Bend.   Sheep-Shank.

Bowline.   Bowline upon the Bight.   Rolling Hitch.   Marling-Hitch

Timber-Hitch.

Half-Hitch.

Clove-Hitch.

27   Different knots, bends and hitches

boat snatched against them. All the local boats in La Coruña possessed large metal springs, or big black plastic snubbers, in an attempt to absorb the constant strain on the ropes. Leighton tried everything he knew to stop the racket: he wet the knots, which worked for a while but then they dried out; he balanced the stress on the warps and that improved matters, but not entirely. After one particularly bad night, during which we'd not slept because of the noise, we vowed to buy some new mooring lines. I had noticed that the boat next to ours seemed to be quieter, and asked the owner where he'd bought his ropes. I told him, in my halting Spanish, that we had only been sailing for two years and that we were on our way to Portugal, and he clutched his head in disbelief and fear, exclaiming '*Madre de Dios!*' which made us feel great.

In 1912, the Neptune Academy in Cardiff used to teach that the way to calculate the strength of a rope is to square the circumference and divide by three for the breaking strain, by four for the proof strain and by seven for a safe working strain. The calculation could be done when you knew what kind of stress you and your rope were likely to face. Modern ropes are much more flexible than the old hemp ones and have a vast range of properties from which you can choose. Some of these are listed poetically in the 1977 *Lloyd's Calendar*:

MAN-MADE FIBRE ROPES

Among the range of fibre cordage on the market today are ropes that will fulfil any of the individual requirements shown below.

High tensile strength
Complete kink resistance

Exceptional repeat load performance
Outstanding capacity to absorb shock loads
Complete immunity to rot, mildew and
    marine decay
Low water absorption
High resistance to 'weathering'
Ease of handling, wet or dry
Light weight
High strength/weight ratio
Resistance to chemical attack
Immunity to degradation from contact with
    oils, petrol or common solvents
Excellent ageing properties, durability and
    long service life
Ability to float indefinitely
Non-rotating – torque-free
Unlimited length without splicing
Versatile winch performance
High or low extensibility

If this were a shopping list of desirable moral qualities, I would rate 'resistance to "weathering"' very highly in myself or in a partner but I'd jettison 'complete kink resistance' as a matter of principle.

A knot in a mooring rope is a weakness and is said to reduce the rope's strength by 50 per cent. Odd that the point where a rope is performing its most important function is exactly where it's most likely to break. Leighton told me never to tie a knot when the rope is wet because you'll never get it undone again. A splice, when the strands of a rope are unravelled and retwined around each other to make a knot-less seam, will never part, but simply become tighter under pressure. The difference lies in where the rope takes the strain: with a knot, the stress is concentrated over a very small portion of the rope, whereas in a splice or a twist, the rope takes the pressure over a much longer portion of its length.

It's no wonder, then, that images for marriage often come from the language of cordage. When I married Leighton, I felt that my commitment to him made me more, not less, free. It simplified the issue of my identity so that I could be more adventurous in other areas of my life. Rather than a narrowing down, our marriage had opened up much wider horizons for me. Under the stresses of the last couple of months, I could only hope that Leighton and I were firmly spliced, that our union did not depend on the much weaker knot.

Cordage is about much more than tying things together; it can also save lives by providing light. Until the advent of electricity, ropes would literally have provided the light for the Torre de Hércules, in the wicks of the lamps kept lit on the point.

I bought a Spanish-language history of the Torre de Hércules, written by the early twentieth-century Galician nationalist and antiquarian, Francisco Tettamancy Gastón. This mustachioed gentleman was Professor of Mercantilism in the Commercial School in La Coruña and wrote a good deal in *gallego*, including long historical poems with erudite dissertations and notes. A reprint of his classic history of the tower was published in 1991 with a preface by Francisco Vasquez Vasquez, the then Mayor of La Coruña, whose poor mother,

I fear, ran out of ideas. La Coruña was very proud of its famous School for Lighthouse Keepers, founded in 1848 and moved, illogically, in 1863 to landlocked Madrid. I was delighted when, at the back of the book, I found a plate showing the outlines of twenty-five different lighthouses, displaying at a glance the tallest and most striking. The Torre de Hércules, listed modestly as being 'early second century', towered above many much more recent lighthouses and was joined by St Ann's and the Smalls, both in Pembrokeshire. Leighton and I felt proud that we had already passed six of the listed lighthouses in *Jameeleh*.

What was most startling about this print, however, was its amassing of lighthouses, which are by definition solitary landmarks. You never see a group of lighthouses – except, perhaps, on the extraordinarily rocky coast of Brittany. The print looked like a rare convocation of lighthouses, like popes gathered together for a momentous discussion of God's will. It made me start listing other objects we only usually see alone: sea captains, hermits, postboxes, dictators.

I was by myself on the day that I visited La Coruña's Archaeological Museum in the old fort, the Castillo de San Antón. The museum's greatest treasure was Phoenician gold jewellery from the third century BC, showing the fantastic wealth that had been generated by their early voyages to the edges of the known world. La Coruña's coat of arms shows the mythical history of the Torre de Hércules, which is portrayed as being founded on a skull and crossbones. The tower was said to have been built by Hercules after he had killed the giant Geryon, whose herd he stole as one of his twelve labours for King Eurystheus. Geryon had three heads, three bodies joined at the waist and fought with six arms.

What exactly did Hercules have to defeat, in order to lay

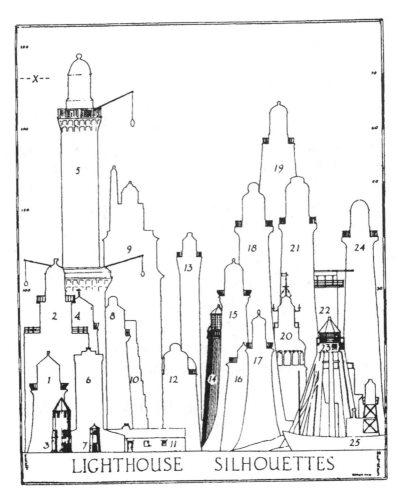

28　Lighthouse silhouettes

the foundations of his remarkable tower? Hercules's slaughter of Geryon is, perhaps, a dramatisation of the Roman conquest over the earlier, frightening and barbaric religions of the Galician peninsula. It was rumoured that the Phoenicians practised child sacrifice in their rituals. The new, rational world order of the Romans was built, therefore, on the defeat of horror. The insight is that civic society can only exist on the foundations of fear confronted. Like the Torre de Hércules itself, safety and ruin can physically occupy the same place and, sometimes, a light can be the only thing dividing the two.

In the museum, I was even more struck, however, by a four-faced head from the same period carved in stone and displayed on a turning plinth. Each face represented a different season and had its own distinct relationship with pain. The first was a death face, with high cheekbones and no flesh. Here was winter, no expression but a dying man with nothing to lose. Spring's head was fully engaged with anguish, rolling his eyes in disbelief at the agony that filled him. Changing sex, the third side of the rotating stone showed summer, an exquisitely beautiful feminine face, in which the hurt of just living was perfectly absorbed, transformed into graciousness. Finally, autumn was trying and managing, just for a split second, to hold sorrow in balance. This evidently required total concentration, and the full masculine mouth was drawn

29 La Coruña's coat of arms, showing skull and crossbones

in a straight line, holding that knowledge. Quartz crystals in the granite glinted in the spotlight that lit the sculpture, making it look alive and, as the head turned, each face was transformed into the next, in a continuing drama of suffering.

This sculpture took my breath away. It told you everything a human needs to know about the different energies needed for living. The head reminded me of the four-sided Torre de Hércules, built on the site of struggle and conquest, presenting a different aspect of danger to each cardinal point of the compass. The figure was astonishing because it didn't divorce beauty from pain, treasure from danger. As I watched the four faces blending into one another time and again, I wondered what nightmare Leighton and I would have to overcome in order to be able to see our way around the mighty Cape Finisterre. What bad dream faced, fought and buried, would be our safety, a foundation on which to build?

The Roman historian Pliny called Finisterre the end of the sky, the water and the earth. The cape has a justified and fearsome reputation as a ship-slayer. Every year, it seems, a large cargo ship is lost in bad weather off the coast and it's not uncommon to hear of smaller sailing vessels being rescued in those turbulent waters. I was so frightened the night before we rounded Cape Finisterre that I went to mass in Santiago Church, one of La Coruña's oldest, to ask for safe passage. On the altar an effigy of Mary was swathed in so many veils that she looked like an exotic jellyfish, ethereal but deadly.

Miraculously, Leighton slept well the night before we sailed. We left La Coruña calmly on the morning tide while it was still dark. The weather forecast had promised a north-westerly, which would have been perfect, but, that morning, the wind was so light that we couldn't sail at all and had to motor along the Galician coast where enormous wind generators stood stalled, like calvaries. A group of dolphins joined us and I spent hours in the bows watching them play alongside us. They were so close that I could hear them opening and closing the breathing holes in their skulls.

Occasionally, one of them would turn on his or her side and regard me and the boat with a dispassionate eye.

During our crossing of Biscay, we had been in the middle of the waves and so could not see their overall pattern, but the Torre de Hércules had given us our first objective look at the dimensions of the swell that might be facing us around the corner of Finisterre. The Atlantic behaves nothing at all like the sea along the British coast. In Aberystwyth, for example, waves simply break rather straightforwardly on the beach. The seas in Biscay are much more powerful and chaotic. *The Times Atlas and Encyclopaedia of the Sea* defines swell as 'residual wind-waves which are no longer under the influence of the forces which generated them'. These are produced deep in the Atlantic depression factory and encounter no resistance until they hit the Galician coast. A swell is much larger than a wave, and is, in fact, the platform on which ordinary waves, as we know them in Britain, come in. It is part of a drama of global dimensions, which sees land as a trifling impediment and cares not for the needs of boats. When you're on the water swell can be extremely deceptive. As we travelled west past the Islas Sisargas and Cabo Villano, *Jameeleh* was travelling along quite smoothly about two miles off-shore. But, looking at the coast, we could see waves crashing in huge waterfalls off the cliffs, throwing up spray like smoke. It looked as if there were bonfires lit all along the beaches.

As we came closer to Cape Finisterre, passing the impressive rocks of Cabo Villano, Leighton and I both started to feel increasingly apprehensive. The wind strengthened but was blowing out of the south-east, which made passing Cape Finisterre much more difficult. We had the feeling that, any second, we were going to round a bend and come face to face with the full brunt of the Atlantic Ocean.

The coast to the west of La Coruña is, cheerfully, called the Costa del Morte, the Coast of Death. In their guidebook to northern Spain, Dana Facaros and Michael Pauls explain:

> the Galicians dubbed this region down to Finisterre the 'Coast of Death', after its number of drownings, shipwrecks and ancient Celtic memories; from the end of the west, from the end of the Milky Way, Celtic warriors would sail out to their reward in the seven-towered castle of Arianrhod. The scenery along this wild land of the setting sun is romantic, the waves are dramatic, only the water is icy cold.

Whenever I heard the familiar name of Finisterre (now renamed Fitzroy) in the Shipping Forecast litany, I had always imagined the end of the ancient known world as a long, low-lying, sandy promontory stretching out into the Atlantic. The real Cape Finisterre is nothing like that. It's a huge head-land, with a rounded top, hunched full of energy like a boar. Stone ribs show through the cape's flesh. During my passage planning I had looked very carefully at the nautical charts of the area and had become concerned to see that each cape had outlying rocks and that these had their own names, like little islands. When Galicians take the trouble to name a boulder, you know it can do you serious damage. Cabo Villano had El Bujardo, and Finisterre a horror called La Carraca, which sounds just like a fibreglass boat being torn to pieces on granite. Finisterre means business; it has resisted weather erosion for millennia and has shipwreck on its mind. La Carraca is its ministering angel.

It was late afternoon by the time we reached Cape Finis-terre, and its cliffs were incandescent with sunset. Once we were abreast of the cape we thought about taking a photograph of ourselves against its rocks, but we immediately dismissed the idea. It seemed sacrilegious, an impiety while we were still in the headland's grip. We looked at the massive rock with awe and I started praying.

The wind still hadn't changed from the south-east. Now we had a north-westerly swell, so the water was becoming troubled. Faced with these new forces, *Jameeleh* slowed. I lined up a stanchion with a wall ashore and watched our progress decrease. Then, suddenly, we were being pushed backwards and there was nothing we could do about it. Our engine was going at full throttle and still we were making no headway. After an anxious twenty minutes, during which we were caught in this adverse tidal stream, we suddenly started to advance against the land. Something had clicked in the mechanism of Finisterre's lock and had let us through. We began breathing again as we pulled away. We had now rounded Finisterre not once, but twice.

As darkness fell, Leighton announced that he would go below to get some sleep, so I took my watch, keeping an eye on the cargo ships further out to sea. The Finisterre light stands over one of the busiest traffic lanes in the world, a key junction where ships come close into land from the Americas, the Mediterranean and Northern Europe. The lighthouse beam swept out over the water like a dragon's tongue, the monster that always guards any mythical treasure. That trove was our safety as we rode over many men's graves in our small boat.

Leighton was always unable to rest when we were motoring at night and soon came up to relieve me. He checked our speed over the ground and was appalled to find that it had dropped to two knots. In the darkness it felt as though the cape were pulling us back towards it, no matter what we did. Leighton exploded. How could I have let the boat slow down so much? Didn't I realise how dangerous these waters were? Hilda the Autohelm was back to her old tricks and was steering the boat badly. He knew she was the wrong model for our boat, he said bitterly. And I hadn't helped by loading *Jameeleh* with so many books that Hilda didn't have a hope of steering accurately even on a good day. I had put us in danger. And, worse still, he was worried sick about *Jameeleh*'s engine. The Perkins motor had never failed us so far but he felt in his water that all was not well.

Riding the wave of his anger, Leighton pulled out the genoa, so that we were motor-sailing, and our speed quickly increased. Gradually, we began to pull away from the magnetic Finisterre and closer to lights further south down the coast, towards our destination, Bayona. On land Leighton was very tactile, always reassuring and concerned for my welfare before his own. This Leighton was so preoccupied that he refused to touch or even look at me. I felt bereft and humiliated.

The dawn sky that morning was ominously red and the wind freshened. We gathered speed now that Finisterre's grip on us had been broken. Bayona is protected by the Islas Cies, stunning granite islands. Leighton wisely decided to change the passage plan and go behind them, so that we could shelter from the stiffening wind that had turned south-westerly. As part of changing the plan, he barked at me, 'What's the time of high tide at Bayona?' I'd forgotten, and gave him the wrong time although I had it written down on my pad below.

'Not good enough,' he said in a severe voice. 'I can't rely on you. I'm going to have to check you from now on.'

I burst out laughing because it was just like a disciplinarian father rebuking a child about her maths homework. My laughter made him even more furious.

As we came into stunning Bayona, all rose and dolphin grey in the livid dawn, Leighton blamed me for adjusting the autohelm wrongly, which I hadn't done. Suddenly the defensive anger drained out of me. I saw in a flash that I would have to take all Leighton's weaknesses and my own on board and sail with them fully. After all, I could hardly argue that I was a good sailor: I wasn't. Sailing was so new to us that we didn't really know what we were doing. And yet, despite all that, we were making our way in this glorious dawn and had reached our goal of Bayona before the winter, despite Woo Sung, despite Graham, despite bad weather, despite Hilda the Autohelm, inexperience, seasickness and, most of all, despite ourselves. Fishermen anchored in the lee of the island waved at us. The sky became even more bruised, the water choppy and black.

Then Leighton began raging at me for giving him an incorrect bearing. I agreed with him that I must be dyslexic and went below to make a cup of tea.

'You're right,' I agreed calmly. 'But that's the least of it. You and I have all sorts of problems.'

Being wrong didn't seem so bad any more. I could see that I no longer needed Leighton's good opinion of me nor, even, did I need my own good opinion of myself. Blame was the narrow game; what mattered was to be open to what was going on – the scarlet dawn, whose clouds had begun to let down their nets of rain, fishing in air – and to make those constant tiny adjustments, which, more than being right, was the only way to get anywhere safely.

By the time we reached the Monte Real Club de Yates in Bayona there was a strong southerly wind blowing. Bayona was Columbus's first landfall on his return from the New World and, as we entered the port, we passed a replica of his ship, the *Pinta*, complete with a plastic matelot climbing the rigging. For some reason the insight of the dawn had freed me from all distractions and, despite having been up most of the night, I was able to concentrate fully on berthing the boat. This was the first time we had moored *Jameeleh* bows-on to the pontoon, a manoeuvre that was doubly tricky because of the high wind. I did it perfectly. Feeling very smug, I thought to myself, 'Not bad for someone who's fucking useless, eh?'

The next day Leighton came back from the marina's shower rooms in shock. A skipper from a British boat had just been found by the cleaner. He had argued with his crew and had slit his wrists in the men's toilets. There was so much blood that you could smell it. As he was leaving in the ambulance he was still saying that he should have cut deeper.

There are precious few idylls, we were learning, at sea.

CHAPTER SEVEN

When does Paradise begin?

The things that affect us stand outside us.
Change your attitude and then, as a
ship entering harbour, you shall find calm.

Marcus Aurelius

'Look at this,' said Leighton, holding the diesel filter of *Jameeleh*'s engine up from the bucket in which he'd placed it. Diesel should look like rosé wine, if you have the red fuel sold to boats in the UK, or like German green wine if sold without the dye. At any rate, it should be clear. The liquid in our bucket looked like stewed tea in which the tea bag had split. Now Leighton couldn't get the engine to start.

It was early November and we were still hoping to make it to the Algarve before winter really set in. We had left the granite Costa del Morte behind us and were now starting to make our way down the Black Coast of Portugal. Safe havens are rare on these shoes, battered as they are by huge Atlantic rollers. During gales, all but a very few of the Portuguese harbours are closed to traffic, as they are deemed too hazardous to enter in a swell. Every year yachts are lost and sailors killed trying to get into sheltered waters in bad weather.

Leixões (pronounced 'Leyshoinsh') is a large commercial port just north of Oporto and enjoys a dubious reputation among sailors. Yachts are warned to look out for floating debris in the water as they round the breakwater. The marina is known to be dirty and, in the pilotage books, sticks out in everybody's mind as the place where dead rats have been seen floating around in the water. Nobody spends more than one night in Leixões, if they can possibly help it. Now we were tied up in Rat Marina with a dead engine.

Things did not begin auspiciously between us and the staff. We had arrived during lunch and tied up at the visitors' pontoon. I had been to the office to complete the paperwork for the boat and this had, as usual, taken an age. By the time I came back, one of the *marineros* was pushing for us to move from the pontoon to our allocated berth. He was wearing a baseball hat and sporting a large Zapata moustache. We were perfectly willing to move as soon as possible but this wasn't fast enough for Moustache. As I clambered on board, and before we were ready, the old man, in a fit of impatience, cast off our ropes, leaving the boat drifting helplessly in the water. I didn't speak any Portuguese but shouted '*Oi, señor! Tranquillo!*' as we switched on the engine – it was still working then – and manoeuvred carefully to the place he had allotted us. The *marinero* took our ropes and made a comment under his breath to a crowd of his friends who were watching us from the quay wall above. I was furious. He wasn't in charge of the boat, *we* were, and he had no right to put our vessel at risk. Had there been the slightest bit of wind or tide running we could have been damaged against the pontoons or other objects. I felt hugely protective towards *Jameeleh* and wasn't going to let a bully put us in danger.

In high dudgeon, I went back up to the office and asked

the girl who the hell the man with the moustache was. She sighed. That would be Manuel, she said, the head of the *marineros*. He was a retired fisherman who had worked in the port for fifty years and thought he owned the marina. With a deadpan Portuguese expression she said that he was out of control and that he had already damaged some visiting boats. The girl clearly disliked Moustache and suggested that I should speak to the manager of the marina about him.

I found the manager outside the office. He was in his sixties, had dyed dark brown hair and wore a sharp suit with an expensive leather coat slung over his shoulders. I explained what had happened and how unprofessionally Moustache had behaved. The manager looked weary, listened and grunted at what I had said. He didn't even take his hands out of his pockets. He clearly wasn't going to deal with the malevolent *marinero*. I went back to the boat full of righteous anger. After all, we were only going to be here one night and this wasn't the kind of service you expected from a commercial marina.

Because we wanted to be off south to Nazaré the following morning, we decided to make the most of our visit to the area and so, that evening, we caught a bus to Oporto half an hour away. The bus took us through Leixões, which was much larger than we'd expected. We could see Portugal's old colonial connections with Africa in the huge piles of hardwood logs unloaded on the quayside. There was coal and bauxite laid neatly alongside cranes that looked as though they were out of a *Tintin* book. It looked like a port from the 1950s.

It was almost dark by the time we reached the centre of Oporto and were lost immediately. It should have been easy to walk downhill to the gorge of the River Douro, but the city was totally bewildering and seemed to go up and downhill in several complicated ways. This prevented us finding the Ribeiro, where the boats carrying port wine were tied up as a tourist spectacle. We walked along mosaic pavements made of white-and-black blocks of limestone laid in swirling wave patterns, past shops with an absurd degree of specialisation. There were *bacalhau* shops selling salt cod, flayed, dried and hung up like snow shoes, with their startlingly bad smell; we passed barbers' shops where men were being shaved with cut-throat razors; button shops, and one that sold nothing but string and religious candles. I was intrigued by this combination and dragged Leighton inside to speak to the owner. He was Turkish and explained that the connection between the two categories of goods was in the wick of the candle, which was made of string. The shopkeeper had Angolan sisal string in all sizes. Leighton, with his bosun's eye for good cordage, bought a ball of very fine plaited and waxed string and I bought two candles to light in churches to give thanks for safe passage when – if – we arrived wherever we were going. I hoped our destination would be the Algarve, the southern coast of Portugal, beloved of the British, but I'd already learned enough to know that, however much you want to get to a place, the sea might have very different ideas.

'Water,' said Paulo, with the sound of doom in his voice.

Leighton had tried everything he knew to start the engine, but still nothing worked. Eventually, the man who ran the diesel berth in the marina phoned a local mechanic and Paulo arrived, dark-haired and stocky in blue overalls and heavy boots. He seemed to know his way around a Perkins engine and tut-tutted at some rust around the head where the engine had previously been repaired.

Leighton explained to me why finding water in the diesel was such a problem. It meant that there was a leak somewhere in the engine and that, possibly, the head gasket was cracked. He had been losing sleep for months over the engine, and feeling sure that all was not well but he had kept his fears to himself until we'd passed Finisterre. We had promised ourselves that we would give the engine a major overhaul once we reached the Algarve for the winter and before venturing further on our voyage. As we were coming into Leixões, however, Leighton had heard an ominous thump in the motor that had made him doubly uneasy. And now here was the result, an engine that wouldn't go.

The situation was bad but we could not be too downcast about it. When we thought about the waters through which we had sailed, the mighty schist of Finisterre, and the fact that the engine could have stopped at any time, we couldn't help but be grateful. Now that the worst had happened we could address the problem. The knot in Leighton's stomach had undone itself. After all, how many sailors are fortunate enough to break down in port, tied up to a pontoon?

We asked Paulo to do what he could with the engine. Before he was able to start anything, we needed to obtain permission from the Port Authority, located in the local fort. I, as the owner of the boat, had to take the ship's papers and make an application with Paulo. This was my first taste of Portuguese bureaucracy and it didn't disappoint. First, we waited outside a window for someone to come. Then the lady behind the desk took a quarter of an hour to find the wrong form for me to fill in. This was accompanied by a great deal of discussion. Portuguese sounds like a mixture of Russian, Spanish and Welsh all spoken with a strong Liverpool accent. Paulo clearly knew what to expect. He chainsmoked until the inefficient lady suddenly became competent and pointed out that he was sitting under a No Smoking sign. I looked at the official letters pinned to the noticeboard, all signed by the grandiosely named head of the Port Authority, one António Manuel de Cruz Tavares Meyrelles, whose job title was *Capitão-de-Mar-e-Guerra* (Captain of Sea and War). I hoped that there wasn't a direct relationship between flamboyance of title and bureaucratic cussedness, but I wasn't optimistic. We waited and waited, smiled at one another and threw our eyes up in despair. We were there for two hours and by the end of the wait we were allies.

That night Paulo came to *Jameeleh* with a translator. I thought to begin with that Keva was a port official, but he turned out to be a businessman who had fallen on hard times and who helped Paulo out with English.

'The right hand washes the left hand, the left hand washes the right and both together wash the face,' he said mysteriously in a heavy South African accent.

Now in his seventies, Keva was born to Greek parents in Mozambique, a former Portuguese colony. His father had once owned a gold mine, though he had lost money in it, but Keva went into shipping. He had a couple of trawlers and used to export prawns to Spain. After Mozambique declared independence from Portugal the government began to arrest white businessmen and seize their assets. Keva lost everything and was now living in Oporto with his wife, hoping for governmental compensation. He hated being poor, hated the climate of Oporto, with its cold wet winters, and hated being old. Through Keva, Paulo gave us a quote for the work he was going to do on the engine. The bad news was that we needed to give him two and a half thousand euros for parts, but the good news was that it looked as though the head of the engine wasn't cracked. We were still optimistic that we could get to the Algarve before winter set in, so we resigned ourselves to a slightly longer stay in Leixões. There was bad weather predicted for the end of the week, so we would not be losing much time while Paulo worked on the engine.

That day, on the quay, I met a German woman of my age who had an eighteen-month-old baby on board her Hallberg-Rassy. We stood outside the marina office in a stiffening wind and looked out at the grey port and the flotsam on the water. She and her husband had been planning a long voyage for ten years, but were finding it hard to get away from Northern Europe. She couldn't believe how awkward boats could be and told me that she had gone sailing for an idyll. I said that I didn't believe there were any idylls on boats and she looked downcast. During an argument with her husband the previous night, she'd asked him, 'When does paradise begin?' He hadn't been able to answer. Now, neither could I.

Certainly, Leixões with its scuzzy water and rampant *marineros* was not my idea of a good cruising destination. I went into town and found Leça da Palmeira to be a poor, ugly place, but with many little corner shops selling food. In one greengrocer's I found a tray of luminous persimmons, so ripe that they looked as though they might explode under your touch. They added some welcome colour to the dull November day and the lowering sky. I tried to find a postcard of the town to send to friends, but there were none to be had. This was non-tourist Portugal. Not even the Portuguese came to Leça on holiday. Nobody came here if they could help it and, had it not been for a broken-down engine, we would not have been here either.

By the following evening, the weather had made us the best of friends with Moustache. The force nine gale predicted for the end of the week arrived early and the *marineros* went around all the boats in the marina, securing them with extra ropes. Bosun Leighton helped Moustache and his crew tie the visiting boats to huge rings in the quay wall. These were springs, lines to stop the boats from being blown backwards. The seriousness of these preparations made us solemn. We began to call Moustache Senhor Manuel and found out that he worked with his brother, Laurindo. Both had been commercial fishermen and warmed to Leighton when they saw, by the way he handled ropes, that he was a proper seaman.

Leixões is famous in northern Portugal for being the only large port that can stay open in all weathers. This doesn't mean, however, that it offers ideal shelter for boats. In *The Mariner's Handbook*, the Hydrographer to the Navy defines a haven as 'a harbour or place of refuge for vessels from the violence of wind and sea. In the strict sense it should be accessible at all states of the tide and conditions of weather.'

The harbour in Leixões had been created by a huge artificial breakwater, but it is known to be open to south-westerly gales. As night fell we began to feel the effect of the swell entering the harbour. Outside, it sounded as though a herd of goats had arrived to graze the marina, each with a Swiss bell hung around its neck and munching vigorously. It was the wind making halyards strike the masts. Later, the sound reminded me of the anvil chorus in Verdi's *Il Trovatore*, except that this forging wasn't musical, but totally chaotic.

We went to bed but neither of us slept as the gale increased steadily in force. The swell was now heavy in the marina and the boat was throwing herself around in a most extraordinary way. Leighton checked the ropes at 2 a.m., and again at 4, when he discovered that we had a problem. *Jameeleh* has a teak toerail, on which fairleads are fixed. These stop the mooring ropes from rubbing against the boat and lead them neatly out to the cleats ashore. The boat was bucking so wildly that the toerails were starting to pull out of the gunwales. If they came apart, it would be very difficult to secure the boat to the pontoon without damaging her. With genius intuition, Leighton had bought some extra-long screws in a tool shop that day, not thinking that they would be so important to us that same night. He dug out his drill and we both struggled to strengthen the toerail, so that the boat shouldn't begin to pull herself apart.

At dawn the marina was a sobering sight. Khaki-coloured waves rolled into the basin like bales of carpet, shaking the walkways as if they were light rugs and bowling the boats from side to side. The wind screamed in the rigging like the sound effects of a bad radio play and the sea was breaking over the sea wall, behind which we sheltered, and on to our boat. With every wave came bits of plastic, syringes, pebbles, all flung on to our decks. The boat was moving so much that I had to take a seasickness tablet. I could read but writing was impossible. Now and again I'd catch glimpses of the boats outside at such unlikely angles that I'd immediately feel sick again, so I decided that it was best not to look. By now the motion of the boat was so violent that we feared that the pontoons were going to break away from their pilings and take us with them. Marina hardware would be as dangerous as any rock to *Jameeleh* and, to me, her hull felt as soft as a new baby's head. We had no engine now to get us out of trouble. Every single rope we possessed was in use, fastening us to any firm surface to which a knot could be tied. I put mental ropes out around us, too, holding us to our berth by a set of imaginary Gulliver moorings.

Around mid morning the weather became even worse. Our wind gauge registered gale force ten, gusting eleven, classed as a violent storm. We had done everything practical that it was possible to do, so we let go and decided simply to wait for whatever would happen. Not a man to scare easily, Leighton began to carry his wallet in his pocket so that we would at least have some cash if we had to leave the boat quickly. I put my notebooks and our documents in a grab bag.

At lunchtime the weather gave us one last squall of almost continuous lightning, torrential rain and an express-train wind before turning, finally, to the west. We were now sheltered by the sea wall, and could heat some soup for lunch. We felt as though we'd been on a long journey in the boat, even though we'd been tied alongside all the while. By four o'clock the *marineros* confirmed that the worst of the storm was over.

So fierce was this gale that, at one point, we thought that we would be shipwrecked in port. During this time, Ellen MacArthur was out at sea, competing in the Route du Rhum race, which she won. She said later that she'd never seen a storm like it in her life. On the radio we heard that a tanker was in trouble off the coast of Galicia, a few miles west of Finisterre. The cape had claimed its first large victim of the year. The oil tanker's name was *Prestige* and she was eventually to break into two, sink, and pollute vast areas of the Galician coast.

I saw the first dead rat in the marina water the day after the *Prestige* storm. It bobbed past the boat, its little paws curled into its chest as if it were begging, or trying to hold up watery bedclothes round its cold neck. It had a friend with it, a bloated fish with all the flesh gone from its head. Both passed *Jameeleh* three times before moving on. Sailors were emerging relieved and shocked from their boats and, together, we looked from the quay wall at the detritus that had collected in the marina basin. In the dock, you could see twigs, logs, branches and trunks, individual shoes, plant pots, mineral-water bottles, a baby's pink potty, half a Castrol Oil container, bits of polystyrene, the backs of sanitary towels, pumpkins, apples, turds, assorted fragments of colourful plastic and the odd doll. Added to this was the general port rubbish – wooden pallets and goods spilt while ships were loading and discharging their cargoes. From time to time we'd pause, squint and ask each other 'What *is* that?' before moving on. Large balls of grease floated in the water and the whole scene formed an ordure that was so disgusting that it made you ashamed even to look at it.

The *marineros*, dressed in wet-weather gear, were starting to clean up. In order to do this they had rigged nets on long poles and were using them to scoop out the mess, which they placed in black plastic bags. These scoops resembled Native American dream-catchers, except that this was nightmare work, sweeping up everything that people felt they could

30 Titan crane on Leixões rocks

throw into water. I stopped to talk to Laurindo and he explained, in pantomime Portuguese, that this only happened in south-westerly gales. Much of this rubbish came down with the Leça River, was taken out to sea and then pushed back into the harbour by the tide. The marina, then, was like a front porch into which the wind blows leaves and packets of crisps, no matter how often you clear it.

The port of Leixões was founded, almost literally, on a shipwreck. Until the nineteenth century, Oporto, on the River Douro, was the area's commercial port. However, rocks and a substantial sandbank made the entrance to the river hazardous and, in 1855, John Rennie reported that some ships were able to make a return trip to Brazil in the time it took others to wait outside the sand bar on the Douro for a chance to sail into the city. Then, on 29 March 1852, the steamer *Porto* was thrown on to the rocks near the entrance, with the loss of sixty-six lives, forcing the authorities to seek a safer solution for shipping. They turned their attention to an area north of Oporto, where a semicircle of offshore rocks had traditionally provided an anchorage in the River Leça. This area became Leixões (originally one of the rocks), which lay between Leça and, on the south side, Matosinhos, named after Amato, the son of Hercules. Clearly Hercules had been busy along the Atlantic coast of Europe.

In 1883, construction of the new port was started, with the foundations of the breakwater literally being built on the circle of rocks that were a major danger to shipping in the area. This was a heroic task, one of the largest civil engineering projects undertaken in nineteenth-century Portugal. In order to raise a breakwater that could resist the Atlantic swell, several gigantic steam-driven cranes were ordered from a French workshop in Lille. Due to their colossal size the cranes were baptised Titans. Two of them remain on the breakwater, monuments to the heroism of heavy nineteenth-century engineering that could make a haven out of the named and lethal rocks.

Later that evening great excitement was caused in the marina by the arrival of a Route du Rhum trimaran that had been damaged in the recent storm. The enormous *Bonduelle* almost blocked the entrance to the marina. Another boat, *Fujifilm*, had broken up in the bad weather and the skipper had been forced to abandon her. A cargo ship had then run over the boat. Luc Coquelin, whom we had met in Lorient, had also been in a collision with a commercial vessel and was out of the race.

The facilities in the marina were minimal – tepid showers

and smelly toilets. Still, we told ourselves, we could put up with discomfort for a short time. After all, we would be off soon. We even began to feel the familiar turmoil of leaving. This included a generalised fear – of having to make decisions, of being unsafe, of making fools of ourselves, of being wrong, of failing, of having to limp back into port, of going backwards, of looking silly, of quitting, of letting ourselves and the boat down. Anxieties crowded in like the crud in Leixões marina. In the event, we need not have been so concerned. We were about to go through a much worse period without ever leaving port.

Two weeks after our engine first broke down, we paid Paulo for his work, settled up with the marina, stocked the boat with food and prepared to leave.

The engine still wouldn't start.

Paulo came immediately and told us we were not to worry. He would rectify the problem and wouldn't charge us any more for the work. He thought it might be something to do with the *'bicos injectores'*, a repair job that had been botched, rather than a whole new area to be repaired.

Keva had taken to visiting the boat during the day when his wife was out teaching English in Oporto. Like all Portuguese, it seems, he loved going to cafés to sip lethally strong coffee and eat cakes. Because he had a problem with his knee, he wouldn't come down to the boat but would call us from the quay wall. As a writer, I treasure my time in the mornings, so I began to dread these summonses from above. They were often to relay bad news abut how Paulo's repairs were going.

However determined we were to think positively and make the most of every day of our trip, our optimism was starting to fade. We were being worn down by the discomfort of living on a bucking boat in a cold climate. A boat is only a luxury dwelling in fine weather. If you can sit outside, you have a patio with prime views of the water. In winter, however, living on a boat was more like existing in an underground corridor that moved like a fairground ride. The windows and bulkheads dripped with condensation; even though we bought ourselves a cheap fan heater, shoes and bags became mouldy because it wasn't possible to circulate dry air in the saloon; our nights were so disturbed by ropes snatching that we bought earplugs. We were driven to playing competitive patience in the small hours if we couldn't sleep.

The weather continued to be turbulent. One day, on my way into Leça to buy groceries, I turned round and saw a waterspout on the open sea, heading towards the marina, a wet tornado. This was followed by a violent hailstorm. I was joined by a lone dog and, soaked to the skin, we both wandered the streets unable to find shelter. When I got back to the boat, with no prospect of being able to dry my clothes, I wept with desolation. I was terribly worried that our struggles in Leixões were going to start me on another downward spiral into clinical depression.

It was clear that, if we were going to survive this stay in Leixões, we could not put off living well until we got to the Algarve, or somewhere that counted. No, we had to look after ourselves in ugly, dirty, frustrating Leixões, and cultivate those qualities that allowed us to be well and for me to stay healthy. If we didn't, we had much more than the voyage to lose. Given the seriousness of my last bout of depression, my sanity – perhaps even my life – and certainly our marriage, might be at stake. The opposite of depression isn't feeling happy but being fully alive, however painful. Awareness of our situation, bleak though it was, couldn't hurt me. In fact, the safest approach seemed to be to increase my consciousness of our discomfort, to understand it fully, rather than avoiding it internally. This insight made a big difference to me and, a short while later, I dreamt that Leighton and I discovered a lion that we had forgotten about living on the boat with us. The creature was looking a bit thin because we hadn't been feeding it. I wondered if it would like its chicken cooked or uncooked, and resolved to start giving it regular food.

For a while that week, it looked as though we were going to get away. Paulo was as good as his word and put right the work that had been badly done in a local workshop. We made our preparations to leave again. By now we were too used to things going wrong to allow ourselves to feel elated as we motored out past the Leixões breakwater. The engine felt sluggish and, after a while, we decided that it wasn't a tidal stream against us but that we still had mechanical problems, so we turned back. There was a party to greet us on the pontoon, and Paulo climbed wearily aboard. He looked at *Jameeleh*'s hydraulic gear drive and found a piece of shattered metal that had sheared off from somewhere, but he couldn't figure out from where.

That night, the manager of the marina dropped dead. He had been, the girl in the office told me, a Salazar man ('You know, like Hitler, only nicer') who had been rewarded with an administrative job in the port. He was sixty-seven, the same age as Leighton, and had suffered a catastrophic heart attack. We had become fond of him over the last couple of weeks as we became marina residents; he and I had developed a banter in French and I found him charming.

We talked about the manager in the yacht club that evening over dinner. I was watching a toddler playing in the restaurant when suddenly she lost control of her limbs and, as if the floor were an ocean liner tilted by a wave, rushed headlong down the length of the room, and full pelt into a potted plant, with which she became entangled. The whole room watched with delight and sympathy as she pulled herself, laughing, out of the palmetto. Clearly we weren't the only ones to have been surprised by a big swell on dry land.

While Paulo was trying to repair our hydraulic gear pump, I began to look more carefully at Leça da Palmeira. We had lunch in the local diner, where a man who resembled Marcel Proust served plates of chicken gizzards and chips to the local workers. I became a regular in the shops and the girl in the post office suggested that I get a job and make a life in Leça. Even the girl in the local Mini Preço, the supermarket, offered me an application for a loyalty card. Superstitiously, I refused to fill it out.

Underneath its run-down exterior, I could begin to perceive that Leça had once been a genteel seaside resort for the residents of Oporto. You could see the structures of old villas with grilles and balconies, testament to gracious living in the past. I discovered the Museo Quinta de Santiago, a stylish arts and crafts house that looked out over the Leixões docks and which must have had stunning sea views before it was boxed in by the port and concrete apartment blocks behind it.

Once I began to notice this old refined Leça, I saw something beautiful every day: a tiled cottage, the remains of a big garden, a glimpse through a door to a terrace full of potted plants, verandas that, in their heyday, must have sheltered the bourgeoisie from summer sun. On the surface our life in Leixões was no better. The water was still dirty, our engine was still broken, but we were gradually able to see good things in the middle of the grime. I began to joke that I never really wanted to go to the Algarve at all; everybody went there. No, I declared to the *marineros*, I much preferred the delights of Leixões. The minute I chose the place, even as a joke, I began to feel much more positive.

I started exercising again and would run up the beach to a rock called Boa Nova. There I found a tiny church dating from 1392 nestled on the headland. A group of men were huddling out of the wind, playing cards. The Portuguese have a rich poetic tradition, and fixed to the side of a rock in traditional blue tiles was a verse from one of the local poets, António Nobre. It read:

> *Na praia da Boa Nova, um dia*
> *Edifiquei (foi esse o grande mal)*
> *Alto castello, o que é a phastasia*
> *Todo de lápis-lazúli e coral.*

> One day, on Boa Nova beach
> I erected (that was the mistake)
> A high castle, which is a fantasy,
> All bright blue and coral.

We were in the middle of ditching our own fantasies about life at sea, so the spectacle of the waves crashing over the rock on which this verse was written gave me great pleasure and satisfaction.

As I went to the supermarket I passed an old church, in

which I was very interested, but which never seemed to be unlocked. Then, one day, I saw that the door was open, so I peeked in. Two women were watching over a body in the aisle. The corpse was covered in netting, as though it were a fish that had been particularly difficult to catch and needed restraining. On the right was a huge ex-voto galleon, placed in the church as the result of a promise by sailors who had prayed for and received safe passage home. I was struck by how the church was, in its own way, a port, both a safe haven and a place of arrival and departure. The nave with its coffin was like a disembarkation hall, where you stopped travelling in a body and continued, after death, by an alternative mode of transport. I nodded at the two lady mourners and withdrew.

Our friendship with Manuel was developing rapidly. He moved us to a more sheltered berth, further up the quay wall. I asked him about his life at sea but his lack of English and my lack of Portuguese made conversation difficult. He had gone to sea aged ten and had worked in the lifeboat service for over fifty years. The walls of his house were covered in photographs of shipwrecks and, on each one, the number of people who had been rescued from each disaster. The first rescue in which he took part was that of a German submarine that had been scuttled at the end of the war with forty-five men aboard. Manuel still had a dinghy from the wreck and had been visited four decades later by the chief engineer and first officer of the submarine. He mentioned helping to rescue the *Maria Ermindo*, the *Urania*, the *Maura*, the *Torbay* – the list went on and on – the *Amethyst*, the *Rui Barbosa* . . . It became clear that Manuel was a remarkable man. He'd lost most of the sight in one eye while rescuing men from a burning tanker. All in all, Manuel had saved the lives of eighty sailors. I felt chastened by this and recalled my complaint about him with guilt. Sometimes the greatest heroes are the most difficult to see.

Because we didn't have a common language, Manuel took to acting out each rescue as he recounted it. I saw how he approached a Dutch catamaran that had gone onto rocks just outside Leixões. Everybody on board, except a ten-year-old girl who was clinging to the mast, had panicked. He brought the rescue boat in close to the rocks and had to withdraw before the next wave wrecked him as well. He and the girl persuaded the crew to jump at the right time. I could see the swell, him revving the outboard engine and his admiration for the child. He replayed it all for us, each rescue a different drama.

Now Manuel was seventy-six but too poor to retire. He still worked in the marina but was no longer part of the rescue services. Nevertheless, he told me, when he was watching television in the house at night, if he heard the wind getting up, he always got dressed and made his way down to the port because he knew when there was going to be trouble.

By now it was very close to Christmas and there was a sudden increase in the number of visiting boats, as sailors headed to the Mediterranean for the new year. We hadn't realised the extent to which our attitude to Leixões had changed until we saw the reaction of these newcomers to the place. One sailor we met on the way back from the Matosinhos market complained that he'd had a bad meal of fish, that the Portuguese were ugly and the buildings hideous, and that there was dogshit everywhere. Nobody knew the reality of life in Leça better than we did and yet I found myself leaping to the defence of the area.

'No, the people aren't grey and boring!' I protested. 'They're just reserved, and that's different.'

I wasn't going to have a word said against lovely, ugly Leça.

Christmas Day, though, was grim. There were four British sailors in port, including us, and we all decided to eat together on a large power boat. We said that we would cook, so Leighton went to the Matosinhos market, selected two plump live cockerels for our dinner and, foolishly, went away while the lady killed and feathered the birds. When we got them back to the boat, we discovered that they had been switched for two stringy hens. Paulo brought us a *bolo de reis*, the traditional Portuguese Christmas cake, and I gave Leighton a lobster pot for Christmas. This was an act of faith that we would soon be in a place where the water was clean enough to contemplate fishing.

Another south-westerly gale blew in on Boxing Day. We were used to the discomfort of living on a bucking boat by now, but I had taken to my bed that day because it was the only way not to feel sick. Paulo arrived in the roaring dark, took one look at our situation in the boat and declared, 'This is impossible.'

'No,' I replied, 'it's possible, but it's not nice.'

He insisted that we leave the boat and drove us up to a *residência* he knew in town. We learned later that, in addition to the gale, the rivers Douro and Leça had both broken their banks. This, combined with spring tides, had caused widespread flooding. We huddled in bed on solid land and were stupidly pleased to watch *Gremlins* on television. We even enjoyed the Portuguese commercial breaks.

The sight that greeted us in the marina the next morning was incredible. The rubbish on the surface of the water was so dense that, if you hadn't known you were looking at the sea, you'd have sworn that the boats in the harbour were embedded in solid mud. A small group of French women who had become stranded in the port over Christmas stood

31 The water in Leixões after a south-westerly gale

around in tears. Staring at the swell breaking over the outer harbour wall, a Belgian lady was getting ready to mutiny. A week in Leixões and these experienced, competent sailors were broken. Wimps, I thought proudly, we've been coping with this for two months.

We all looked on in awe as a tanker left the harbour. Under commercial pressures, such cargo ships have to sail even in rough weather. We watched as the westerly swell caught the ship and, as she struggled to turn north, flung her around at impossible angles. The stern lifted so that we could see the propeller turning in air. It was as if the sea were showing the ship to a potential purchaser. The tanker made her turn at the second attempt. The Belgian lady muttered something to herself and went to make a phone call.

Keva's wife had told me about a local saint called Santa Rita, who specialised in difficult cases. I promised myself that I'd make a pilgrimage to her shrine in the new year and announced my intentions to the *marineros*. They approved and said that Paulo was especially fond of Santa Rita. Manuel had been to Fatima three times, once on his knees, to ask for help. We were getting desperate.

Then Paulo made his biggest breakthrough yet. After the gear pumps had been repaired and reinstalled, the engine was still not right. So then Paulo removed the heat exchanger and discovered the explanation for all our technical problems. What we saw in Manuel's workshop made our blood run cold: the U-bend of the exchanger was so corroded that it looked like a Roman soldier's sandal in a museum. The metal looked so ancient that you could have carbon-dated it. The real extent of our engine problems was now clear. Unbeknown to us, there had been no anodes on the engine to stop a current forming between the machine and the sea water. Over many years the water had literally eaten away at the metal. With the engine in this condition, it was a miracle we had ever got out of Cardiff, let alone reached Portugal.

When Leighton saw the heat exchanger he whistled, then said, 'Forget Santa Rita; we're going to need Jesus Christ for that.'

I went on my pilgrimage to Santa Rita all the same. She told me that our problems would take some time to sort out, and I left with two medals bearing her image, one for the boat and one for Paulo. He lent us a car for a few days and we took a break in the mountains.

When we got back, however, I was beginning to struggle. By now Keva was becoming fed up with us. He had taken to calling Leighton 'Thing', which didn't help matters. One afternoon, he declared, 'You people are welcome to come back to Leixões any time, but don't bring your engine.' I felt as though we had both been bailing emotional bilge water out of *Jameeleh* for a long time. Keeping up our spirits in these circumstances was exhausting and I was tiring rapidly. I began to cry and feel helpless, and Leighton persuaded me to take a quick trip home. My instinct was to stick it out, but I was so frightened of becoming depressed again, and thus making our trip even more difficult, that I gave in. After all, it would take a couple of weeks to make a new heat exchanger and Paulo still had plenty of work to do. My computer had crashed and the terms of its warranty required it to be serviced in the UK. I assumed that Leighton could look after himself and that he would be able to keep up his morale alone. In the end I couldn't resist the prospect of seeing friends and taking hot baths at my sister's house.

I should never have left Leighton alone in that terrible place. Halfway through my trip home I phoned him. There was another gale blowing and, because of the work Paulo was doing, Leighton had no power on the boat. The thought of him on the boat with no heat or light galvanised me. What was I thinking, abandoning him there? We were in this together, and being apart was worse than anything Leixões could throw at us.

I changed my ticket and rushed back to Portugal the following day. We could no longer let fear of depression be a factor in our decisions. That brief separation changed the balance of power in our marriage. In the past Leighton had mainly been the one looking after me. I'd had a short break and my spirits were, for once, in better shape than his. For the first time I was the one rescuing him.

The night I got back we were blissfully happy, even though a new south-westerly gale was forecast. No matter, we would go back to the *residência* if things blew up. Everything looked better because we were together again. Leighton lay on my nightshirt before I got into bed, to warm it up. The swell rocked us to sleep. It wasn't balmy but it was a kind of paradise.

As *Jameeleh* seemed to be in a state of total nervous break-down, we took the opportunity to sort out the autohelm once and for all. I wrote a long letter to the manufacturers and a local dealer came to investigate Hilda. We weren't surprised to find that Graham had installed the fluxgate com-pass – which helps the steering mechanism determine which bearing it should hold – back to front. The unit was also suffering from 'intermittent power to the head', a fate that, in our view, had similarly afflicted Graham. The dealer replaced the unit and we were astonished by the new autohelm's stronger grip on the steering wheel. I sent a post-card to the Hilda after whom we'd named the first autohelm, telling her she'd been too neurotic and that we'd had to replace her. Then we renamed the properly functioning unit Rita, hoping that she would be made of sterner stuff. We needed a saint, not a pensioner, at the helm.

By now it might have been cheaper for us to have bought and installed a brand new Perkins engine into the boat, but because our mechanical problems had been discovered piece-meal, we had no choice but to persevere with Paulo. In a last attempt to get us out of his life, he arranged for the whole engine to be hoisted out of the boat. He ordered brand new piston rods, cylinder sleeves, material to repair the crankshaft and new gaskets. By the time he had finished, he promised us, we would have a 'reborn engine', an 'engine for life', if we changed the oil regularly. In his workshop he showed us all the parts meticulously laid out and sprayed bright green. He then showed us where the anodes were fixed, so that we could make sure the same thing didn't happen to the engine again. Then he sent us away.

A ship is an entity, whereas a port is simply a collection of activities. We had certainly learned a good deal about the types of activity it took to survive a place like Leixões, which, after Lisbon, is Portugal's second busiest port. Throughout the months that we had been in Leixões, we had been acutely aware of the volume of marine traffic in and out of the docks. This was because every time a ship entered or left, its wake would wash into the marina and rock *Jameeleh* from side to side. The pilot boats, which were berthed in the same basin as us, would ignore the harbour's own speed limits, enter at a lick and, performing an expert handbrake turn in the water, make our boat pull even harder at her mooring ropes.

I loved watching the slow ballet of the tugboats helping large cargo vessels to their berths. Ports and seamanship are about nothing if not the controlled movement of objects. Like children guiding clumsy adults into a miniature den, the tugs would patiently nudge the ships into place. They lay their foreheads against the cowlike flanks of the ship and pushed gently. They only ever shifted quickly if a cable snapped or something went wrong. Even when tugboats towed ships it seemed as though no force was being used. The towing rope was never taut because, once the ship had begun to move, the weight of the rope's bight (or slack end) did the pulling. Thus, the tugs pulled huge ships with slack reins. I found the care of these manoeuvres very touching. This seemed to me an admirable image for marriage. Don't use force, let the other person follow, if they want to, on a very long leash.

By the end of January, I felt so worn down by the protracted works on our engine that I'd lost all interest in travel, in Portugal, certainly in anything to do with the boat. I found it impossible to feel enthusiastic even about leaving Leixões. This was no life for us, and yet I didn't have the energy to envisage any other. I was sick to death of the voyage and its difficulties.

'Going to sea' is a vague and romantic notion, and one that costs nothing to entertain as a fantasy. The sea as an idea is great – glittery and abstract. But going to sea in reality leaves you totally open to doubts, fears, injury, worry, feelings of inadequacy – everything you usually take a good deal of trouble to avoid on land. Our time in Leixões had been about learning to accept the downsides of sailing – being pissed off, angry, frustrated and helpless – and to carry on, dead rats and all. There was no point waiting for someone else to be kind to us or fair or loving; *we* had to be those things to ourselves and one another or be starved of them completely. We'd been hard-pushed, but we'd survived three months in a filthy commercial port without moving. I recalled that Zen swordsmen can spend the first three *years* of their training simply learning to breathe properly. Like Zen pupils, Leixões had given us a long apprenticeship in the sea without ever allowing us to sail.

One day I came back from shopping for food in Leça and was astonished to see exhaust coming out of *Jameeleh*'s stern. I dropped my bags and ran to the quay wall. The *marineros* laughed as I did a strange disco dance of victory. I never knew

I could dance like that, whooping at the sound of that heavy engine. It's surprising how the will to live returns once you have a working engine in your boat.

In the paper we read that Ellen MacArthur was starting another sea race after her victory in the Route du Rhum. We read her daily mileage and were chastened to notice that she had covered in a day the distance we had come in eight months. Three of those months had been spent in Leixões. We did a quick calculation. Since the previous May we had averaged 37.8 nautical miles a week. That was 5.4 nautical miles a day and an average speed of 0.225 knots. We really must be the slowest cruisers in the world.

We took the boat out to the main harbour for a test drive. Paulo stood in the cockpit grinning broadly. 'Engine good?' he asked, 'or engine very good?'

'I don't know,' I said cautiously. 'Engine good, I think. We'll see.'

The staff of the marina were so used to us trying to leave Leixões that nobody made much of a fuss when we decided to attempt it one day in the first week of February. That morning we asked Manuel what he thought of the weather and he said it was a fine day to leave. He and Laurindo helped us cast off. Both brothers mimed hugs and kisses at us and I waved hard at my new Portuguese uncles. They made us promise that we'd 'phone home' when we reached Nazaré.

As usual, things began to go wrong as it was getting dark. I had just cooked our meal when what looked like smoke began pouring out of the cockpit vents. It wasn't smoke but steam. The engine was boiling dry, and, as he opened the radiator cap to check the water level, Leighton burned his hand. Worse still, he dropped the cap into the engine so we couldn't find it again. Even if he succeeded in restarting the engine, we couldn't run it without the radiator cap and we didn't have a spare.

While Leighton was working on the engine, I did everything I could think of to make the boat safe. I plotted our position on the chart and logged our drift. I noted mentally where the fishing vessels around us were, so that I could call them on the radio if need be. We were now abreast of Aveiro, a port with notorious shoals at its entrance. There was no way that we could sail in there in the dark without an engine. In the livid dusk, we decided that we couldn't just drift. Our best bet was to sail overnight to Nazaré and hope that we could be helped into port by daylight.

It was a bleak night. A squall blew up and Leighton put two reefs in the sail. Slowly but surely we began to pull away from the dangerous coast. Neither of us said anything but we were both thinking the same things. We had spent all that money and still didn't have a working engine; those months of discomfort in Leixões had been for nothing; the boat was breaking us both; we had been fools to think we could make such a voyage.

Then, suddenly, in the middle of it all, the night became astonishingly beautiful. I was beginning to understand the Zen of the boat. You do something that's difficult, that shows up all your awkwardness and helplessness and then, because there's nowhere to go except onwards, no one to blame while you're out at sea, you start surprising yourself. After you've wept with rage and frustration and vowed never to leave land again, things start unfolding and showing themselves to you.

My despair flipped into exultation. Here we were, sailing through black velvet water, with phosphorescence in our wake. We saw the Nazaré lighthouse from a very long way away, and its beam seemed to drag us towards it. Phosphorescent dolphins, like radioactive torpedoes, charged at the boat and still we didn't sink.

Once it became light and we and the engine had cooled down, Leighton retrieved the radiator cap, refilled the water tank and started the motor. Rita did her work perfectly and we entered Nazaré harbour under our own steam.

Later, I emailed Leixões to let the *marineros* know that we had arrived, but that we still had engine problems. My poetry publishers had been trying to contact me and I dashed off a reply:

> Sorry not to get back to you sooner. I've been up all night sailing down the coast of Portugal with a dead engine.

The words startled me, then made me laugh with joy. I'd been waiting all my life to write that sentence.

CHAPTER EIGHT

Knots and Unknots

A *tangle* in a knot or link projection is a region in
the projection plane surrounded by a circle such
that the knot or link crosses the circle exactly four
times. We will always think of the four points
where the knot or link crosses the circle as occur-
ring in the four compass directions, NW, NE, SW
and SE.

Colin C. Adams, The Knot Book

After Leixões, Nazaré looked like heaven. Mind you, anywhere would have made a favourable impression on us after
a winter in Rat Marina. A fishing port and summer resort,
Nazaré reminded me of a happy Aberystwyth, with its tall
sandstone cliffs and small-town eccentricities. The local
women still wore traditional Portuguese costume every day:
a wraparound skirt with a decorative apron, socks, clogs and
a knitted shawl tied tightly around their waists. In a seafront
store, where tartan shirts were also for sale, I bought a cream
jumper identical to an Aran sweater. These people, I decided,
weren't Phoenicians at all, they were Celts, and evidently
practised the same knitting habits.

Our favourite thing in Nazaré was how calm the water was

in the harbour. The town is protected not by a spit of land or a sea wall – which is usually the case with a good port – but by its opposite, a trench in the sea floor. This chasm, thousands of metres deep, smothers the Atlantic swell more efficiently than any solid barrier. *Jameeleh* was berthed in the fishing port, opposite local boats named after different aspects of the Virgin Mary – *Senhora da Piedade* (*Our Lady of Mercy*), *Senhora da Visitação* (*Our Lady of the Visitation*) – or other generally religious themes, such as *Viva Jesus* (*Jesus Lives*) and *Príncipe da Paz* (*Prince of Peace*). These fishermen only worked during the week and we would usually hear them leaving before it was light. One morning I watched the crew of the *Sonho de Amor*, the *Dream of Love*, preparing to leave. Nazaré fishing boats are decorated in bright colours, with crosses painted on the hulls, as if gaudiness were a defence against danger. Not one of the ten men who piled on board the old green and white boat was under fifty. They had clearly been fishing together for years and they pulled on their oilskins and waterproof sleeves with an ease that came from long practice. One fisherman ate a sandwich, while others gossiped in groups or smoked. It was all so calm and beautiful that the men looked as though they were sleepwalking. The helmsman crossed himself, started the engine and the men rode out to sea, using their faith as a means of transport.

Every evening small boats returned like iron filings to the magnet of the market. One day Leighton and I wandered over to the fish auction held in a shed on the quay. The ladies in their aprons sat in rows bidding for the cartons of squid, conger eel, sea bass and octopus that filed in front of them. All down the Atlantic coast, fishermen mark their lobster pots and nets with home-made Dan buoys consisting of a float with a flag attached to a pole. These poles mark out the prairies of the sea, hanging it with nets that stretch for miles under the surface. Often the flags make the water look like an empty but particularly challenging golf course, on which avoiding a hole in one is essential, as a yacht can easily become caught up in the nets. Through an open door in the auction shed I watched the stern of one of the fishing boats bobbing on the tide. A pile of markers with their flags was gathered in the back of the boat and looked like a heap of chivalric lances.

Heraldry was an important element of the local patron saint's story. A medieval knight was chasing a stag on the top of the formidable Nazaré cliffs. In its desperation to get away from its pursuer, the stag jumped and plunged towards the sea. The prince was too intent on following his quarry to stop his horse at the edge of the precipice and it seemed certain that both would fall to their deaths. Suddenly, the Virgin Mary appeared and prevented one of the horse's hind legs from leaving the ground. To this day you can see one rear hoofprint in the rock above Nazaré, 'proving' that a knight was saved by a miracle. I had a horrible feeling, though, that the Virgin Mary had forgotten about the stag that the knight was hunting and that its back was broken on the rocks below.

We had already glimpsed what such a miracle might mean in real life. While I was back in Wales and Leighton was alone on the boat in Leixões, he had made friends with Fernando, the garbage man, who wanted to practise his English. Fernando had mental problems but was obviously taking the pills. He was mocked by everybody else in the marina, who called him crazy and would have nothing to do with him. One day Fernando came to Leighton, very excited, because someone had given him a dog, whom he'd called Estrela, Portuguese for star. Fernando soon discovered that the dog

32   The miracle of Our Lady of Nazaré

was blind, but this made him even more determined to keep
her. The bitch responded to his kindness. Fernando told
Leighton to walk the dog on her lead to the edge of the quay

wall. About eight feet away, she dug in her heels and wouldn't budge. Then Fernando took the dog's lead and walked her to the edge. The dog followed and, furthermore, walked right over the drop. Fernando caught her but that dog's front paws walked on thin air safely, such was her trust in her new owner.

A marriage requires this type of mutual trust. In the past, Leighton had caught me many times when I'd run out of solid ground, but since Leixões he had been very despondent. Nothing I could say seemed to cheer him up. Perhaps it was my turn now to catch him emotionally by the scruff of his neck and hold him above the crashing waves.

Until we reached Nazaré, we hadn't realised how much energy it had taken us to stay positive in Leixões. We were both exhausted and traumatised by our latest engine breakdown. Leighton tracked down the slow leak that had helped drain the engine of water and we bought a spare radiator cap. We called Paulo and he came down one Saturday to look at the engine again. He tried to charge Leighton eight hundred euros for the visit, even though he was correcting work for which he had already been paid. Leighton gave him his travel expenses and threw his invoice in the dock.

We consoled ourselves with the thought that we had learned a great deal about maintaining boat engines since we had left Wales. The crash course had been beneficial, said Leighton, trying to be upbeat.

'Yes,' I replied brightly. 'I even know how to bleed an engine, which I didn't before.'

There was a long pause while I tried to remember the right sequence of movements.

'Leighton?'

'Yes?'

'I've forgotten.'

'I know, love, I know.'

'It's something to do with loosening some screws and using the finger pump. But what if I loosened the wrong one? That could be disastrous.'

Leighton sighed and concluded wisely, 'Better leave bleeding the engine to me.'

It was while I was reflecting, once again, on my shortcomings as a sailor, that I read about the Portuguese water dog. This marvellous creature

> is a medium-sized dog with a wavy or curly coat . . . It has a fluffy mop of hair around its head, a long curled tail, and resembles a cross between a standard poodle and an Irish water spaniel, both of which probably contributed to the breed. The dogs, now few in number, are black, brown, white, black and white, or brown and white. Developed along the Algarve coast by fishermen who trained them to retrieve fishing nets and tack as well as to guard their boats, the breed is recognised by international kennel clubs.

My *Portugal: The Green Guide* had no photograph of the dog and I was instantly obsessed. I looked it up on the Web and discovered that this breed was also used by fishermen to herd schools of fish into traps and carry messages between boats and the shore. If a fishing boat were caught in fog, the dog would stand in the bows and bark, a canine foghorn. It's rumoured that these *cão de água* sailed with the Spanish Armada. According to the American Kennel Club it is an 'animal of spirited disposition, self-willed, brave and very resistant to fatigue. A dog of exceptional intelligence and a loyal companion, it obeys its master with facility and apparent pleasure. It is obedient with those who look after it or with those for whom it works.' It seemed that Portugal's Hornblower came on four legs and I was desperate to see one.

Everybody I asked about the dog described it differently. The woman in the tourist office said it was smaller than a St Bernard and, like her sweater, close-haired and curly. Nuno in the market said, 'It has webbed feet, is thinner than a Labrador but sturdier than a retriever.' The lady in the pet shop didn't have any but, if we came back later, the vet could tell us how we could buy one. I looked and looked but nowhere could I see this ideal mariner. I had a suspicion that a good *cão de água* would be much more use to Leighton on the boat than I was.

In the marina we made friends with a German couple who had been sailing since they were children and who possessed, between them, eighty years of experience on boats. They were astonishingly efficient. Leighton looked on in awe as Ralf prepared to change his engine oil wearing white trousers. When Leighton had last done this in La Coruña, oil had exploded everywhere and had even ended up in his mouth. Ralf had an electric pump and didn't spill a drop on his outfit. We were invited to tea one afternoon and the boat was so perfect – coordinated dishes, towels, cutlery, shining brass, the couple even wore matching neckerchiefs – that it made me furious at our own makeshift domestic arrangements. In the past, Leighton would never let his own spirits be affected by my mood swings. Now, for some reason, he wasn't able to shrug off my dejection and sank even lower than I did in a crisis. It was as if I'd used up all my depression credit with him. He left me to it. One thought did comfort me, however: for all their years of sailing and matching fenders (ours were bashed and battered after Leixões), the Germans confessed that they never put to sea at night nor did they venture out of port if there was a swell running. Some of our most memorable sailing had been done in such conditions, so I concluded that we were simply on different voyages.

Slowly the knots in our stomachs from Leixões unravelled. By now it was the middle of February and we were in Nazaré for the Mardi Gras parade, a huge event in the local social calendar. We watched children playing on the beach, dressed as Spidermen, wizards and princesses, all having forgotten their roles because real sand was more interesting. The adults dressed up as Smurfs, Mexican peasants, a neolithic tribe and, on my favourite float, the characters on the famous Memorial to the Discoveries in Lisbon. At the top of the wooden monument stood a very drunk Henry the Navigator in his big hat, singing a catchy pop song into a karaoke machine. The fishermen of Nazaré had their own float, which they had built in the yard near us. It was a boat and they had dressed up as fishermen. This seemed to me a new definition of happiness – that, when given the choice of any fantasy role in the world, you would choose your own daily job. Either that, or it showed a staggering lack of imagination.

During the day, if they weren't out at sea, the fishermen had plenty of work to do repairing nets. I'd often see them walking backwards along the grass pulling long reels of line, untangling them. The fishermen's hands were so swollen from being immersed in salt water that they looked like bunches of bananas, but the men worked quickly and deftly. I found the sight of the men tackling this snarled cordage, stretching out the kinks, a profoundly hopeful one, as if chaos could always engender clarity. In *The Knot Book*, I began to read about the science of knots and discovered that, at a most basic cellular level, our bodies are built up from such long spools of information:

> If the nucleus of a cell were the size of a basketball, the DNA within it would be equivalent to 200 kilometers of fishing line. And it's not as if we had carefully wound the fishing line up before we stuffed it into the basketball. It's a tangled mess.

I suddenly had a vision of the Nazaré fishermen inside our bodies pulling out miles of DNA, teasing out misinformation, and keeping us from genetic diseases and cancer.

Tying and untangling ropes is very much an art in my mind but the theory of knots is an important field in mathematics. Knots can be identified as pretzel knots, satellite knots, torus knots, hyperbolic knots and two-bridge knots. Every braid can be a knot but not every knot can be a braid, especially if it's a writhe. Many scientists believe that knot theory might help describe the vast forces of the universe. String theory, which imagines knots in ten dimensions, is being used in the attempt to reconcile general relativity with quantum mechanics. Superstrings have been described as wormholes, which, some scientists have argued, might make time travel possible. So, when Leighton encouraged me to practise tying knots in the dark, I was dabbling in the fundamental fabric of the universe.

Leighton had taught me that the best way to untangle a rope is to keep loose hands and to throw the end away from you.

He told me that if I started threading ends through the maze, I would make the bundle even tighter. Even with a bird's nest, all I had to do was pat it and, somehow, it would free itself. The mathematical theory of knots, writes Colin Adams, is much more precise about how to do this unravelling:

> We say that a knot K has *unknotting number n* if there exists a projection of the knot such that changing n crossings in the projection turns the knot into the unknot and there is no projection such that fewer changes would have turned it into the unknot.

An unknot is simply a circle, with no ties in it. The author adds that 'in general it's very hard to find the unknotting number of a knot'. I felt sure that, given our difficulties in unwinding after Leixões, Leighton and I now had a very high unknotting number.

Our next breakdown happened as we were crossing the mouth of the River Tagus (the Tejo) near Lisbon. I was on watch and had been surprised by the strength of the tide going out. Despite my best efforts, we had been swept over a fishing buoy. I thought we'd got away without a rope wrapped around our propeller, but, shortly afterwards, the engine stopped again.

It was a calm day and we sunbathed and drank tea as we waited for the Polícia Marítima of Cascais to come out to our assistance. When they arrived, both wearing back-to-front baseball hats, Officers Silva and Cunha (who looked like James Belushi and Pippin from *The Lord of the Rings*) threw us a rope and towed us sedately at two knots into the marina. There, a diver checked our propeller, which, unfortunately, was clear. That meant more engine problems. A local Perkins engineer was called and pronounced that the hydraulic gear pump, which had been repaired in Leixões and which had already let us down once before, was still not working. The boat was beginning to feel less like a means of transport than a magic carpet that stopped unpredictably and was driven by forces entirely beyond our control.

I phoned Paulo, who was, initially, very reassuring.

'Queeneth,' he declared, *tranqüila*. If pomp not working, no more money.'

We sent the pump back up north and waited. Cascais was a lovely town on the River Tagus, half an hour away from Lisbon by train. We knew, from bitter experience, that there were far worse places in which to wait for engine parts.

Leighton was beside himself with worry. His stomach was now constantly upset and he had difficulty sleeping. I noticed that he'd developed small lumps under his skin but he dismissed them as benign fatty deposits, which he'd had removed before, and which, he insisted, were nothing sinister. A larger swelling on the side of his neck concerned me but Leighton flatly refused to visit a doctor. He had, he told me, more important matters on his mind. He felt that he had dragged me into this trip and that it was his fault that it was going so wrong. I pointed out that there had been no coercion involved and, besides, he was taking far too much upon himself. We were both equally responsible for this voyage.

'Why don't you take a walk to the Mouth of Hell?' suggested Sandra, who worked in the marina. 'It's only twenty minutes away, and gives you a good view of the coast. Be very careful, though, on the rocks. Many people fall.'

In our state of mind, the Mouth of Hell sounded positively idyllic. We took her suggestion and found that the Boca do Inferno was a series of limestone caves and gullies eaten into the coast by the sea. The stone was so soft that it looked like ice being melted by spatters of hot water. Later, we went back to the Boca during a storm registering fifty knots of wind, and saw the Inferno in full action mode, the puppy sea transformed into a Rottweiler. Walls of water crashed on the rocks, throwing up spray like temporary trees and soaking the hundreds of onlookers who had come to enjoy the melodrama.

By now things had started going seriously wrong with Paulo. Having assured us initially that the pump would be repaired for free in the factory, Paulo began to change his tune. He became evasive on the phone and then, when we tried to clarify the situation, abusive. Leighton remonstrated with Paulo who told him, 'So sue me,' and put the phone down. Things deteriorated further when Keva told Leighton to fuck off. We managed to get Paulo to return the pump and began investigating other means of repairing it in Lisbon.

We were walking along the marina later the same day when we passed a chandlery that had been recommended to us. Leighton was so low that he didn't want to go in to ask if they would repair our pump, but I insisted that we should do everything in our power to solve our problems. The engineer asked us how old the pump was and, barely bothering to turn to speak to us, said arrogantly, 'Get a new pump, we don't repair the old.' Another fuck off. As we left we were asking ourselves if we had 'Kick Me in the Teeth' written on our foreheads.

Once we were back in the privacy of the boat Leighton really lost his cool. I'd never seen him so distraught. He was finished, he said, he had nothing left to give. He was furious with me for having exposed us to another rejection when we were already feeling so down. He grabbed the poles that provide handholds for when you're in rough seas so hard that I could see them flexing. It wasn't my fault that I had been so ill, he continued, but he was all used up. I was bossy and wilful and didn't leave any room for him; I wasn't a real wife. He wanted to sell the boat, go home and get a divorce.

I was stunned. I knew Leighton had been down for a while, but it was a huge leap from dealing with engine trouble to the end of a marriage. I immediately assumed that this was all my fault. I felt terrible that I had made Leighton so unhappy but I was also desperately hurt by what he had said. I had kept going for years by telling myself that I didn't mind having depression or struggling with myself. But if it meant that I had become unbearable to live with, if it was going to lead to me losing Leighton, then I *did* mind desperately. I felt suicidal. For two days I walked around Cascais, sitting on park benches crying, thinking, 'My husband is going to divorce me.'

All my assumptions about this voyage now lay in tatters. I no longer knew if we were going to go on or head back to the UK. We had an engine that, even after months of expensive work, still wouldn't go and we didn't know how to repair it. For the first time I realised that travelling is not a question of will at all. We had done everything within our power to make our boat move, but still it would not. All we could do was encourage that to happen, but something other than us would have to provide the means and the expertise to repair that pump and allow us to start sailing again safely. We were sitting in a boat with an unknot where a gear pump should be and a marital knot that looked as if it had come undone.

As we began to talk again over the next couple of days,

Leighton became very remorseful and said that the last thing he really wanted was a divorce. I resolved to listen more carefully to him and to try to be better crew on the boat. We thought through all our options. One day, on the train to Lisbon, I asked Leighton, 'Couldn't we sail without an engine?'

'No,' answered Leighton. 'How would we get in and out of port?'

'Hornblower never had an engine,' I countered.

'Hornblower always seemed to have a favourable wind.'

It seemed to me that, if our dreams of a smooth voyage had unravelled so easily in the face of difficulties, they couldn't have been sustainable in the first place. Our hope for a good place where we could live cheaply and away from hassles was clearly a false one. I saw the same thing in a Danish couple we had met, who had returned early from a voyage to the Caribbean because they were so disillusioned by the residents trying to take advantage of visitors. They had sailed towards an idea of paradise, and had been shattered to find it was a tourist destination. We had been aiming for Brazil but, after our time along the coast of Portugal, I no longer believed in Brazil. There are no good places, I argued to myself, there was only this constant struggle with problems and the need to keep going, though I had no idea how we could do that. By now we knew for sure that our marriage was the main engine of the boat and, with that broken, we were no longer going anywhere.

The wonderfully kind Cascais Marina staff put us in touch with a consumer association that was expert at putting pressure on unscrupulous businessmen. The membership fee was, I felt, considerably cheaper than Leighton going to Oporto, hitting Paulo and ending up in jail. The staff arranged for our boat to be moved to a better berth, close to the office, because it was clear we were going to be in Cascais for some time. They introduced us to Taka and Junko, a Japanese couple, and we became friends. One afternoon, Junko tied me up in a different type of knot, the Japanese ornamental sash called an *obi*, which I loved. Taka, teasing us, said that I was an empty cup and Leighton was good strong tea. Sitting on Taka's boat, eating sushi one night, and discussing our engine problems, he told us that there was a Zen saying that proposed that heaven and hell are identical. The proverb imagines both as a group of people sitting around a table trying to eat with very long chopsticks. The people in hell are the ones who are trying and failing to feed themselves. The people in heaven are all feeding each other and, therefore, being fed.

The very next day, still in the pits of misery, I finally saw a water dog. Leighton and I were walking out of the marina to go into Cascais, feeling very low and wobbly. We rounded a corner by the fort and whoa! – there it was, a bundle of energy wrapped in a jet-black, curly coat. The dog wasn't at all like a poodle and its limbs were firm and athletic. It had lovely dark eyes and big feet, which, its student owners told us, splayed open when it swam. This dog was very nervous and, because it was always afraid, had been named Scooby-Doo. I was elated. Seeing a water dog was no practical help to us at all, but it was comfort from a unexpected direction. It gave me faith that, in the depths of despondency, an ideal of seamanship could manifest itself, even if it was in the form of a neurotic dog and an increasingly shaky couple on a yacht called *Jameeleh*.

Gradually, by asking advice and phoning the original manufacturers in the UK, we began to work out what we should do about the hydraulic gear drive. The Mark I Nicholson 35s feature an unusual engine configuration, with a hydraulic drive to a propshaft that exits at the keel root. This was why the boat was sometimes difficult to handle at low speeds. The arrangement was a sturdy one, but much more unusual than the V-drive gearbox that was installed in the later models. By now we had given up on Paulo, who had turned out to be our third and most costly siren, enticing us to stay with him until he could fix all our engine problems when he must have known that this was beyond his abilities. Leighton tracked down the original manufacturers of the pump in England and asked them to make us a new one. This came at a fraction of the price we had already paid Paulo for the repair of the original. We were told sternly by other boat owners in Cascais that it was imperative to stick with reputable agents in Portugal, so we gave the fitting work to the Perkins dealers in Lisbon.

When Ricardo and Adrian came aboard *Jameeleh*, they were intrigued by the hydraulic drive set-up and asked where our oil filter was. We don't have one, we replied. You must do, they insisted. And, sure enough, we did. It was hidden away in the cockpit locker – Leighton had always assumed it was part of the fridge. We were all silent as we looked at the disgusting filter, which crackled with metallic fragments and strange bits of blue glue. Our engine had been going wrong in parts we didn't know existed. We felt like rank amateurs and were embarrassed by our ignorance in a place with so venerable a history of seafaring.

Nearly everything important in Lisbon came to the city as a result of the fifteenth-century Voyages of Discovery. This had been my favourite history topic in school and now I was staying on the coast that had been the Cape Canaveral of its day. There are basic physical reasons why the first voyages across the Atlantic and down to Africa set off from the coasts of Portugal and southern Spain. The trade-wind system begins south of Lisbon and means that ships can rely on steady winds to propel them westwards and southwards, at predictable times of year. Boats still flock through this revolving door of the trade winds when crossing the Atlantic today. Areas like the Tagus estuary and Andalucía are highly favoured slip roads on to the Atlantic wind motorway. Historians are, however, still at a loss to explain why the discoveries happened when they did, given that no startling new sailing technology was developed in the period. What did change was the development of a new culture of exploration and adventure, sponsored by kings and fuelled by chivalrous ideals.

Going round the Maritime Museum in Belém it was easy to see how dashing the pioneering explorers were. Seen collectively, I was impressed by the beards they sported, like facial sails. My favourite explorer in school had always been Vasco da Gama, because I liked the sound of his name. He also had the best beard in the museum, shaped like a shovel and clearly destined for great things. In Portugal, the name Vasco da Gama is used all the time, by taxis, building companies and plumbers. Further up the Tagus was the Vasco da Gama centre, a huge shopping mall, where the Portuguese are urged to venture out on to a sea of designer labels, a sad debasement of the heroic ideal of sailing into the unknown. This did, however, make certain historical sense. When the Portuguese reached India via the Cape of Good Hope, they didn't have the bullion or manpower to establish a trading monopoly by force, as the Spaniards had attempted to do. What they did was to establish a totally different concept of empire, which depended not on the acquisition of territory but control of the seas. They made the system pay for itself by levying tariffs on trade from the strategic ports they established in East Africa and Macao. Thus the Portuguese were the first to establish the idea of a global trading system, one of the fruits of which was the chain stores in the Vasco da Gama shopping centre.

The Portuguese poet Fernando Pessoa went so far as to claim that Portugal invented the very concept of sea exploration:

> You can forget about Columbus and Cabot. Columbus is sociologically Portuguese, because the Discoveries were a Portuguese initiative, just like their scientific conception and the construction of the whole as a fact of civilization, and as a result everyone who has contributed to them has for that reason become Portuguese.

Pessoa even saw his own work as a poet as a continuation of Portuguese maritime exploration, in a way that made a good deal of sense to me as a writer. Dedicating a book to Prince Henry the Navigator, he wrote:

> Your initiative, Sir, led to the discovery of the Real World; mine will lead to the discovery of the Intellectual World. I too have finally arrived at the furthest void, at the intangible edge of the limit of being, at the uncertain door, of the remote abyss of the World. I passed through that door, Sir. I sailed, Sir, on that sea.

During his life Pessoa hardly left his flat, let alone the city of Lisbon, and yet he asserted that he'd undertaken vast interior adventures. We weren't making much progress down the Portuguese coast either, but I believed I was making my own discoveries all the time. Reading a book in the Cascais public library, I learned that the word for yacht came from the Dutch word, *jagen*, which means to hunt, to look for, or to follow. Our yacht was, I felt, a vehicle in which Leighton and I were hunting an ever more elusive existence – our own lives, not as we had imagined them, but a richer, more rewarding reality. I could only hope that some benign force would catch us before we went over the edge of a marital cliff.

Things were going from bad to worse on the boat. By now it was May and the mosquitoes were out. I carelessly left the front hatch above our bed open one night. We woke to discover the forepeak covered in squadrons of insects, which were biting us viciously. These females were so bloated with our blood that they could hardly fly. I wouldn't let Leighton spray insecticide and hunted the bitches by hand.

'You are totally unsuited to this way of life,' he screamed, before moving to sleep on his own out in the saloon.

While we were in Cascais, I had read that King Carlos I of Portugal had been one of the first oceanographers and had assembled a significant collection of marine life. The king used to vacation in Cascais and the Museu do Mar in the park exhibited a film that showed him on the royal yacht trawling for specimens. And there, in the gunwales, was a water dog, alert, intelligent and eager to retrieve any creatures that might escape from his master's nets. I saw a similar breed in São Roque's church in Lisbon, depicted as part of a sacred story. I had gone in just before closing time and was having difficulty working out exactly what had happened to the saint. I asked the curator, who replied, 'He died.'

'Yes,' I replied, 'they all do.'

'Of cancer of the leg.'

I learned, months later, that São Roque had, in fact, caught the plague, but cancer made sense from the pictures.

'And the dog?'

'The creature brought him food because São Roque was so ill he couldn't do anything.'

'A great dog,' I reflected.

'Yes,' replied the curator, wistfully, 'better than some people.'

By now the frustrating wait for the new pump and the rows with Leighton had meant that I was starting to feel the symptoms of depression again. The marina had installed an innovative sound system as part of its fight to keep seagulls from shitting all over the pontoons. This broadcast alternated the cry of a dying seagull and that of a young chick being tortured. The recordings were played at regular times of day but the birds never seemed to get used to them. Neither did we. We'd sit in *Jameeleh*'s saloon and wince as we heard the electric pain strike up at dusk. I felt I had just as repetitive and repelling a pain inside myself. Much against my will but obedient to my old enemy, I started to take anti-depressants. In a calm moment, Leighton confided to me that he thought I had changed since I'd been depressed the last time and that his worst fear was that he had lost me. I told him that I had never been more present in my own life and that I thought I was *more* available to him, not less. He didn't seem to believe me.

I was determined to see as much of Lisbon as I could while we were in Cascais. Leighton, however, had withdrawn into himself and wasn't interested in sightseeing. This was unusual because, in the past, he was always more than happy to go anywhere with me. I found myself wandering around the Alfama or Belém on my own. He didn't come with me on the day that Emilia, the Cascais customs officer, invited us on a picnic in the public gardens. Nor was he there on the day I went up to visit Sintra, a town in which the Portuguese aristocracy, flush with the wealth of global trading, had built its summer residences. Sintra's summer palaces look down on the sea from wooded hillsides and are gorgeous follies, showing nineteenth-century extravagance at its most fanciful.

I decided to keep away from the tourist crowds and visit a house called the Quinta del Regaleira on the outskirts of town. This house and gardens were built by Italian architect Luigi Manini for the fabulously wealthy Dr António Augusto Carvalho Monteiro, so rich that he was known as 'Money-bags Monteiro'. On the wooded hillside of Sintra, Monteiro commissioned a work that was more like a dreamscape than a summer retreat. He asked the architect to realise his fantasies about the spiritual journeys of the Knights Templar and the Masons. What resulted was a fabulous park, populated with crenellated turrets, grottos, chapels and mythological beasts. The walk around the garden itself was designed to mimic the *vera peregrinatio mundi*, man's pilgrimage through the labyrinth of life.

'Be sure you ask for a torch,' advised the manager of the hotel where I asked directions for the house. At the entrance, I was told that they were waiting for new torches. The curator was cheeky: 'Face your fears,' he said, 'you're *meant* to go through in the dark. Put out both arms and you won't hit your head.' Mystified, I made my way up the slope, past the Fountain of Abundance, the Egyptian House, Leda's Cave, the Grotto of the Virgin and the Threshold of the Gods. A large stone iguana guarded the entrance to the Terrace of the Celestial Worlds. I climbed higher up the hill until I found what I was looking for, the Well of Initiation. It was deep and gloomy and a spiral staircase sank into the earth. A young Romanian couple peered down the shaft at the same time as me. As I walked into dusk I was soaked by drips of water. At the bottom I peered into the totally unlit gallery. I couldn't even begin to think about entering the passage. I was stuck.

'Please wait for my wife,' said the man as he descended the staircase behind me. I assumed that he wanted me to take a photograph of them together, so I waited. But no, he wanted us all to go through the tunnel together. I relayed what I had been told about the passage: that there were two turns and then we'd see the light.

'Put your hand on my wife's shoulder,' he commanded as he disappeared into the void.

We followed, blind.

The labyrinth wall seemed to make many odd turns and, as time went on in the watery blackness, we became convinced that we were in a dead end.

'Two turns and then the light,' I repeated.

'Are you sure?' asked my new friend.

No, I wasn't sure, but just as I was turning to look back, his wife shouted that she could see sun. Shortly afterwards I could see the couple, like monarchs' heads on a stamp, against the light of the cave entrance.

'We have passed the test!' we laughed triumphantly. It did feel as though something important had happened. Going into the dark we had been strangers, but because we had trusted each other, we had made our way through. I felt wonder and gratitude for such landscape theatre, a present to us from a nineteenth-century Italian architect. It had given me hope that, even though Leighton and I didn't know where we were, we would be fine as long as we kept moving together.

'Gwyneth, come and look at this,' Leighton called down into *Jameeleh*'s saloon, where I had been working. Curious, I hurried up to the sea wall, only to see a blue tug moving rapidly away. In the entrance to the marina was an upside-down trimaran and, sitting astride one of its sponsons, Ellen MacArthur in sunglasses. Every now and again she would disappear into the inverted hull of the boat. She had been sailing on Alain Gautier's sixty-foot trimaran, *Foncia*, on a Mondiale Assistance race from Cherbourg to Rimini when, in the middle of the night, the boat's leeward hull hit something. A wave lifted *Foncia*'s stern and the trimaran bore away out of control and capsized sixty miles off the coast of Portugal. She was towed by tug with the crew still on board and here she was now, stuck on a falling tide just outside the harbour. The yacht's mast had touched bottom and was preventing the boat from getting in.

We all watched as a diver was sent under to cut off the mast before the boat was damaged further. Some of the *marineros* we knew told us that this was the third time this crew had been in Cascais with problems.

'Last time they went the wrong side of a buoy and hit some rocks. I don't think they're very good.'

We could feel the crew's concentration on bringing *Foncia* in safely to the salvage area. They made very little noise but were intensely aware of one another and of the boat's movements. They exuded calm and capability.

33   Ellen MacArthur on the overturned *Foncia*

'Do you realise,' said Leighton, in awe, 'that we're not the only ones to have been towed into Cascais? Ellen MacArthur did the same thing.' This was an encouraging thought. Since we'd left the UK the previous autumn, Ellen MacArthur had passed us three times on her international races. I looked at her carefully. She was smaller than I had expected and prettier, with tiny white teeth and blue eyes. I became shy, but Leighton went straight down on to the pontoon and shook her hand. He invited her for a cup of tea aboard *Jameeleh* and she said that she might take us up on the offer. He explained that we had been brought in with engine problems and she wished us luck with the repairs.

A few days later I met Ellen MacArthur myself. She was sitting on a wall waiting for a crew member to take her into Lisbon. I asked her if she'd ever read the Hornblower books and she confessed that she hadn't. She was more of a *Swallows and Amazons* fan. I repeated Leighton's invitation to tea on the boat and she repeated her acceptance. We arranged a time the following morning. She took down *Jameeleh*'s name but not mine, which seemed a very seamanlike thing to do.

I went back to Leighton beside myself with excitement. I felt as though I had finally met Hornblower. Forget the Portuguese water dog; Ellen MacArthur, with her youthful fortitude and easy manner, was the very embodiment of the seafaring virtues. I felt that, if she were able to come on board *Jameeleh*, she would, in some way, make us real sailors. Leighton made the ropes on deck look professional and I went shopping for bread, croissants and two kinds of jam.

The following morning Ellen MacArthur didn't show. Clearly something had happened.

'I'm sure she's very reliable,' said Leighton, as we sat down and ate three croissants each.

I tried to be reasonable, but I was gutted. I felt that we had missed a blessing that I desperately wanted, some kind of assurance that things would be all right and that our voyage could continue.

I took a photograph of Ellen's empty place at our table. After this encounter, all I could tell you was that she's very quiet and she doesn't take sugar.

To take our minds off our disappointment, we went into Lisbon together and walked round the cool streets of medieval Alfama. Seamanship is something you have to do for yourself, it's not an attribute you can discover in someone else and hope to 'catch'. Buddhists say that you should kill the Buddha if you meet him on your way. Any Buddha that looks like one is going to be a fake, contrived from your own stock ideas. Like Hornblower, the Ellen MacArthur I had

34   Morning tea without Ellen MacArthur

wanted to meet was a fiction, though she is, of course, real to herself. That morning's no-show began to take on a certain rightness.

The next day the mobile phone rang and Leighton answered it.

'Ellen who?' he asked pleasantly, and then, calling her sweetheart, passed her on to me.

Ellen was phoning to apologise for not having kept our appointment and we talked for about twenty minutes. I explained some of the difficulties we'd faced and she told me, 'If sailing were easy, then it would be very busy out there.' Most of her strength comes from the fact that she simply loves being on the sea. 'I'd paddle a plank across a lake if I had to,' she confessed.

As preparation for every race she would tell herself at the

start, 'This is going to be harder than I can ever imagine but also better.' Spoken by Ellen MacArthur, it wasn't a platitude but a matter of experience. Then, as we ended the conversation, she said simply, 'Never give up, never stop learning.'

Not long after that, things came together quickly with the engine. The Perkins engineers installed the new hydraulic drive, checked everything and announced that we could leave. Just as we were ready to go, Leighton caught gastric flu. After a couple of hours I piled him into a Vasco da Gama taxi and took him to the local doctor. I sat on the boat, watching him sleep and feeling lonely. More cruisers came and went and Leighton slowly recovered.

It was a great day when we finally passed the sacred Cape St Vincent and turned the corner into the relatively sheltered waters of the Algarve. Leighton was still weak from his illness and went below, leaving me in charge of the boat for the last few hours into Lagos. The wind was a brisk thirty-five knots and the seas lively, but I had begun to understand how to trim the sails. Rita held her own against the swell, giving me enough leisure to enjoy the school of dolphins that swam with us.

I watched in fascination as they talked to us and each other by means of the angles at which they approached the bow wave, their sudden accelerations and joyful leaps into the air. Even if I'd wanted to, I couldn't have counted them, their repeated passes at and returns to the boat multiplied their number endlessly. In a way, they were one dolphin infinitely duplicated. I was so happy that I started to sing them Welsh hymns. They loved 'Calon Lân', a rousing song about wanting a pure heart, but they weren't so taken with 'Onward Christian Soldiers'.

That evening and only six months late, Leighton and I

brought *Jameeleh* into Lagos marina. We were greeted by some sailors we'd met in Leixões. They'd had a lovely easy and sociable winter in Lagos, with plenty of ex-pat company. We, on the other hand, been through a crash course in port survival.

CHAPTER NINE

The Nature of the Bottom

A wrecking sea is part of what we all dream ourselves to be every night; and the ship becomes
our own puny calculations, our repressions, our
compromises, our kowtowings to convention,
duty and a dozen other idols ... A psychiatrist
tells me that a morbid obsession with disaster is
a common defence against depression; its enjoy-
ment brings a vicarious sense of manic triumph
over normal reality. So the shipwreck is not only
what we are thankful will never happen to us; it
is also what we secretly want to happen, and
finally to ourselves.

John Fowles, *The Shipwreck*

We loved Lagos. The sun was noticeably hotter and Leighton
rigged an awning over the cockpit so that we could sit in
the shade. June 13 was the Feast of Santo António, widely
celebrated in Portugal because the saint was born to a noble
family in Lisbon. I had seen a poster advertising what I
thought was a brass-band concert in the Philharmonic Society
of Lagos but it turned out to be a dance with an accordion and
hundreds of local people eating salted sardines and *bifana*
sandwiches in a square at the top of town. Ladies with

formidable bosoms danced together and a huge fuss was made of a young baby, who looked up in unfocused awe at the fairy lights, tissue decorations and a wet moon stuck in an acacia tree. On the way back to the boat, we met another black *cão de água*.

We spent a week in Lagos before heading down towards Gibraltar, where we wanted to prepare the boat for an Atlantic crossing. Despite our brief holiday in Lagos, when we started sailing again things seemed worse than ever between us.

'Jesus, Gwyneth!' screamed Leighton. 'When I say tack, I don't mean maybe!'

The combination of seasickness pills and anti-depressants had made me drowsy. A rope slipped on the traveller, making the boom swing wildly. I could only watch as it happened, unable to respond. Leighton snapped the line into its cleat and glared at me. I felt total indifference towards anything to do with the boat. We were in the middle of a field of fishing nets, requiring extra vigilance, but I couldn't have cared less.

That night, in the Spanish port of Mazagón, where Christopher Columbus provisioned his ships for one of his voyages to America, Leighton voiced his fear to me.

'We cannot carry on like this. You're a liability. We both need to be wide awake at sea.'

The pills, it seemed, dulled my emotions, which was useful when they were a constant agony, but a disadvantage when we needed to sail. Reluctantly, I had to agree that what Leighton was saying was true. I decided that I would taper myself off the pills.

'In sailing, you've got to be alive, or you're dead,' Leighton declared profoundly.

As for boats being anti-depressants in themselves, I had

long ago stopped believing that particular myth. We met one Welshman in Sines who had suffered from depression and went for psychotherapy. His therapist asked him what was his delight, and he replied that it was his boat. It was suggested that, when he was feeling anxious, he should think about his yacht as a refuge from his bad feelings. He did so, but immediately started obsessing about a problem with his keel and worrying about his mast and what if . . . In a trice his mood had spiralled down with anxiety and back into depression. That's how therapeutic boats can be.

There was another matter that needed addressing, however, in the way we sailed together. I could no longer pretend that our arguments were the result of inexperience. We had now been sailing long enough that we should have adapted to our new roles on the boat. And yet, as we came into Rota, just north of Cádiz, we had another fight. Leighton had asked me to skipper the boat into port and I'd made a bad choice by furling the genoa far too early. Leighton had not wanted to offend me at the time by challenging my call, but then he couldn't let it go and fumed at the seemingly endless time it took us to reach the marina. I wept with resentment and frustration.

When the American composer and conductor Leonard Bernstein was asked which orchestral instrument he would most like to have played, he answered: 'Second fiddle.' This, he reasoned, was the most difficult instrument of all, for temperamental reasons. Nobody likes to be second in line. I resolved to make more of an effort to become crew for Leighton. There had to be clarity of decision between us and I needed to learn not to become offended when I was told that I'd done something wrong.

We were by now in the Bay of Cádiz, an area dense with history and which has been sailed for centuries by British sailors, especially during the Napoleonic wars. We were astonished, however, when we met a French couple who told us that they had been attacked by pirates off Cape Trafalgar. They had been fishing near the notorious shallows that surround the cape and the weather was thick. Out of the fog came a RIB with men dressed all in black, their faces covered. The boat circled them, their fishing lines were cut and then the men demanded money. The husband went below to broadcast a mayday. A nearby cargo vessel diverted to their position, and was seen to do so by the pirates, who swiftly disappeared back towards Morocco.

As part of the preparation for our voyage I had read quite a bit about piracy in foreign waters, but I'd never heard of such an incident in Europe. The International Maritime Organisation's *Guidance to Shipowners and Ship Operators, Shipmasters and Crews on Preventing and Suppressing Acts of Piracy and Armed Robbery* informed me that the smell of stale urine in a secluded part of a ship is a clue that you might have a stowaway or potential pirate on board. The IMO does not recommend that cruisers carry firearms, although many yacht owners do so in Pacific or Caribbean waters. Again, awareness is the key to self-defence:

> Maintaining vigilance is essential. All too often the first indication of an attack has been when the attackers appear on the bridge or in the master's cabin. Advance warning of a possible attack will give the opportunity to sound alarms, alert other ships and the coastal authorities, illuminate the suspect craft, undertake evasive manoeuvring or initiate other response procedures. Signs that the ship is aware it is being approached can deter attackers.

The guide suggested the use of high-pressure water hoses to repel boarders – not an option on *Jameeleh*, though my pee bucket was always close at hand. We were now a mere fifty miles from Africa, in an area notorious for drug smuggling and illegal immigration. The Frenchman told us that we might see marooned migrants clinging to navigation buoys, signalling to passing boats with mirrors. He warned us that it was illegal to go to their aid. These were waters in which anything could happen.

We decided to stay a few days in Rota, a small resort and fishing village located next to an American naval base. As we first came into the port, we thought we could hear the sound of a muezzin. This call to prayer was, in fact, an auctioneer in the fish market selling the day's catch. We went into town and ate a meal of octopus salad. Every day at noon the town's clock played Beethoven's 'Ode to Joy' in a minor key.

This part of Spain is rich in minerals and so attracted the ancient Phoenician traders. The Greek writer Diodorus Siculus wrote that the supply of silver from Huelva (one day's sail up the coast) was so prolific that, when there was no more room for precious metals in their ships, the merchants replaced their lead anchors with silver ones. I had to leave Rota for a couple of days to take part in a festival in Germany, but, before I went, Leighton gave me a present, a gold anchor and chain purchased in a *joyería*. (Was there ever a happier noun for a jewellery shop?) It was an intricate piece, and had a Christ figure carved on the back of the anchor, which was also a crucifix. To be a saviour, this Christ had to drown himself. I loved it.

Sailor and novelist Joseph Conrad outlined, from a seaman's point of view, why an anchor makes such a powerful symbol:

An anchor is forged and fashioned for faithfulness; give it ground that it can bite, and it will hold till the cable parts, and then, whatever afterwards befall its ship, that anchor is 'lost'. The honest, rough piece of iron, so simple in appearance, has more parts than the human body has limbs: the ring, the stock, the crown, the flukes, the palms, the shanks.

Conrad goes on to comment that the anchor is the heaviest object that a sailor has to handle on board ship and is used mainly at the beginning and the end of a voyage. I hoped sincerely that Leighton's gift to me was not a portent that our voyage together was already over.

I returned from Germany to find Leighton in a state. When I'd left, he had been desperate to rest, but had been unable to do so because some kindly Brits on the same pontoon had undertaken to 'look after' him while I was away. I was surprised that he was so upset by their well-meaning invitations to dine, go out for a drink or play boules. Normally more than capable of looking after himself – indeed, he's usually robust – he had been unable to draw a line between himself and the couple and so felt even more exhausted. I took over the role of gatekeeper as soon as I got back and, as a result, we enjoyed a peaceful couple of days, waiting for a favourable wind to enter the Strait of Gibraltar.

My paper preparations to enter the strait made us quite apprehensive. Southern Europe and North Africa are separated by a body of water only fourteen miles wide. This is partly why Napoleon once declared, 'Let us only be masters of the Strait for six hours and we shall be masters of the world!' The entrance to the Mediterranean Sea is one of the busiest shipping junctions in the world, with a traffic separation scheme and designated lanes for commercial vessels, so we needed to be very careful that we weren't run down by a large ship. We had already learned from the Bristol Channel that, when water is forced through a narrow geographical feature, you can expect lively sailing. The charts of the strait mark vigorous tidal currents that change direction with every hour that passes after high tide. Thus, when the current in the middle of the strait is east-going, the stream closer to land might flow westwards. Not only do the tidal streams on the surface change during the day, but the strait currents thrust in opposite directions at various depths in the water because of the different salinity of cold Atlantic and warmer Mediterranean water. During the Second World War, German U-boats used this to their advantage and avoided the Allied fortification of the strait, by drifting in and out of the Mediterranean on favourable deep currents while the tidal flow on the surface might be flowing in the opposite direction.

In Barbate, our last port before Gibraltar, we asked advice from the marina staff and from sailors who had passed through the strait before. One boat owner told us to remember that wind over tide creates rough water and to use that principle as a guide to finding the currents most favourable to us. This meant that, going east on a westerly wind, we should keep to the smooth water, which was itself moving east. I was most reassured by a British builder who told us that he always planned his strait passages meticulously on paper but had found that, no matter when he left on the tide, he always seemed to wash up in Gibraltar. In this, we would be helped by the dominant easterly current caused by the evaporation of the Mediterranean, which draws in water to replace it from the Atlantic.

We left Barbate at the crack of dawn, with the morning

shift of local fishermen. We all sailed together, lit up like individual stars in the dark. It's well known that the strait has a funnelling effect on winds and we had been warned by many sailors not to attempt a passage on anything but a fine weather forecast. What might start off as force four in port would very likely be a force seven or more in the strait. Huge wind turbines line the coast near Tarifa, making turbulent weather productive. I found the sight chastening; those turbines were there for a reason.

By the time we had reached Tarifa and entered the strait, we began to experience the full complexity of the seas. The turbulent area outside Milford Haven was called Five Tides, but this was more like Fifty-Five Tides. Around us the surface of the water jumped, as if it were being fried or pelted by invisible rain. As we went through some of the rough eddies, I was horrified to see the echo sounder fluctuating wildly and registering some depths of under two metres. *Jameeleh* draws 1.6 metres, which means that the keel extends down about six feet beneath her. I looked at the surface and it reminded me of how tide behaves in the shallows over a sandbank, so I shouted out to Leighton, was he sure we were sailing in a safe depth? He was furious with my question. Of course we were. Didn't I remember that the echo sounder goes crazy when registering depths of more than a hundred metres? Didn't I trust him at all? Was I stupid or what?

I went cold. Given the evidence before my eyes, I felt that I was completely right to check our position and to query it with Leighton. This wasn't a matter of personality, but of safety. I had been trying to do my job as crew and still things weren't right. Perhaps I had been concentrating so hard on playing second fiddle that I hadn't realised the degree to which the lead violin was out of tune. For the first time I could see that our problems might not be mainly due to my incompetence.

There was no mistaking the Rock of Gibraltar when it appeared before us as we rounded the last peninsula in the strait. The Rock dominates the area, rearing up above the narrows like a slowly breaking limestone wave. This was the ancient mountain of Calpe, answered geologically on the Moroccan side by Mount Acho. Together, these were the twin pillars of Hercules, the route out of the ancient world of the Mediterranean into the Atlantic, the unknown realm of the gods. It was even rumoured that one of the Gibraltar caves contained an entrance to the underworld. These two rocky mountains, facing one another across such a narrow stretch of water, appeared as twin columns on the design of the early pieces of eight shipped to Spain from South America. Later, these were transformed into the parallel lines down the S of the American dollar sign, representing the gateway between the old world and the new. It has been argued that the twin towers of the World Trade Center echoed this iconography. Thus, the Pillars of Hercules are at the symbolic centre of the global capitalist economy, and now Leighton and I were sailing right in between them.

I hadn't been prepared for the beauty of Gibraltar. As we drew closer, we could see colourful tankers anchored out in the bay. There seemed to be very little flat ground on the peninsula, so the residents had built vertically. I knew that packs of Barbary apes lived in the scattered green foliage of the peak, stirring like hidden thoughts on the slopes. I was still steering the boat and, in order to avoid the high-speed ferries thundering between Algeciras and Ceuta, I took us behind one of the bunkering ships into less frequented water. Leighton complained loudly that this was unnecessary and that I ignored everything he told me to do, so I ignored him and concentrated instead on the stunning rock ahead of us.

Because of unique weather conditions in the strait, sailors sometimes have to wait weeks for a favourable wind to go east or west. In the ancient world sailors tried to increase their chances of safe passage by offering sacrifices to the gods. In a Gibraltar cave, archaeologists have found evidence of a shrine to Hercules, dating from the eighth century BC with offerings of Phoenician pottery, incense, perfume and ointment bottles, finger rings and dozens of figurine pendants. I could see the psychological, if not nautical, sense of this. Sometimes, in order to continue a voyage, you have to sacrifice your own illusion of control. Ellen MacArthur has written that she would never dream of crossing the Equator without throwing something overboard to the gods of the sea. I had already given up any idea of the 'success' of our voyage, but the fact that things were still so difficult for us suggested that even more needed to be relinquished. I had been trying very hard to be the crew that Leighton wanted but nothing pleased him. He was projecting huge amounts of rage at me and I had soaked it up willingly. No wonder I had been feeling depressed – I had been carrying Leighton's bad feelings and mistaking them for my own. This latest row on the boat made me decide to jettison an attitude that had been a huge liability for me. I had no idea what was going on with him, but I refused to keep taking the blame for Leighton's anger.

We had been travelling at a speed of eight knots or more, a tearing pace for heavy *Jameeleh*. As the builder in Barbate had promised, Gibraltar sucked us in like a long piece of spaghetti. Soon we passed Rosia Bay, where Nelson's ships used to anchor. On one visit, Nelson had sent his laundry into town but, receiving unexpected news of the French Navy, had sailed abruptly, leaving his smalls ashore. It was to Gibraltar that Nelson's body, pickled in a casket of brandy, later changed to spirits of wine, was carried after the Battle of Trafalgar before being returned to England.

Gibraltar is known as a good port to buy cheap boats, partly because it is such a busy sailing intersection. We had also been told that it is the place where many sailing wives jump ship. Women who are new to sailing and who've not enjoyed their Atlantic crossing (whether due to meteorological or emotional storms), or those who've experienced a rough time in Biscay, abandon ship there, leaving various Captain Bastards short of crew. Although Lord Nelson didn't have the problems of modern cruisers in mind, he once wrote that, after Gibraltar, every man becomes a bachelor.

As we rounded the corner into Waterport, where we planned to tie up in the world-famous Sheppards marina, I noticed a RIB full of divers anchored at the entrance to a harbour. Divers always look sinister to me, as if they are investigating the scene of a crime, dragging a lake for a body. Later that evening, I finally lit the candle I had bought in Oporto, to give thanks for arriving safely at our destination.

'Remember,' I said firmly to Leighton, who had calmed down again, 'Gibraltar is where the couples part.'

He looked at me uncomfortably.

Aside from its strategic position at the gateway to the Mediterranean, Gibraltar was crucial to the British Empire as a bunkering station. Supplies of coal exported from the UK were deposited at key points around the world to enable the navy and merchant navy to refuel in hostile waters. Indeed, without coal and the telegraph wire, the empire might arguably not have existed. Writing in 1905 about the British Oceanic Empire, and the challenges it faced in the near future, Gerald Fiennes noted:

> The one serious question is coal. Modern warships can steam for 8,000 to 15,000 miles without re-coaling; but in war time it is desirable to keep a reserve in the bunkers. Although it may not be absolutely necessary to take advantage of them, it is desirable to have coaling stations within a thousand miles or so of every area of sea within which a fleet is likely to operate.

Fiennes's map of the Ocean Empire (see Figure 35) and its highways shows the reliance of British possessions around the world upon the coal ports that supplied them with fuel. Regulating a steamer's coal consumption was, therefore, a major preoccupation for her engine-room crew in this period. *Reed's Useful Hints to Sea-Going Engineers*, published in 1921, notes that any second engineer should pay particular attention to economy of coal consumption and 'to the Firemen and their methods of working', urging the officer to 'insist upon the fires being worked in his own manner. With good firemen he will have little trouble, but unfortunately good men are scarce . . . He should examine all the fires each watch, and see that the Trimmers keep a good supply of coals on the plates. He should also see that unburnt fuel is not thrown overboard with the ashes.'

This anxiety about getting the maximum mileage out of the coal available on board reminded me of an account I'd read about the first British steamer to cross the Atlantic. The

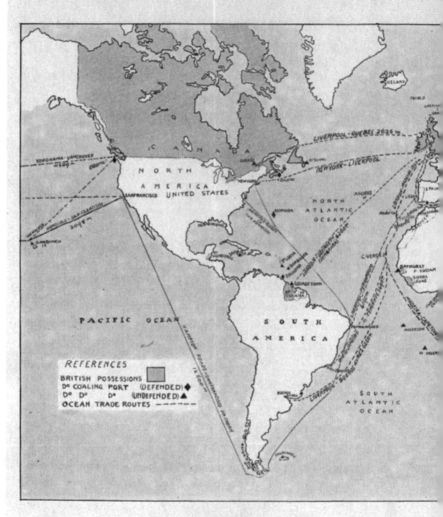

35 Strategic ports of the British Empire

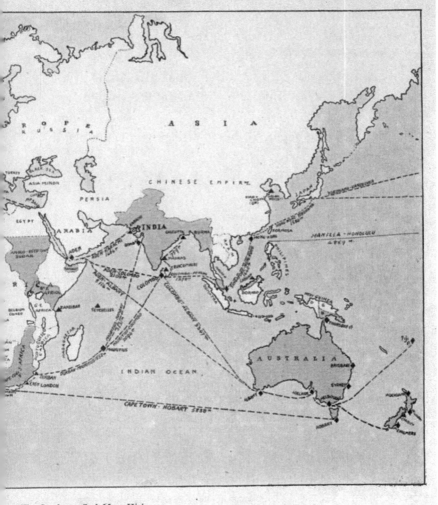

"The Lord our God Most High
He hath made the deep as dry,
He hath smote for us a pathway to the ends of all the Earth."

KIPLING—"A Song of the English"

Sirius burned twenty-four tons of coal per day and produced a speed of eight and a half knots. The crew nearly mutinied when they began to doubt the ship's capacity to reach her destination on the fuel available. By the end of the voyage, the engines had to be fed with all the vessel's furniture and spars. Over the past few months on *Jameeleh*, Leighton and I had been running very low on our usual fuel. Quite a few pieces of emotional furniture had already disappeared into the boiler and I was worried about what more we could find to burn before the engine of our marriage finally sputtered and cut out.

'There!' said Darren Fa, of the Gibraltar Museum. 'A piece of Welsh coal from the bottom of Gibraltar Bay.'

I opened the ziplock bag he'd placed in front of me and pulled out its contents, a large cobble of wet coal. The mineral was cold and slightly greasy to the touch, old energy that had refused to stay dead. On its side the calcareous tube of a marine worm showed that the coal had been under the sea for some time.

'There's not much of that Welsh coal left,' added Darren. 'Most of the stuff retrieved from the bay has already been burned in Gibraltar.'

Darren was a passionate diver and, with a friend, was working on a book cataloguing and describing the major wrecks of Gibraltar Bay.

Darren showed me where coal used to be loaded in Gibraltar, part of the docks still called Coaling Island. Space has always been scarce in Gibraltar, so bunkering steamers would often be serviced by hulks out in Gibraltar Bay. The job of refuelling a coal-fired ship was formidable and so broke down the usual racial and social hierarchy on, say, a First World War battleship. When a ship was ready to be refuelled

36   Coaling Island, Gibraltar, early 1900s

the whole crew, including officers, changed into their oldest clothes and put Vaseline into their nostrils and around their eyes. If they didn't do this, no matter how much they washed later, their eyes would be left ringed with coal kohl. Often a band would be assembled to help lift the spirits of the crew as they shovelled the coal into the hold. *Reed's Useful Hints* reminds engineers that they should check a new consignment by sending some of their heaviest men to tread over the heap, in order to discover any hollows cunningly built up in the coal by unscrupulous merchants. According to Leighton, one of the worst jobs in the merchant navy of the late 1950s was cleaning out the hold of a ship that had discharged her cargo of coal and was waiting to load grain, as was the case on the regular run between Cardiff and Buenos Aires. The men would strip to underpants and flip-flops to hose down the pervasive dust.

Welsh coal was not a uniform product but came in many different grades, all of which were suitable for different purposes. Moreover, the coal was called various names according to its size. Cobbles were up to five inches in diameter, French nuts up to three. Then, in descending order of size, were: stone nuts, pea nuts, beans, peas, grains and duff, which would pass through a screen with holes of three-sixteenths of an inch in diameter. (When I asked if I could look at documents relating to coal in the Gibraltar Archive, I was presented with three boxes of council correspondence about the price and quality of coal. The papers were damp and mouldy, and when I commented on this to the staff, I was told, 'Ah yes, there was a flood in the council offices in the 1970s.' The papers had still not dried out. I was inhaling 1970s mould.) In 1909, in order to save money, the Gibraltar authorities decided to start burning cheaper coal. This led to huge problems in the Gibraltar electricity supply boiler, in which 'nutty slack' from Nottinghamshire collieries had been tried. A weary official conceded that the more pricey Welsh coal was best because, ultimately, 'cheap coal is expensive coal'. Leighton and I had clearly been running on some sort of inferior nutty slack for quite a while.

Darren told me about the wreck of a Cardiff-registered steamer, the *Rosslyn*, that had been sunk off Gibraltar in February 1916. She was returning in ballast from Malta and was anchored off the Gibraltar South Mole when a south-westerly gale caused her to drag her anchor. The ship was damaged against the breakwater and foundered the following morning, and she now lies in twenty-three metres of water. Darren told me that the wreck's boilers could still be seen, with a small donkey boiler sitting on top.

Marked with crosses, the Admiralty chart for the area shows hundreds of wrecks below the surface, each one a personal, if not historical, disaster. In addition to this, the chart noted,

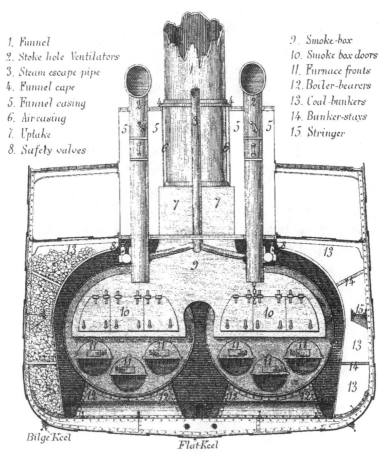

1. Funnel
2. Stoke hole Ventilators
3. Steam escape pipe
4. Funnel cape
5. Funnel casing
6. Air casing
7. Uptake
8. Safety valves

9. Smoke-box
10. Smoke box doors
11. Furnace fronts
12. Boiler-bearers
13. Coal-bunkers
14. Bunker-stays
15. Stringer

Bilge Keel

Flat Keel

37   Mid-ship section of a steamer

the strait holds 1,448 unmarked wrecks at depths greater than twenty-eight metres. I hoped very much that our marriage wasn't going to end up yet another uncharted wreck on the bottom of Gibraltar Bay.

The reason Leighton and I had decided to come to Gibraltar was to take advantage of the dependency's status as a VAT-free port. We needed to buy equipment – such as wind steering, a non-electrical back-up to Rita, and a satellite phone – before we ventured out into the Atlantic. We spent the first few days frantically busy, ordering work to be done on the boat. This included constructing a new steel A-frame for the stern, so that we could mount our solar panel, radar and Navtex aerials out of our way. It would also provide a framework for a canvas bimini, which would be crucial for the hot climates we were hoping to reach next. We asked an electrician to sort out a couple of problems for us and ordered a Hydrovane from the UK. After this first flurry of activity we finally had some time to look around. We did the usual tour of the rock and saw where the waters of the Atlantic and the Mediterranean meet at Europa Point. In St Michael's Cave preparations were under way for the annual Miss Gibraltar competition. Being dripped on in a bathing suit couldn't be very glamorous, I thought, but at least the caverns would be mercifully cool out of the July sun.

I saw my first Barbary ape in the car park near the entrance to the cave. A custodian told me that the ape was called Lonely and that he had stolen four packets of crisps from the shop and become very thirsty. Given a choice between crisps and apples, the apes would take the junk food every time. Higher up the Rock, at the Ape Den, we looked down at the ships anchored in Gibraltar Bay. I fell into conversation with a student from Leeds University who was monitoring the social life of the ape pack for a degree project. He pointed out the alpha male, called Wolf, who had a wise and distracted look on his face. I moved closer and suddenly realised that the ape was masturbating.

'Actually, they masturbate quite a lot,' said the student, who was in a position to be scientific about such matters.

Leighton had been nagging me to learn how to scuba-dive since Lisbon. In Gibraltar, I finally agreed that we should do a course together. To begin with the dive master had been reluctant to take Leighton on because of his age. They didn't see many sixty-seven-year-olds who wanted to learn to scuba-dive. In response, Leighton jumped up and down, touched his toes, then did a few press-ups.

'Can *you* do that?' he asked.

The dive master admitted that he could not and proceeded to fill out the form.

The following morning we set off in a battered old car for our first dive in Camp Bay. Our teacher was Tony, an immensely experienced British Sub-Aqua Club teacher and examiner. He looked like a benign Terry-Thomas and made us laugh, saying that the most dangerous part of the day was the drive to the beach. The overloaded boot of the car wouldn't close and Tony suggested reversing up the hills. He was a sailor, too, and lived on his boat in Marina Bay. When not diving, he worked part-time as a virtual bouncer, vetting clients in an online casino, which he hated. Diving was the joy of his life and his enthusiasm was infectious.

We carried the heavy gear down from the car to the beach

and I sat in the shade to wait, as Leighton went first. All around us relaxed families were setting up their sun shades and picnics, gazing distractedly at the sea. I watched as Tony and Leighton pulled on their wetsuits and kitted up. They walked down to the water, stood for a moment adjusting their mouthpieces and then, suddenly, they were gone.

It was at that moment that the full horror of diving struck me. Leighton had disappeared completely under the sea, which looked as solid to me as a field of earth. How could he possibly be breathing under that soil? There was no sign of him, nothing to show that he was there. It was as though he had been buried alive.

Tony had told us that he would try to show us a wreck that was sunk just off the beach. After about fifteen minutes, I saw two seals' heads bobbing just above where the wreck should be. Leighton is unusually buoyant in water so, in addition to the lead on his weight belt, Tony had put extra stones in his pockets. The stones had fallen out and so Leighton had shot to the surface. He had, however, seen the wreck on his first dive and couldn't stop talking about it when they got back to the beach.

By now it was mid morning and very hot. I was exhausted by the time I'd pulled on my wetsuit, and the weight of the belt and air tank made me feel sick. Panting, I entered the water with Tony but couldn't see how this breathing underwater could possibly work. Patiently, Tony took me through each step and I finally managed to get under the surface. I breathed and turned on my front and suddenly it was like flying, so beautiful and comfortable that it took my breath away. I willed myself to carry on inhaling and watched as tiny cuckoo wrasse came towards us, suspended like colourful clouds in the water. A little further on I could see a school of larger, silvery fish. On the sandy bottom, I found a substantial golden wedding ring and picked it up. The next instant, for some reason, my normal breathing reflexes kicked in; I tried to inhale through my nose, panicked and had to surface in a hurry.

On that dive I went hardly any depth at all, because I couldn't clear my ears, to equalise the pressure either side of my Eustachian tubes. But I'd seen enough to know that I had to do more. Back on the beach Tony gave me a present – the ring I'd picked up from the bottom and dropped when I stopped breathing. I was touched by his attentiveness. The ring turned out to be cheap, although it had looked like a high-carat piece underwater – even grains of sand suspended in the waves look like golden glitter below the surface – and I accepted it gratefully. It was my wedding ring to a magical world of which I'd caught a glimpse, and which I was desperate to see again.

I've always had a hunch that travelling is less a matter of seeking out new experiences than of moving towards your own past. After all, on our voyage, Leighton had returned to the sea after four decades on land, I was following my father's maritime connections and, together, we were retracing historical trade routes from Cardiff. Once I'd met Eleri in the Gibraltar Tourist Board's office, I was sure of it. When I had gone there to book our tour of the Rock, I had commented on her strong Welsh Valleys accent. It turned out that we had been at school together and we ended up speaking in cascades of Welsh, catching up on the past twenty-five years. Like me, Eleri had married a seaman.

'It's great. He cleans, washes and irons. I'm spoilt.'

She was head of human resources and her current preoccupation was with the twenty-eight lifeguards who supervised the Gibraltar beaches in July.

'Living in Gibraltar is like being in a small Welsh village,' Eleri told us a week later, as she led us into the rear of the Garrison Library. 'If you do something wrong, they know up the street before you've even got there.'

Eleri had invited us to a read-through of the pantomime that she and her friends would be performing at Christmas, and for a pot-luck buffet afterwards. The pantomime was *Little Miss Muffet* and Leighton was given the part of the villain, Jasper Grasper, a wheeler-dealer and conman. There was no part for me, so I was the audience, booing and cheering in all the conventional places. Leighton has a lovely deep voice and had once fancied himself as an actor. He can be a terribly hammy Welshman and played the villain's part with relish. We read until it became too dark to see the scripts under the palm trees. Above us, aggressive Gibraltar gulls screamed at the sun for daring to go down.

That weekend we started our diving course in earnest. The first two days took place in a swimming pool and Leighton and I were joined by teenager Jason, who would fling himself into the water from time to time out of sheer joy for being there. I was delighted that I was finally able to clear my ears, so I joined the men at the bottom of the deep pool, kneeling like a religious supplicant, as Tony taught us the basics: how to clear our masks of water, how to solve any problems with our gear and how to go to the assistance of another diver with our spare breathing apparatus.

On land, Tony was a bowed, slightly harassed person,

easily given to exploding into rants against Gibraltar traffic, the immigration authorities, the press and many other targets. Underwater, his personality was very different. There he had infinite patience and taught us with gentlemanly attention. In his black wetsuit, which somehow reminded me of a dinner jacket, he stood, waiting for us to perform the tasks he gave us, hands folded like a butler. Then he would bow to us, applaud success, or make us perform a botched action again.

Being underwater automatically makes you do everything the easy way. Force won't work so care and elegance have to take their place. I wished it were possible to live equally calmly on land, doing everything slowly, deliberately, grateful for each individual breath. It struck me also that the principles of diving are an exaggerated version of the kind of seamanship required when sailing. In both activities you brave an inhospitable terrain, in which danger is a constant. Safety procedures have to become habitual because in water you need to be ready for everything to go wrong, because it always does. Diving is far more extreme an activity than sailing because you are letting a hostile environment much closer to your body; instead of having a boat to protect you, all the security you have underwater is your wetsuit and your breath. The level of awareness required for diving is so high that it's like meditating.

Leighton continued to have problems with his buoyancy. Every now and then I would see him streak past my face mask, on a trajectory for the surface. He would battle his way back to the bottom and stay with us until, without warning, he'd shoot off again at a different angle.

That night, when we returned to Sheppards marina so tired we could barely walk, we passed a group of residents. At dusk, after the fierce heat of the day, the old folk would come out with the cats to talk in the cool evening air. As Leighton passed they applauded him for learning to dive at his age. 'Hey, Hercules!' they called after him, and he wasn't displeased.

If Hercules continues to make his presence felt in Gibraltar, Lord Nelson is, without doubt, the presiding deity for the British there. On the back of every Gibraltar ten-pound note is a dramatic etching of HMS *Victory*, bearing the body of Nelson after the Battle of Trafalgar. Nelson valued initiative, boldness and independent action in his sailors. In Bell Books in town, I found a copy of C.S. Forester's biography of Nelson in which he summarised the latter's revolutionary new brand of heroism: 'A fleet commanded by Nelson was equivalent to a fleet manned by Nelsons.' A diagram in Forester's book showed the opening gambits of the Battle of Trafalgar, with the British, Spanish and French ships approaching each other like blood cells attacking a virus.

Part of Nelson's greatness was his attention to detail. He once sent a consignment of flannel shirts back to the Admiralty, requesting longer ones, because they rode out of the seamen's trousers as they leaned over the yards to work sails. Even as he was dying, Nelson was thinking what was best for his ship, giving orders for the tiller ropes to be repaired and telling Hardy that, after the battle, he wished the fleet to anchor, in order to ride out the coming rough weather.

In Sheppards marina, Leighton was working like a demon on *Jameeleh*. I tried to persuade him to take things easy, that

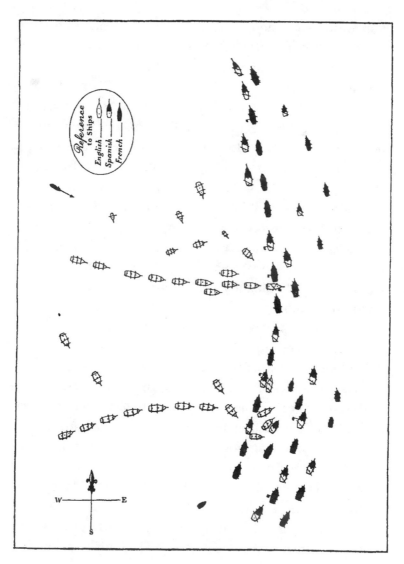

38   The Battle of Trafalgar

there was no need to drive himself so hard, but he wouldn't listen. He was obsessed with the idea that he had to get the boat ready and nothing I said would dissuade him. Helping him wasn't an option, as that seemed to create even more trouble between us. He was so bad-tempered that I took to going ashore during the day, to avoid him.

One day a catamaran arrived and moored behind us. As we helped the couple on board to tie up, the skipper announced that they were Mary and Joseph and what did we think of that? We talked for a while and the subject of who was master at sea cropped up. Joseph declared, forcefully, 'Nobody is master at sea, only the sea. You have to do what it tells you.' We couldn't disagree but Leighton began recounting some stories of my stroppy attitude towards him on the boat. I questioned Mary further about her partner's conduct under the sea's mastership on their recent Atlantic crossing. She admitted that he had almost broken her spirit. Then, in a moment of rebellion, she shouted out after us as we left, 'You hang on to that bad attitude, Gwyneth; it's important to keep it!'

It seemed to me that Leighton was labouring on the wrong project. By now, I couldn't care less where or when we went in the boat. The basic mechanism that drove it – our marriage – was in serious need of attention and yet, no matter how I tried to get him to sit down calmly and discuss it, Leighton would not admit that anything was wrong.

Matters came to another head when, having fixed the wind-steering system, Leighton found that the vane guiding the rudder hit against a part of the newly constructed and installed A-frame. We looked and looked at the glitch and everything I suggested to remedy it was rejected. It was the end of Leighton's world. During one of our heated exchanges about the device, he managed to drop a crucial pin into the dock water. I duck-dived for it but failed to find it; our neighbour, with sub-aqua gear, retrieved it for us.

Feeling desolate, I took myself off to sit on a bench in Main Street, where crowds of British tourists shopped for booze, cigarettes, perfumes and electrical goods, along with toy monkeys that you could drape around your shoulders. I sat there crying, hoping I wouldn't see anybody I knew. I was in a street selling nothing I wanted and on a voyage that had gone horribly wrong. I watched a family we knew from the marina walk in the shade up to Saturday-evening mass. They were taking all their weaknesses together to church. We, I felt, no longer had anywhere to go.

Above the town, the Rock glowed in the sunset like a dying lump of coal.

The only activity that brought Leighton any pleasure any more, it seemed, was diving. As we were about to do the sea-diving part of our course, I caught a cold and so Leighton went out alone with Tony. He would come back euphoric with fatigue and full of the joys of wreck diving. When my cold cleared it was my turn to go ocean diving with Tony. I had been practising clearing my Eustachian tubes, as you do on ascents and descents in aeroplanes, so now I had no difficulty following him underwater, down the sandy slope, past the breakwater rocks and on to the sea floor just beyond the Camp Bay beach. Tony pointed out some flounders, with strange swivelling eyes, hidden in the sand. And there, in the distance, was an octopus. As we approached, it morphed from gonad to arrow, intent on flight, white now with fear. We followed it to a rock, where it did its best to pretend it wasn't there, wearing the greens, browns and purples of the local stone. In a matter of minutes, this octopus had shown itself to be three separate creatures.

We swam out to the first wreck, a car, its windscreen like a television broadcasting a telegenic shoal of sardines, showing off their silver flanks in the light. Sea cucumbers lay around like big turds, and the fish were wearing outrageous fashions. One sea slug looked like a crocheted pineapple, and in every hole I looked, something peered out at me, placid but curious.

I was so enchanted that I didn't want to let Tony check my air, but he signalled to me that we should make our way back to the surface. Reluctantly, I obeyed. As we approached the beach I could hear the roar of the surf, like a rock concert or vast applause, the sea congratulating itself on its own wonders. There, suddenly, were the legs and fat bottoms of the Spanish grandmothers treading water. When I ripped off my mast, all I could say was, 'Wow, wow!' and Tony replied genially, 'You've got snot all over your face.'

In order to gain my Ocean Diver licence, I needed to perform at least four dives, one of them to a depth of twenty metres, and to demonstrate a controlled buoyancy lift of another diver. Tony took me down to a sunken barge called the 482 to do this. We flew down together and into a world that looked like an underwater Poussin painting – greenery alternating with architectural ruins. Under the hull of the 482, Tony pointed out a scorpion fish with the tail of another hanging out of its mouth. Fish flew like flags in the underwater currents, and a shoal of bream hung above us like a mobile. On the metal of the wreck, anemones stretched open orgasmically, temporary flowers, and then snapped shut. I remember kneeling on the deck of the wreck and reaching up above me in sheer joy to where a group of red anthia fish swam. By the time our air had come to an end, I was exhausted, not with the physical effort, but with the constant struggle to make myself ever more conscious; with telling myself to remember everything I saw, to be here more fully. I was blissed out when we reached the beach, where the swimmers had no idea of the cool rooms that extended just beneath them.

On the way back to the marina, Tony commented that a boat could be the biggest heap of shit ever known on the surface, totally unseaworthy, and yet make a wondrous wreck below. That evening both Leighton and I received our Ocean Diver certificates.

'Not bad,' said Leighton, 'for an old-age pensioner and a swot!'

Mrs Rubenstein could hardly have accused me now of not living my life to the full.

It was late August and Leighton and I had worked our way through the list of jobs to be done on the boat. It was time to leave.

Located at the meeting point of warm Mediterranean and cooler Atlantic waters, Gibraltar is often prone to fog. *Jameeleh* was abreast of Rosia Bay when we saw it billowing over Europa Point. A large vessel was coming towards us and we saw her quickly blotted out by a fog bank, except for her mast. The ship sounded her horn, as if she were in pain.

Of course, we went back into Sheppards. There was no question of us risking the strait blind. We were disappointed but there was one thing that I had desperately wanted to do in Gibraltar and which might now be possible. Once we were moored in the marina, I called in at the chandlery and asked if could I dive with the Sub-Aqua Club that evening. And were they, by any chance, diving the Cardiff wreck, the *Rosslyn*? They were and I could. Ecstatic, I raced back to the boat to tell Leighton. He was withdrawn and depressed because we'd failed to leave and, uncharacteristically, didn't even want to dive that evening, though he insisted that I went.

I was half an hour early meeting the members of the diving club at the boat. Tony had managed to sprain his arm and so Fred, a tall man from Derbyshire, was going to be my diving buddy. We were hoping to leave Gibraltar on the morning's tide so this was my one and only chance to see what had happened to this ship from my home town. All the club members pitched in to help me, sorting out my equipment, assisting me in getting dressed and into the water, which was slightly awkward over the hard edge of the boat.

Once we were in, Fred took me by the hand and led me down like a child. Almost straight away we saw an octopus's elegant curled arm in a rock crevice. We sank down further and further, Fred waiting patiently for me to clear my ears and then suddenly, like a catastrophe, the *Rosslyn* loomed above us.

Fred showed me the ship's rudder and, together, we swam through the gap where the propeller used to turn. This was now a beautiful arch planted with soft lavender-coloured corals and sea lilies. The propeller lay on the seabed, ruined.

Disaster seems to be, but never is, the end. We were now looking at every sailor's worst nightmare, a sunken ship but, because we were diving, the vessel's story was continuing. As

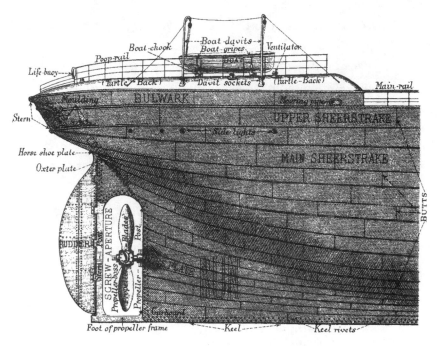

39   After-body of a screw-steamer

we passed, a large spider crab on the surface of the wreck
reared up, shooing us away. At best, this environment was
totally indifferent to us and still it was stunning. A school of
sardines above us suddenly changed pace and direction, like
modulating music.

Fred led me patiently into the *Rosslyn*'s engine room, filled
with mysterious grilles, pipes and ligatures. The beams of our
torches looked like pink light and picked out the 'snow', or
particles, suspended in the Gibraltar water. I noticed that the
bubbles from Fred's mouthpiece hit the roof of the room and
scuttled along it like lively jellyfish or empty speech bubbles.
Using divers' sign language he then showed me the *Rosslyn*'s
emergency steering and spare prop. Then we flew up and saw

two other divers from the club above us, gliding over us like large birds.

Back on the surface, it felt as though I was lifted out of the water and into the boat by many hands. I couldn't stop grinning. I had never imagined when Darren Fa first told me about the *Rosslyn* that I would actually see her with my own eyes. The way Fred had guided me reminded me of the couple I'd met in the Well of Initiation in Sintra. The dark's not so bad when you can trust the strangers you meet.

The thing about history is that it never stays in the past. Leighton and I went for a meal with the club divers afterwards and I was astonished to learn that Patrick, who'd been with us on the dive, was the first cousin of the Marquess of Bute, who owned Cardiff docks.

'If his mother had been his father then he would have been the Marquess of Bute,' someone deduced, leaving me confused. I told Patrick that his family had exercised a strong influence on our lives in Cardiff because the Butes had constructed not only the docks but also the city behind them. The streets of Cardiff are named after the Bute estates and managers – Mount Stuart, Ryder, Talbot, Sneyd and Tyndall. There is even a Bute mausoleum in the parish church at the bottom of our street. I had read the whole history of Patrick's family and told him my favourite Bute story, which involved the Second Marquess, who built the glorious folly of Cardiff Castle. In 1846, he sent his agent a telegram, commanding, 'Order four horses for my carriage at Chepstow and at Newport. Air the castle.'

The following morning we left Gibraltar to start our Atlantic crossing. Three weeks later, Leighton was diagnosed with cancer.

CHAPTER TEN

Sailing without a Boat

I feel that my vessel has stuck
Down in the depths
Upon some huge thing.

And nothing
Happens! Nothing . . . quiet . . . waves . . .

Nothing happens, or has everything happened
And we are already tranquilly in the new?

Juan Ramón Jiménez

We had no intention of visiting Africa when we left Gibraltar, but the wind blew us there. We were aiming for Cádiz, on the Atlantic coast of southern Spain, but when we emerged out of the bay into the strait, we could make no headway against an unexpectedly strong west wind. Rather than returning to Gibraltar for a second time, we decided to nip across to Ceuta, a Spanish enclave on the coast of Morocco, for what we thought would be a couple of days' sightseeing. In the marina office I used my O-level Spanish to attempt a conversation with the young receptionist and she told me that the wind this year had been '*loco*'.

251

Ceuta is a Spanish possession but was first conquered in the fifteenth century by the Portuguese Prince Henry the Navigator. This allowed the Portuguese access to caravan routes deep into Africa and a way of controlling exploration along that continent's Atlantic coast. Ceuta was controlled by means of a spectacular fort built on a narrow isthmus, where a moat links the Mediterranean with the Atlantic, giving Ceuta a front and back door to the sea. In July 2002, the enclave shot into world consciousness when some Moroccans who wished to celebrate the king's birthday reclaimed Perejil, an uninhabited island just off the coast. I believe there was a goat on the rock and, after much diplomatic shouting and flag-waving, the Parsley Island goat, who was briefly Moroccan, returned to being Spanish.

In the marina, Leighton and I had spotted a Portakabin with the words 'Club Kraken' on it in Greek lettering. Pepe, the dive master, agreed to take us diving. As we motored under the citadel's walls in a RIB, Pepe pointed out the still-visible gashes made by cannon balls in the fortifications. The cut, he explained, had been lined with marble paving stones, to prevent the anchors of enemy ships from gaining any purchase on the bottom and so launching an attack on the walls from below.

Pepe stopped the boat on the Mediterranean side of Ceuta and led us down the anchor line to the bottom. I found my neutral buoyancy immediately and spotted a moray eel poking its ugly head out of pubic seaweed. Its body was swathed in wildly fashionable yellow curlicues, and looked like a leopard-skin ribbon. The decorative accessories had been left off its head, which was mean and unfinished, like the chewed end of a biro. The sea is full of eyes and mouths and exhibits a terrible hunger. At least in a boat you have a wall between you and the water. Diving, we ventured time and again into the lion's mouth.

Our dive with Pepe was cut short unexpectedly when Leighton noticed that his air supply was running out. Leighton normally has an extremely low pulse rate and in Gibraltar had been complimented on his frugal consumption of air while underwater. We assumed that his bottle had not been full at the start of the dive, but when the same thing happened during the second dive with Pepe, we began to wonder. After we'd washed our gear and hung it out to dry – our wetsuits looking like corpses, or spare lives, dripping in the sun – we sat in the Kraken clubhouse talking. Pepe, it turned out, was a bomb disposal officer in the *guardia civil*. He and his friends told us a legend that Hercules had come over to the African side of the strait and fallen in love with a local nymph. When he left to pursue another of his labours, she died of grief and turned into a rock now called the Mujer Muerta. You could see the shape of the dead woman, they told us, as you sailed out of Ceuta.

The Strait of Gibraltar is dominated by two winds of distinct temperaments. The *levante*, an easterly wind, brings damp, cloudy weather and can be recognised instantly by plumes of cloud that form over the Rock of Gibraltar and the Rif mountains on the African side. The *levante* creates a hot, sticky atmosphere, making everyone bad-tempered, partly because it's difficult to sleep at night. The *poniente*, or westerly wind, on the other hand, brings clear, fresh weather but can, like the *levante*, be strong enough to pin a boat in port for weeks on end; that is, if you're going the other way. This *poniente* showed no sign of letting up, so we went on a day trip to Morocco. As we were walking along the streets of Tetuán I noticed that, under his tan, Leighton was looking grey. I began to watch him more closely.

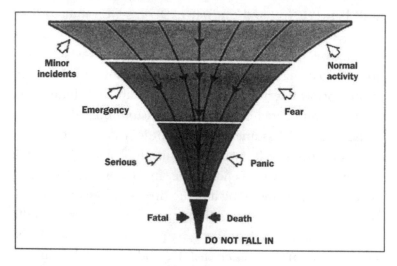

Minor incidents

Normal activity

Emergency

Fear

Serious

Panic

Fatal

Death

DO NOT FALL IN

40   The incident pit

The souvenir we carried away from Morocco was a tummy bug. Soon my stomach settled, but Leighton's became worse. We were anxious to move from Ceuta, but, after a few days of intense abdominal pain, Leighton finally conceded that he needed to see a doctor, so we went along to the local hospital. There, Dr Sanchez, the surgeon on duty, palpated Leighton's abdomen and said he was ready to whip out his appendix, but before operating he wanted to do an ultra-sound scan. We saw him flinch as he noticed the soles of Leighton's feet, which were black from going barefoot on *Jameeleh.*

'We're not dirty people,' said Leighton defensively, 'it's just that we live on a boat.'

At this point, the news didn't sound too bad. If Leighton had an inflamed appendix, it needed to come out before we attempted an Atlantic crossing in December. I did have a copy of the *Sea Captain's Medical Guide*, which tells you how to treat immersion foot, piles and gonorrhoea. I didn't, however, fancy operating on Leighton's intestines from a manual if peritonitis set in hundreds of miles from land. There was still time for him to recover from an operation before the hurricane season made crossing the Atlantic unwise.

I sat outside the X-ray department and waited. I noticed that there was a postbox there in the shape of a lion's head and I wondered if this was the Nemean lion, a symbol of death, that Hercules had hunted and killed. I started chatting to a middle-aged Spanish gentleman sitting next to me and told him how reluctant Leighton had been to come to the hospital.

'*Es valiente*,' he said with approval.

'No,' I countered, '*es stúpido*.'

The ultrasound was inconclusive and so Leighton was given an outpatients appointment with a gastric surgeon in a week's time. Then we went back to the boat to see if he would recover.

On *Jameeleh*, Leighton went deeper into his pain. He was now permanently angry with me. He raged at me for not agreeing to use the wind-steering on the way over to Ceuta, and accused me of opposing him as a matter of course. I argued that we should go back to Gibraltar so that he could be treated in an English-speaking hospital.

'No,' he snapped viciously. 'I want to be here.'

There was no way I could move the boat on my own.

It was lonely without Leighton. Though he was physically present, the man I'd married hadn't been with me for a very long time.

Every night I'd hear a group of men singing heartily, just as dusk fell. I did my best to find them but the direction from which their voices came was distorted by the water in the port. I looked behind the *guardia civil* cabin, searched for any Spanish Navy boats moored in Ceuta and whose crew, I thought, might be singing while the national flag was being lowered at dusk. No matter how many people I asked, nobody could tell me whose voices they were. I felt as though I was hearing my own private sirens.

On the day before we were due to see the gastric surgeon, I had to collect the results of Leighton's blood tests from the clinical analysis department of Ceuta Hospital. I was already feeling apprehensive as I tried to decipher the result of the tests, and matters were not improved when I was introduced to the head of the department, Dr Morte, whose name I mistook for Muerte: Death. Leighton's blood showed that he was very anaemic. We already knew that his liver and spleen were enlarged but not why. Dr Death asked me if there was anything he could do to help. I thanked him and he commented on the hat I was wearing, which looked like something out of *Death on the Nile*.

'*Chica!*' he said pleasantly before going back to his work.

It seemed that the entrance to the underworld, which Hercules had found in the Strait of Gibraltar, was still open and functioning.

That night I finally found the Ceuta sirens. I followed their vigorous music single-mindedly until I was in front of the Club Kraken cabin. There I met one of the club divers and I asked, not a little madly, who was singing. I was relieved that he could also hear the song; he told me that it was a group of local lads on the sea wall, practising for next year's carnival. We were now in September and carnival isn't until early spring, so they were keen. I remembered that Ellen MacArthur said that she never wore wax earplugs when she was at sea because she needed to tune into, rather than tune out of, the requirements of her boat. If these were the worst sirens we were going to hear in Ceuta, then I saw no call for earplugs at all.

That night I finally understood that there must be something seriously wrong with Leighton. In an attempt to shake his fatigue, he disappeared early to bed. I went out last thing to check the ropes only to find that a brisk *poniente* was pushing the boat's bow uncomfortably close to the pontoon. I stood at a loss. I didn't want to wake Leighton, but how was I going to push a twelve-ton boat back against the wind and adjust her mooring ropes all on my own?

At that moment two big Germans appeared from a neighbouring boat and asked if they could help. I explained that my husband was ill and they immediately saw the necessity of moving *Jameeleh* back. One of them jumped on board and in five minutes we had the boat tied securely, with a double spring to stop her from moving forward again. I thanked them profusely and went back below.

If Leighton had been well he would never have let anybody else touch *Jameeleh*'s mooring lines. A substantial German had been clomping around above him on deck, barking loud orders to his friend, and yet Leighton hadn't even stirred. His awareness of the boat's needs had been blotted out by something more compelling. He was the bosun on our boat and I knew that he would not have deserted his post willingly. I sat on the head and cried. Even this didn't wake him.

As the bosun's mate, I would now have to take over looking after the boat's welfare and, more importantly, looking after her skipper.

The following day, Leighton was admitted to hospital. Dr Gastón took one look at him, said he still suspected appendicitis and arranged a bed for him on a surgical ward. By now

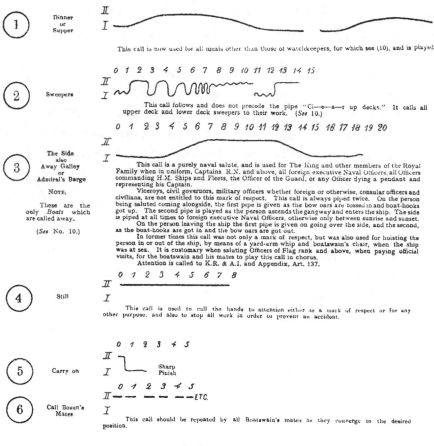

1. Dinner or Supper

This call is now used for all meals other than those of watchkeepers, for which see (10), and is played

2. Sweepers

0 1 2 3 4 5 6 7 8 9 10 11 12 13 14 15

This call follows and does not precede the pipe "Cl—e—a—r up decks." It calls all upper deck and lower deck sweepers to their work. (See 10.)

3. The Side
also
Away Galley
or
Admiral's Barge

NOTE,

These are the only *Boats* which are called away.

(*See* No. 10.)

0 1 2 3 4 5 6 7 8 9 10 11 12 13 14 15 16 17 18 19 20

This call is a purely naval salute, and is used for The King and other members of the Royal Family when in uniform, Captains R.N. and above, all foreign executive Naval Officers, all Officers commanding H.M. Ships and Fleets, the Officer of the Guard, or any Officer dying a pendant and representing his Captain.

Viceroys, civil governors, military officers whether foreign or otherwise, consular officers and civilians, are not entitled to this mark of respect. This call is always piped twice. On the person being saluted coming alongside, the first pipe is given as the bow oars are tossed in and boat-hooks got up. The second pipe is played as the person ascends the gangway and enters the ship. The side is piped at all times to foreign executive Naval Officers, otherwise only between sunrise and sunset.

On the person leaving the ship the first pipe is given on going over the side, and the second, as the boat-hooks are got in and the bow oars are got out.

In former times this call was not only a mark of respect, but was also used for hoisting the person in or out of the ship, by means of a yard-arm whip and boatswain's chair, when the ship was at sea. It is customary when saluting Officers of Flag rank and above, when paying official visits, for the boatswain and his mates to play this call in chorus.

Attention is called to K.R. & A.I. and Appendix, Art. 137.

4. Still

0 1 2 3 4 5 6 7 8

This call is used to call the hands to attention either as a mark of respect or for any other purpose, and also to stop all work in order to prevent an accident.

5. Carry on

0 1 2 3 4 5

Sharp Finish

6. Call Bosun's Mates

0 1 2 3 4 5 —ETC.

This call should be repeated by all Boatswain's mates as they converge to the desired position.

41   The boatswain's call

Leighton was nearly demented with pain and general dread. He swung violently between worrying that he should look after me and saying that he didn't care at all. I wanted to get him a fresh towel and he accused me of being a spoilt brat. I mentioned again that I thought we should get ourselves to Gibraltar, and he told me to fuck off. I could see now that, whenever he attacked me, Leighton was describing how he felt himself: full of guilt and fear of what might be the cause.

Much later he told me that he thought he had a brain tumour.

Leighton was put on a drip and immediately looked more relaxed. At least now he was properly hydrated. While he was waiting for a CT scan he was given a place in a tiny three-bed ward, which he shared with another patient. Juan was paralysed down one side by a stroke, had heart problems and more than a touch of Alzheimer's. He had been admitted to have a severely infected eye removed. Juan was bedridden and couldn't speak but every now and again would shout something that sounded like 'Potato!' but which, we were assured, was his way of calling for a nurse. He reminded me of Buddhist drawings of a laughing old man, except that he wasn't laughing. His daughter joked that if he became any more noisy, we'd have to put him on our boat. I would have preferred to put his large and extremely loud family there, away from us. They seemed to see his illness as an occasion for a constant low-key party at his bedside. Juan lay next to the window, his loins wrapped in a sheet so that he looked like a bald Roman senator, except that he was constantly trying to pull out his catheter or masturbate, I wasn't sure which.

Mamma, Juan's wife, insisted on having the television on all the time. When Leighton politely asked her to switch it off at midnight, she glared at him and just said, 'No!' The nurse Leighton summoned for help was too frightened to stand up to Mamma, so Leighton, still attached to his drip, ended up confronting her, saying in English, 'You are a horrible, horrible woman,' until she switched the set off and turned her back on him in a sulk. In this hospital, members of the patients' families were expected to help with the nursing, so, over the next eight days, we came to know Juan's family very well indeed.

Maria, Juan's daughter, was much nicer than her mother and she and I became friends. I also took to Najah, the family's Moroccan maid, who used to look at me and laugh. One day she dragged me out of the room for a break on the hospital's fire escape. This structure faced the sea and, because it was the only place where you could catch a breeze, it was very sociable. Seeing us outside, a Moroccan lady from a nearby ward came to warn us that it wasn't safe to stand on the fire escape. A man with his arms bandaged up to his armpits joined in the conversation. He had been bitten by a dog he knew and severely injured. His friend went down to look at the metal bolts fixing the fire escape to the building and, sure enough, they looked inadequate. But, said the man with the bandages, if anything happened, we were already in the right place for emergency treatment.

Leaning over the parapet, it felt as though Najah and I were on the stern deck of an ocean liner. We looked at the people down in the street walking past the hospital. They had been lucky enough to get off the hospital cruise ship before the whistles blew and she moved away from the quay of ordinary life. I would have done anything to be able to find the gang-plank and leave this dreadful vessel. There must have been a mistake; I hadn't bought a ticket for this particular cruise. The lights stayed on all night as the hospital steamed on with its cargo of illness and pain. It felt as though some malevolent god had hijacked our voyage.

Each evening, before it became too dangerous to walk home alone, I went back to the marina to sleep on the boat. There, they were getting ready for the arrival of sixty-seven tuna fishing boats, which were to take part in a competition that weekend. At the office I met two of the judges, both of whom were pessimistic about the prospect of a large catch.

'Many fishermen, few fish!' they lamented.

If the *levante* that was now blowing continued, the tuna would simply refuse to come into the Mediterranean, swimming past Ceuta and on down the African coast.

As we were speaking, we were suddenly astonished to see a school of fish break the surface of the water in the marina. They were extraordinary creatures, petrol blue with a black plaid hologram on one side, silver on the other, like two different fish in one. The oddest thing about them was their fins. They swam by means of two pairs of flanges, one at the top and one at the bottom of their tails. These worked either in the same or in opposite directions. Every now and again the fish would jump together, flashing like a knife blade in the sun.

The tuna competition judges were stumped. They thought these might be moonfish, but they weren't sure. Certainly they'd never seen them in Ceuta waters before. The cleaner, who fell into conversation with us as she passed, thought they were very *graciosos*. I thought that they signified the start of the end of my world.

I was in a morbid mood. Earlier in the day, Dr Gastón had come back with the results of Leighton's scan. He didn't have appendicitis, but a lymph gland in his stomach was enlarged. He needed a colonoscopy and a visit from the blood doctor and then we would see. In the meantime, he was to have nil by mouth, in case they needed to operate quickly.

When I got back to the hospital, Juan's bed was surrounded again by strident family members. There was a new girl whom I didn't know there, dressed in white. I asked if she was a nurse.

'No. I'm a butcher,' she said.

That evening, Juan, who had been constipated for four

days, suddenly shouted '*Caca!*' and produced a turd so pungent that it drove us all out of the room and into the patients' waiting area. Maria and I sat laughing together and soon Leighton shuffled in, pulling his drip stand behind him. Even Mamma's wifely dedication wasn't strong enough to ride out that smell and she joined us. From then on, whenever Juan shouted out '*Caca!*' we all ran.

By now, Leighton had been on a drip for five days and was getting extremely hungry. He looked at his feet and commented that even his toes had lost weight. Our fight with Mamma and the television was ongoing. Other members of Juan's extended family were reasonable about keeping the volume down so that Leighton could rest, but Mamma was implacable. We did notice, however, that Juan had stopped shouting in the afternoons when the television was off, and we thought that he must have hated its constant noise as well. One evening, Juan's brother and his wife came in straight from a holiday in the Caribbean. They stood in the middle of the room, shouting loudly at Juan and telling him and Mamma – and us – all about the lovely place they'd just been. Najah had told me that Mamma had been nursing Juan for ten years, so this conversation can't have made her feel any better. Sister-in-law, who looked at me as if I were dog dirt on her shoes, had her hair plaited in cornrows and long white beaded plaits, which jangled as her head moved. Suddenly, Juan shouted '*Puta!*' so loud that sister-in-law had to leave. Even Leighton, with no Spanish, recognised the word for whore. Internally, we both cheered.

I would stay with Leighton all day, to make sure that his drip was replenished and to try to understand the rapid medical Spanish spoken by Dr Gastón. Occasionally Dr Sanchez, who spoke very good English, would pop in to see us. He was a snappy dresser and possessed a surgeon's sexual charisma. I swear his teeth glinted with a diamond flash every time he smiled. *Ting!* Even his glasses were glamorous.

Poor Juan had little allure but I became very fond of him nevertheless. Time passed especially slowly in the afternoons. I would often look up to find Juan staring at me, so I began to play a game with him. When he blinked I would blink back, and so we held long silent conversations. We'd spend hours looking at each other, making sure that Mamma didn't catch us. She was always too busy watching bullfighting on the television or leaning out of the window to notice. One evening, as I left the hospital, I automatically waved at Juan and said goodnight. To everybody's astonishment, he waved back and said '*Hasta luego*' so sweetly that everybody in the room was stunned. Clearly, Juan understood a good deal more of what was going on than anybody had suspected.

When I got back to the marina that evening, I could see the strange fish moving under the water, like the internal workings of a watch. A group of boat owners stood on the quay watching the school. José Luís, who lived on a motor sailer near us, said that they had not appeared in Ceuta until four years ago. They would come for about ten days in the autumn and then depart. They were called *pez de luna*, moonfish – sunfish in English – and grew into adults as large and as round as a satellite dish. Meeki, the commodore of the yacht club, told me that their Latin name was *mola*, and that they ate jellyfish. My admiration of them increased. Anything in the animal kingdom that eats jellyfish has to be a good thing. '*Extraño, curioso*,' mused José, and it was hard not to feel superstitious about these uncanny visitors.

When I arrived at the hospital the following morning, I

found two armed guards posted at the door of the room next to Leighton's. Just after I'd left the night before, a drug-crazed member of the local mafia had gone berserk, attacking a nurse with a drip stand and smashing up his ward. Leighton said that the Moroccan women who accompanied the gangster had nearly caused a riot, running up and down the corridor ululating. Ceuta is one of the wildest border towns in Europe, and the local authorities have been struggling to contain the drugs trade from Africa into southern Europe, not to mention the smuggling of consumer goods and humans. From the fire escape in the hospital, Najah had pointed out the tall ebony-black Africans – illegal immigrants to Ceuta, who had swum there and had to live without official papers.

'See that?' Pepe had said when we were out diving one day, pointing at a group of black RIBs with powerful outboard engines. 'Drug boats,' he told us, adding that they had been impounded by the *guardia civil*. With the strait only eight miles wide at its narrowest point, and Europe in plain sight, the temptation to venture across these dangerous waters at night proves irresistible for many.

Leighton was due to have a colonoscopy the following day. The procedure involved air being pumped into his intestines and a camera shoved up his backside to see any evidence of tumours. Even though he'd not eaten for a week, he had to drink a litre of strong emetic so that his gut was completely clear. By now he was becoming seriously worn down by the barrage of noise in the room with him. Leighton tried to calm himself by spelling out the names of our family in the phonetic alphabet we'd learned on a radio operator's course back at home: Golf, Whisky, Yankee, November, Echo, Tango, Hospital. I brought him some wax earplugs to help blot out the racket of Juan's family, but they were only partially successful against their machine-gun Spanish. There was nothing I could do to comfort Leighton.

'I'm the one who's ill,' he'd hiss at me.

'But I'm here too,' I replied helplessly.

Somehow or other the nurses botched the preparation and the next morning his gut wasn't clear enough for a colonoscopy even after three enemas. Poor Leighton had to go through the same horrible process again. I sat on the bed as he downed yet another glass of the emetic.

'How do you feel?' I asked.

'Full of shit.'

'You never said a truer word.' This was the first sensible thing he'd said in a very long time.

When I returned from the hospital that night, the marina waters were eerily quiet. As quickly as they'd arrived the sunfish had disappeared.

For some reason they performed a colonoscopy on Leighton without using a muscle relaxant. I was standing outside in the corridor and could hear him shouting with pain. I was about to burst into the room and assault the consultant when a Spanish man who was waiting in the corridor told me very quietly not to go in. I don't know how I stayed out, but I did. When the air was released from his gut, Leighton soon recovered his composure. In a flash of his old humour he said that he was now doubly sure that he could never be homosexual.

On his last night in hospital I stayed with Leighton, to shield him from Mamma. He was now so low that I was prepared to abandon my Welsh reserve and become very Spanish if necessary. Somehow Mamma sensed this and left us in peace. In the dark, Leighton's drip twitched, like a jumping nerve in my eye. Suddenly I felt a sharp longing for Leighton's body – for the firm flesh of his instep, the baby-soft fold between his groin and his hip. Something was now happening to change him against our will. I had a very clear perception of what we were losing. Without knowing it, we had been carrying a stowaway on board. Pirates are not just men with guns. They can, just as easily, erupt from the cells inside your body and take over a voyage. I didn't sleep until three and spent the time looking down a very dark abyss.

The next day Juan was prepared for the operation on his eye. Even though he was unconscious, his family came out in force to be with him. The atmosphere was festive. At one point we counted fifteen of them in a room designed for three patients. Leighton was beginning to crack under the strain of their sociability. We begged the surgeons to discharge him but there was one more test that needed to be done. The doctors had noticed the swelling in Leighton's neck that had worried me in Cascais, and they decided to do a biopsy of the lymph gland. Then we were free to go back to *Jameeleh*.

By noon the next day Dr Sanchez had obtained a preliminary result of the lymph gland biopsy. I phoned him from Mendoza's, the local diving shop. Dr Sanchez was brisk. Leighton, he told me, was suffering from advanced cancer of the lymph glands.

'Oh hell,' I said, after a pause.

'Quite,' said Sanchez matter-of-factly. 'But he's not going to die right now.'

As I rushed from Mendoza's to the boat I caught sight of four of the sunfish, which had come back for a last time. I jumped for joy when I saw them, even though I'd just received the worst news of my life. Perhaps the only good use for pain is that it wakes you up.

I blessed them, then ran to find Leighton.

'A little bit of chemo and I'll be all right,' said Leighton shakily, as we sat in the cockpit of *Jameeleh* trying to come to terms with the news.

I disagreed. I thought this changed everything.

I had spoken to my sister Marian, who is a doctor, and she'd reassured us somewhat by saying that lymphoma is a very treatable cancer. Leighton had non-Hodgkin small lymphocytic lymphoma, at least stage three. We learned that low-grade non-Hodgkin lymphoma is not curable but can often be managed by ongoing treatment for years. It was hard to feel that this was good fortune when all we could think of was that Leighton had cancer. Where was the luck in that? We had thought ourselves daring for keeping death at bay underwater by only the thickness of a wetsuit. Now the enemy had passed under the guard of Leighton's skin and was inside his body.

The area where the lymph gland had been removed for the biopsy had filled with fluid, so Leighton now looked like Frankenstein with a bolt in his neck.

'You know,' I ventured, 'I would rather do this journey with you and cancer than an Atlantic crossing as we've been in the last few months.'

Leighton said nothing. He was working on a length of rope that had been badly spliced by a visiting sailor for our neighbour José Luís. He unpicked the mess and respliced it, tight and taut.

'I hate people who waste a good length of rope,' he said vehemently.

Later, I learned that strands of DNA can become super-coiled, like rope. This supercoiling is a means by which the DNA is protected. Every time a cell divides, the DNA has to make a copy of itself; first, it has to uncoil and is thus exposed to potential damaging influences from chemicals, radiation and so forth. Cancer starts when a cell's DNA mutates and the damage remains unrepaired by the body. When such a mutation occurs the DNA still resumes its supercoiled struc-ture, thus protecting the mutation within the new supercoil. Chris Woolams explains:

> The original rogue cell with its unravelled ball of DNA string can simply copy itself repeatedly. And the message to the cellular system is often to do this very rapidly in much the same way as foetal cells divide. Perfect copies of the new slightly looser ball of string are made from the original, because the body normally does copy perfectly. So suddenly there are many cells all with the new-look ball of string. Theoretically, if the environment of this cell is main-tained . . . the rogue string becomes the norm in an area of the body.

If this was right, Leighton was going to have to undo the most important tangle of his life and attempt to resplice the snarled cordage in his blood cells. I hoped that remembering to keep his hands loose and to throw the bird's nest away from him would be good enough advice to see him through.

Day by day Leighton said little but I could see that he was concentrating on keeping calm. That took all his energy.

42   Leighton splicing

Leighton was so weak from eight days without food that we clearly couldn't depart without giving him time to rest. I booked us a flight home from Gibraltar a week later, and began to prepare to leave the boat in Ceuta.

One night I dreamt that we were diving again with Pepe. We were already underwater when I saw him signalling for me to go down deeper. I was afraid but he was telling me that downwards was the only safe direction, although it seemed the most dangerous.

As we prepared to go back to Britain, the people we had met in Ceuta could not have been more helpful. Meeki arranged to move our boat next to his own and promised that he would keep an eye on *Jameeleh* while we were away. He introduced us to his friend Agapito, who undertook to start our precious engine every week and check the bilges for water. José Luís offered us the use of his van.

'How is Lion?' he'd enquire anxiously every day.

I went to have my hair cut and coloured. A large Spanish woman came up to me and asked me how my husband was. Then I recognised her as one of the receptionists at the hospital (*'Sí, el hospital fatal'*). We both agreed that you couldn't possibly face a fight with cancer without getting your hair right first.

At this point I felt that I had lost everything. The man I'd married had been replaced by a lookalike. Once described by a friend as 'delicious, like a meringue – crispy on the outside, soft and chewy on the inside', this Leighton didn't move or think in the same way. He even smelt strange to me.

When I'd tidied the boat up and left her ready for the winter, packed my books and our clothes and paid six months' mooring fees in advance, we were ready to fly back to Britain. We boarded the huge ferry that crosses from Ceuta to Algeciras. We reached home just before the end of September, at the start of the university year. I felt like a student at the beginning of a new term and the course we were enrolled on was cancer.

Cancer has taught me how to be crew on a boat. The secret is to treat the skipper as though he were seriously ill. Your job is to do everything you can take the weight off his shoulders so that he can devote himself to the navigation and healing that only he can do for himself.

This wasn't easy when we first arrived home. We had rented out our house while we were away and returned to discover that the tenants seemed to be breaking the terms of their lease by running businesses from the premises. One of them was making South African sausages in my kitchen and selling them to local pubs. When asked by the agent, they agreed to move out, given our circumstances. Then, instead of leaving as promised, they sat tight, telling the neighbours that they couldn't be bothered to shift. I had to stop Leighton from going over to smash his own windows. We didn't have the energy for a legal fight, so we let them be to concentrate on Leighton's recovery. My sister heroically said that we could live with her in Radyr, a suburb of Cardiff. In an odd way, as long as we were not in our own house we felt that we were still on the voyage together. This was to be our Atlantic crossing, and the most challenging part of the journey so far – except now we were sailing without a boat.

Within a week Leighton was referred to Dr Chris Poynton, consultant haematologist in the University Hospital of Wales at the Heath. A bone marrow biopsy showed that his lymphoma had reached stage four. There is no stage five. The bone marrow was very compromised, with hardly any normal cells in it. No wonder he had been feeling awful and behaving like a monster.

'Did you not feel ill before you left?' asked Dr Poynton.

'No,' said Leighton.

'That's not true,' I said. 'He's been a bastard for a whole year. I was about to divorce him.'

'When do we start the chemo?' asked Leighton.

Dr Poynton didn't hesitate. 'Today.'

He explained that the chemotherapy would attack Leighton's immune system, and that we needed to watch carefully for infections. These were more likely to kill him than the cancer during treatment. I asked how aggressive Leighton's chemotherapy would be. Dr Poynton thought for a second.

'Gale force eight, not a hurricane.'

Leighton was given his medication in the form of tablets, which he was to take at home, thus avoiding the need to be in hospital. Before he swallowed the first dose, I kissed him, exactly as I would have done had we been on *Jameeleh* and about to go out to sea.

Of course, our journey into cancer had, unbeknown to us, started a long time ago. We had thought that we were in a certain narrative – one concerned with sailing, in which marital unhappiness seemed to be playing an increasingly large part – but it turned out we were part of a completely different story about cancer. Only now was the plot of our lives becoming clear. We had been pulled off-course by a magnetic force that was impossible to resist – no wonder the whole voyage had been such a fight. All the clues had been there but only now did they make sense. Perhaps I should have challenged

Leighton sooner and attempted to reach the root of the problem, but I had been too close to him to see, until the end, the full extent of his illness.

Leighton's white blood count was already low, but chemotherapy would decimate it further. At a certain point in the cycle, when he was neutropenic, he would have very few defences against infection; these were hazardous shallows that needed the most careful pilotage. When a boat goes aground you can drag her off by rowing out in a tender with her anchor, dropping it in deeper water and then winching the boat off the bank by her anchor cable. This is called kedging and was my job while Leighton was ill.

I went to see an old friend who burst into tears when I told her the full story of what had happened.

'Don't cry,' I urged her. 'Don't even worry. Cancer is going to be part of the answer for us.'

I had already started kedging.

Everything we had learned at sea now came into its own as a way of navigating on dry land. Before leaving, I'd copied out advice on survival from a 1954 Admiralty *Manual of Seamanship* in case it came in handy:

> The qualities which are essential to the survival of the crews in boats or rafts when adrift in the open sea are discipline, confidence, cheerfulness, willingness, and a determination to win through, and the man in charge must be a good leader . . . He must maintain strict but sympathetic discipline.

Leighton had only kept going for so long because he had driven himself, despite feeling lousy. He had tried to use this aggression against me whenever I reminded him of his problems. That could not be allowed to continue.

43   Life saving for beginners

One night I dreamt I was swimming in big seas, rescuing Leighton. A tornado was coming in and I was pulling him as hard as I could away from sharp rocks. A life saving handbook that my mother owns shows various different methods for releasing oneself from the grip of a drowning man. Each looks like an erotic dance in the weightlessness of water, and the aim is for two bodies to move along stretched full-length together, both breathing calmly. I feared our marriage falling apart much more than I dreaded cancer. If humanly possible I would not be letting go of Leighton. I put my foot down and let Leighton know that it was not acceptable to lash out at me, however ill or angry he might be feeling. Things immediately improved between us.

In another book on life-raft survival, written by Captain Michael Cargal, I learned that it is wise to treat all jellyfish as dangerous. I thought that the photograph of Leighton's abnormal cells, dyed pink for analysis, looked like a particularly threatening species of jellyfish (see Figure 44).

Cargal also has an invaluable insight into the survival uses of a solar shower, which is basically a plastic bag of water heated in the sun, with a tube and nozzle attached: 'If you reach a point when the only water you have left is too disgusting to drink, you can absorb up to a pint a day (enough to keep you alive) by enema.' I include this information here because it might, one day, save your life. Poor Leighton had already undergone more than his fair share of enemas. Captain Cargal's most important advice is the following: 'Stay calm; conserve body heat; do not waste energy. You will need it later.'

On the day after Leighton began his first course of chemotherapy, we were nearly killed in a car crash. A complete wheel came off a transport lorry, bounced across the central reservation of a dual carriageway and on to our bonnet. I was driving and there was nothing I could do to avoid it. We sat there, stunned, in the eerie silence of the stopped car. A few minutes later we heard ambulance sirens and thought that there must have been another crash, but the accident was us.

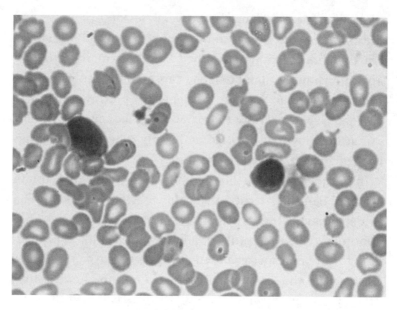

44   Two of Leighton's lymphoma cells

We were unhurt, except for whiplash, and we stood looking at the damage with the paramedics, who pronounced that another six inches and the wheel would have gone through our windscreen. Everybody urged us to be grateful. Grateful? Two minutes ago I had a car, now all we had was a write-off. PC Hoole gave me a little sermon in his Volvo. He told me that we had both been given a second chance and that we should live our lives accordingly. I pointed out to him that, before cancer, we had been in the process of sailing round the world. At the roadside I turned to Leighton and said, 'I'm sorry, love, you're going to have to continue with the chemo.' He laughed.

For the first time, Leighton began to know what it was like to feel seasick, but he managed the nausea of chemotherapy with the drugs Dr Poynton prescribed. Leighton began his six-month course of chemotherapy in the autumn, the very worst time of year for infections. Just before Christmas he caught a dose of flu and ended up in hospital, where we celebrated our tenth wedding anniversary.

'You know how to show a girl a good time,' I commented, as a chesty Leighton drew deeply on his oxygen. On the walls of the haematology ward are a number of sea views painted as *trompe l'oeil* windows. Leighton was in an isolation ward and our painting showed a yacht sailing just the other side of a lighthouse. We spent hours looking at the scene and I knew he was improving when he suddenly pronounced: 'With clouds like those, there would be a much bigger sea running.' I felt that an element of reality had returned to our life together. That night, while he was sleeping, I timed the drip by the side of his bed, as if it were the flash of a lighthouse.

Back in my sister's house, I found an old photograph of Leighton when we'd started to sail in the Bristol Channel. In it he looked relaxed and very happy, tanned in shorts and totally comfortable at sea. I put it on the mantelpiece. It marked a new – or was it old? – place that we were working hard to reach, although sometimes it looked impossibly far away.

Nursing someone through a serious illness is an exercise in memory and hope: a recollection of what they once were to you and the hope that they will be that person again. On the old windjammers, when the weather was so rough that carrying canvas was too dangerous, the old masters used to send the hands aloft, so that their bodies acted as sails, giving the ship some steerage way. This is what Anson did in order to round Cape Horn on his terrible voyage round the world in search of Spanish gold in 1740. Of the 1,900 men who

45   Leighton in the Bristol Channel

sailed with Anson, 1,400 perished. Despite their suffering, Anson's patience and stoicism in hardship meant his men loved him and he was known as 'lucky Anson'. For all our difficulties, we felt fortunate in that we had discovered how seriously ill Leighton was before we had left Europe to cross the Atlantic. I was grateful that I hadn't left Leighton. Now I could stand as a sail for him in the gale now blowing through his bloodstream.

During the winter I saw a good friend and he commented on how different I looked physically. The fat on my face had gone; I had more cheekbone and less mouth, as if there were less to say and more to know. One day in the hospital Leighton met an old friend and his wife, who was having chemotherapy by intravenous drip. They mentioned that they had seen us both in the haematology unit the previous month and then, with sympathy, one of them asked, 'It's the wife who's got cancer, is it?' Leighton was delighted because it showed that he was looking better. I, on the other hand, felt as if I had aged a century.

One of the few freedoms we still had that winter was noticing the world. A white cat had taken to visiting my sister's garden from across a busy road. The cat – who we discovered was called Philly, as in Philadelphia, after her creamy colour – stopped traffic regularly and we greeted her with joy every day because she hadn't yet succumbed to the inevitable road accident. Her visits became one of the things that kept us going. I began to see that there might be a major principle involved here in life: anything that increases your consciousness of each day is a good thing, even if it is cancer. The cancer perspective simplified things radically. This was a new dark way of seeing life, but I began to use it extensively as a way of admitting or rejecting different thoughts. Pain was in, but alcohol to dull it was definitely out. Feeling badly done by was out, or thinking that other people had done us harm. If we couldn't eject the tenants from our house, we could at least dismiss them from our minds.

Things became easier when, after three doses of chemotherapy, I could see Leighton begin to thaw out of his illness. Because we were facing the unspoken prospect of him dying, our relationship began to take on some of the quality it had possessed when we'd first met. One Sunday, for the first time, we found ourselves chatting in bed and laughing in a way that we hadn't for a very long time. In the middle of chemotherapy, Leighton had stopped being Captain Bastard and was now Captain Very Pleasant If a Little Subdued.

The need for privacy is greatest when you're living in the most confined spaces, and in our lifeboat, we gave one another as much emotional room as possible. One evening when we were watching television and flicking channels, we came across a documentary about new treatments for cancer. Leighton didn't want to watch it but, while he was out in the kitchen, I switched channels and sneaked a look at the programme. It showed various couples, one of each fighting cancer, in consultation with their doctors. From their expressions I understood exactly what these people were feeling – worry, concern and fear of what might be ahead – because we were now living the same experience. Each couple had an emotional restraint born of the desire above all not to upset one another. They held themselves carefully so that the thorns of their grief, held deep inside them, didn't shift and cause them pain. They had hope, because they had to. They lived by an optimism that might turn out to be fiction, but they held on to it anyway for the other person's sake. What I didn't expect to see in the faces of these couples was how full of grace they were, especially when they couldn't stop themselves from shedding tears, run-off water from the glacier around their hearts. As Leighton came back into the room I quickly switched channels.

David Lewis, the sailor who documented the vanishing maritime tradition of the Polynesian islanders, was the first man to sail single-handed to Antarctica. His book of the voyage, *Ice Bird*, makes fascinating reading partly because of his attitude to hardship. Going through chemotherapy, which sometimes seems worse than the cancer it's designed to treat, required huge amounts of endurance. Keeping up morale (not unrealistically, but in a credible way) was an important part of the journey for both of us. In one particular passage, which should be given out to everybody who suffers from depression, David Lewis writes:

I tried clumsily to express these thoughts in the log. 'Earning membership of humanity – must earn it every day, to be a man.' I proceeded to try for that day's quota by laboriously and painfully emptying out twenty-four bucketfuls of bilge water, clearing the jammed halyard in a snowstorm and hoisting another sail to assist the little jib.

For us, bailing out bilge water meant getting rid of everything that distracted us from living each day, illness or not, to the full. In doing this, I discovered a basic orientation towards optimism in myself, a drive to live richly that went much deeper than the bleakness of our current situation. We had not reached the tropics as I had hoped, but, for the time being, we seemed to have left the depression factory behind.

As I write this, Leighton is in unconfirmed remission. This will not last for ever. We have been told that Leighton's type of lymphoma tends to return. But he is coming back to himself. One morning, in bed, he woke me up and I swore at him.

'I must be getting better if you're talking to me like that,' he said.

'Yes, now sod off and let me sleep some more.'

As we had hoped at the start of our voyage, Leighton and I have been changed by the sea and, even more, by our sailing without a boat. We have been facing death, a blank region but one full of vast energies by which we are learning to navigate. One of this journey's greatest gifts has been a seamanlike state of mind, not unlike the one we experienced on our four-day crossing of the Bay of Biscay. Above us we can see that there might be heavy weather on the way, but the world unfolds rapturously in front of us, ignoring our terror. In these moments, you watch as, with each minute's changing light, your past emerges from your subconscious. People appear from every period of your life – the kind, the cruel, the liars and the deceived – so vivid that you're pleased to see them. They present themselves as they were when you first loved them, under the shade of a summer tree, or wearing a certain coat. They come in a parade, like guests at a wedding or couples into the ark that's about to float. Above you is a carnival of clouds, a low-pressure system coming in, but something like forgiveness is happening and you are able to sail.

In the meantime, we're practising internal sailing at home, in the way described by the samurai *Book of Five Rings*:

> 'Crossing at a ford' means, for example, crossing the sea at a strait, or crossing over a hundred miles of broad sea at a crossing place. I believe this 'crossing at a ford' occurs often in a man's lifetime. It means setting sail even though your friends stay in harbour, knowing the route, knowing the soundness of your ship and the favour of the day. When all the conditions are met, and there is perhaps a favourable wind, or a tailwind, then set sail. If the wind changes within a few miles of your destination, you must row across the remaining distance without sail.

The wind did change unexpectedly for us on our voyage, and we've had to do a lot of rowing. But the wind will change again. As soon as Leighton is recovered from his chemotherapy, we plan to return to our boat in Ceuta and cross the Strait of Gibraltar, tracing a new route between the Pillars of Hercules. Dr Poynton has told us that an Atlantic crossing may not be out of the question for us, even now. And will we be able to sail together happily then? I don't know.

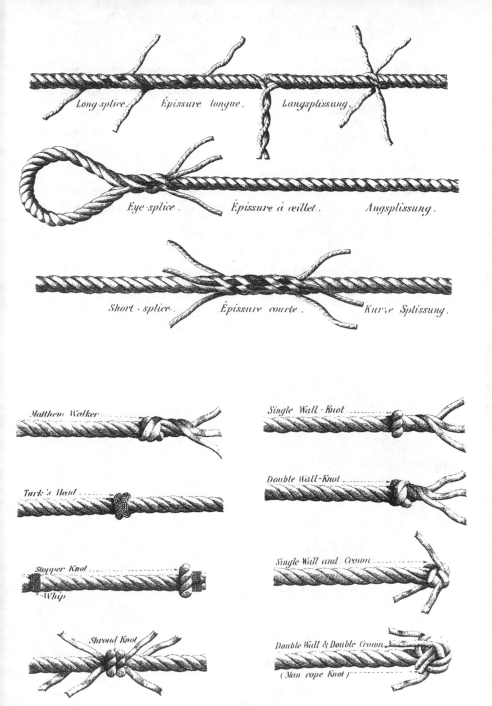

Long-splice.   Épissure longue.   Langsplissung.

Eye-splice.   Épissure à œillet.   Augsplissung.

Short-splice.   Épissure courte.   Kurze Splissung.

Matthew Walker.

Turk's Head.

Stopper Knot.
Whip

Shroud Knot

Single Wall-Knot

Double Wall-Knot

Single Wall and Crown

Double Wall & Double Crown
(Man rope Knot)

46   Splices

I have, at last, become a kind of Hornblower myself, the servant of our boat, our marriage. I dreamt not long ago that I was summoned to the Admiralty to collect new charts. Perhaps I have now received my inner commission to be a sailor. The central discipline of the dry-land seamanship we are now practising requires total focus on the present moment. This, I have learned, is a truly safe port. This sea wall keeps out the swell of fear and despair. It's the only destination worth travelling towards, and the greatest surprise is that, boat or no boat, house or no house, health or no health, Leighton and I are already home.

BIBLIOGRAPHY

Adams, Colin C., *The Knot Book: An Elementary Introduction to the Mathematical Theory of Knots* (New York, 2001)

Admiralty Manual of Navigation, Vol. I (London, 1955)

Arthur, Max, *The Navy 1939 to the Present Day* (Hodder & Stoughton, London, 1997)

Attwood, Edward L., *Theoretical Naval Architecture* (London, 1931)

Black Book of the Admiralty, quoted in Commander Hilary P. Mead, *Trinity House* (London, no date)

Cargal, Captain Mike, *The Captain's Guide to Liferaft Survival* (Seafarer Books, London, 1990)

Cleto, Joel, *Port of Leixões* (Port Authority of Douro and Leixões, 1998)

Conrad, Joseph, *The Mirror of the Sea* (Dent, London, 1946)

Cornide, Don Joseph, *Historia de la Torre de Hércules* (1792, reprinted Libreria Arenas, 1947)

Davies, John, *The Artless Yachtsman*, drawings by John Jensen (Pelham Books, London, 1964)

Facaros, Dana, and Michael Pauls, *Northern Spain* (Cadogan Guides, 2001)

Fernández-Armesto, Felipe, *Civilizations* (Pan Books, London, 2001)

Fiennes, Gerald, *The Ocean Empire: Its Dangers and Defence* (London, *c.* 1905)

Forester, C.S., *Lieutenant Hornblower* (Michael Joseph, London, 1954)

Forester, C.S., *Lord Nelson* (Simon Publications, Florida, 1929)

Gastón, Francisco Tettamancy *La Torre de Hércules* (La Coruña, no date)

Fowles, John, *The Shipwreck* (Jonathan Cape, 1974), quoted in Jonathan Raban, ed. *The Oxford Book of the Sea* (OUP, 2001)

Gastón, Francisco Tettamancy, *La Torre de Hércules* (La Coruña, no date)

Hague, Douglas B., and Rosemary Christie, *Lighthouses: Their Architecture, History and Archaeology* (Gomer Press, 1975)

Hill, Christopher, *Maritime Law*, fifth edn (Lloyd's Practical Shipping Guides, 1998)

IMO's *Guidance to Shipowners and Ship Operators, Shipmasters and Crews on Preventing and Suppressing Acts of Piracy and Armed Robbery*, quoted in Katrina Davis, 'Sharks of the Sea: A New Perspective on Twentieth-Century Maritime Piracy (BSc thesis, Cardiff University, 2000)

Jiménez, Juan Ramón, *Selected Writings of Juan Ramón Jiménez*, ed. Eugenio Florit (Farrar, Straus and Cudahy, New York, 1975)

Lewis, David, *Ice Bird* (Fontana, London, 1977)

Lisboa, Eugenio, with L.C. Taylor, eds. *Centenary Pessoa* (Carcanet, Manchester, 1995)

Lloyd's Calendar 1977

Lovell, Captain Rob, 'Managing Pilot Fatigue', *Seaways*, March 1998

Manual of Seamanship 1937 (The Lords Commissioners of the Admiralty, London, 1938)

Manual of Seamanship, Vol. III (Her Majesty's Stationery Office, 1954)

The Mariner's Handbook (Hydrographer of the Navy, 1973)

Musashi, Miyamoto, *A Book of Five Rings*, trans. Victor Harris (HarperCollins, London, 1995, and Profile Books, 2004)

Nicholson 35 Owners Handbook

Noble, Peter, and Ros Hogbin, *The Mind of a Sailor* (Adlard Coles Nautical, London, 2001)

Ocean Passages for the World (Hydrographer of the Navy, 1987)

Portugal: The Green Guide (Michelin, 2001)

Reed, Thomas, and Peter Youngson, *Reed's Useful Hints to Sea-Going Engineers: And How to Repair and Avoid 'Breakdowns'* (Sunderland, 1921)

Robinson, Tim, *My Time in Space* (The Lilliput Press, Dublin, 2001)

Royal Life Saving Society Illustrated Handbook of Instruction (London 1981, reprinted 1946)

Segelhandbuch für den Atlantischen Ozean (Deutsche Seewarte, Hamburg, 1910)

Sleightholme, Joyce, *The Sea Wife's Handbook* (August & Robertson, London, 1970)

Thomas, Captain R.E., *Stowage: The Properties and Stowage of Cargoes* (Glasgow, *c.* 1948)

The Times Atlas and Encyclopaedia of the Sea, ed. Alastair Couper (Times Books, 1987)

Tzu, Lao, *The Tao of Power*, trans. R.L. Wing (Doubleday, London, 1986)

Whybrow, Peter C., *A Mood Apart* (Picador, London, 1999)

Woolams, Chris, *Everything you Need to Know to Help You Beat Cancer: The Ultimate Guide for People who have Cancer and Everyone who wants to Prevent It* (Health Issues Ltd., 2002. For more information please call 01280 815166)

LIST OF ILLUSTRATIONS

Every effort has been made to trace owners and copyright holders, but we would be grateful to receive any further information on missing credits.

Cecil H. Fox, *1904 Manual of Seamanship for Boys' Training Ships of the Royal Navy* (London, 1904)

15   The Milford Haven Giant Squid
     Courtesy of Milford Haven Museum

16   Odysseus and the Sirens
     From an Attic polychrome-figured white lekythus, fifth century BC, now in the Central Museum, Athens. Reproduced in Joseph Campbell, *The Hero with a Thousand Faces* (Fontana, 1993)

17   *Jameeleh*'s Atlantic Voyage

18   What happens to men on boats
     John Davies, *The Artless Yachtsman*, illustrated by John Jensen (Pelham Books, London, 1964)

19   Section through warm front and cold front
     George Kimble, *The Weather* (Pelican, 1951)

20   Definitions of horizon
     Captain Robert E. Sharpley and Captain William C. Aubrey-Rees, *'Neptune' Memory Book* (Cardiff, 1912)

21   Sectional view of a squall
     From *Segelhandbuch für den Atlantischen Ozean* (Deutsche Seewarte, Hamburg, 1910)

22   No longer seasick

23   The rolling of ships
     Edward L. Attwood, *Theoretical Naval Architecture* (London, 1931)

24   Cardiff Port Authority 1960s Rat Harbourage form

25   La Coruña, *Torre de Hércules*. Engraving by Ruidavets, 1880
     Reproduced in Francisco Tettamancy Gastón, *La Torre de Hércules* (La Coruña, no date)

26   Torre de Hércules
     © Douglas B. Hague, in Douglas B. Hague and Rosemary Christie, *Lighthouses: Their Architecture, History and Archaeology* (Gomer Press, 1975)

27   Different knots, bends and hitches
     Paasch's Illustrated Marine Dictionary

28   Lighthouse silhouettes
     © Douglas B. Hague, in Hague and Christie, *op cit.*

ACKNOWLEDGEMENTS

Neither a voyage nor a book can be undertaken without accumulating debts to many people. Some of these are practical – like the help given to us by Crest Nicholson Marinas in Penarth, Cardiff. Leighton and I will never forget the kindness shown to us by the staff at Cascais Marina in Portugal. I can't find the words to thank our friends in Ceuta, especially Laarbi Hamed Meeki and Agapito Calvo Fontecha, who looked after *Jameeleh* for a whole year. Their kindness was astonishing and much appreciated.

Many people helped me with the research for this book. Julia Young and Tony Lewis at the Butetown History & Arts Centre in Cardiff Bay shared their historical and social knowledge of the area and the communities living there. Associated British Ports gave me a useful tour of the modern Cardiff docks. Anthony Beresford, Lecturer in international transport at the Cardiff Business School, gave me access to the department's materials about sea commerce and answered many of my questions. Staff at the Milford Haven Museum were extremely helpful in tracking down the photograph of the Giant Squid, and Mike Howe, Information Officer in the Cruising Association's library in Limehouse Basin, London, also helped with illustrations. The Kinsale Regional Museum gave me permission to reproduce 'A Fitting Out', by an anonymous English sailor, and Padraig O'Callaghan helped with information about the poem. Jeremy Lines, Voluntary Archivist for Camper & Nicholsons, supplied plans of the Nicholson 35 and checked my facts about the boat. I would also like to thank Darren Fa at the Gibraltar Museum, Lorna Swift at the Gibraltar Garrison Library and staff at the Gibraltar Archive. Jim Hewitt helped with fact-checking, while Marguerite Harrison was kind enough to correct my Portuguese.

I'm grateful in a much larger way to Philip Gwyn Jones, who commissioned this book. Nicholas Pearson became a generous foster-parent and Silvia Crompton has saved me from myself many times with her accuracy and clarity of thought.

I'm hugely grateful to NESTA (the National Endowment for Science, Technology and the Arts), who awarded me a five-year fellowship and supported me in many other ways. I also want to thank Academi for a bursary that helped me to complete this book.

Thanks are due to Dr Chris Poynton, Leighton's consultant in the Department of Haematology, University Hospital of Wales at the Heath, not only for his skill and humour as a physician but also for casting his eye over the last chapter of this book. Sol Davidson, whose wisdom and knowledge of the frustrations of sailing boats have made him a great support, will be able to hear echoes of our conversations throughout this account.

My sister Marian proved to be the most important port for us during the worst storm of our voyage. Her tolerance and generosity will be difficult to repay but I'd like to make a start here.

Not one page of this book could have been written without Leighton. If you've read this far, then you know exactly why the book as a whole is dedicated to him.